Understanding Internet Policies and Complexities

Also from Westphalia Press
westphaliapress.org

The Idea of the Digital University

France and New England Volumes 1, 2, & 3

Treasures of London

The History of Photography

L'Enfant and the Freemasons

Baronial Bedrooms

Making Trouble for Muslims

Material History and Ritual Objects

Paddle Your Own Canoe

Opportunity and Horatio Alger

Careers in the Face of Challenge

Bookplates of the Kings

Collecting American Presidential Autographs

Freemasonry in Old Buffalo

Young Freemasons?

Social Satire and the Modern Novel

The Essence of Harvard

Ivanhoe Masonic Quartettes

A Definitive Commentary on Bookplates

James Martineau and Rebuilding Theology

No Bird Lacks Feathers

Gilded Play

Earthworms, Horses, and Living Things

The Man Who Killed President Garfield

Anti-Masonry and the Murder of Morgan

Understanding Art

Homeopathy

Fishing the Florida Keys

Collecting Old Books

Masonic Secret Signs and Passwords

The Thomas Starr King Dispute

Earl Warren's Masonic Lodge

Lariats and Lassos

Mr. Garfield of Ohio

The Wisdom of Thomas Starr King

The French Foreign Legion

War in Syria

Naturism Comes to the United States

New Sources on Women and Freemasonry

Designing, Adapting, Strategizing in Online Education

Gunboat and Gun-runner

Meeting Minutes of Naval Lodge No. 4 F.A.A.M

Understanding Internet Policies and Complexities

Vol. 2, No. 2 of Internet Learning

Edited by Melissa Layne

WESTPHALIA PRESS
An imprint of Policy Studies Organization

Understanding Internet Policies and Complexities: Vol. 2, No. 2 of Internet Learning
All Rights Reserved © 2014 by Policy Studies Organization

Westphalia Press
An imprint of Policy Studies Organization
1527 New Hampshire Ave., NW
Washington, D.C. 20036
dgutierrezs@ipsonet.org

ISBN-13: 978-1941472927
ISBN-10: 1941472923

Updated material and comments on this edition
can be found at the Westphalia Press website:
www.westphaliapress.org

Internet Learning
Volume 2 Issue 2 Autumn 2013

Table of Contents

Academic Libraries & Others: Hunting for the Overlooked in Online Learning _____ 1
Fred Stielow

Current Issues with Copyright and Higher Education: Lawsuits, Legislation, and Looking Forward _____ 4
Kay Cunningham

Virtually Yours: Online Embedded Librarianship in Higher Education _____ 21
Denise Landry-Hyde, Laureen P. Cantwell

Continuous Improvement and Embedded Librarianship in Online Learning Environments: A Case Study _____ 38
Jeneen LaSee-Willemssen, Lisa Reed

"MOOL" in a MOOC: Opportunities for Librarianship in the Expanding Galaxy of Massive Open Online Course Design and Execution _____ 47
Laureen P. Cantwell

MOOCs for LIS Professional Development: Exploring New Transformative Learning Environments and Roles _____ 83
Michael Stephens

Efficiency, Economy, and Social Equity in Online Education at America's Community Colleges _____ 100
Marco Castillo

Mindful Meditation for Online Learning: Lighting the Fire by Dimming the Lights: Helping College Students Relax and Focus to Prepare for Online Learning _____ 111
Brenda Freshman, Carol A. Molinari

Curriculum Design for Flexible Delivery: An Assessment of E-Learning Approaches _____ 121

Jayanath Ananda

Rethinking Distance in an Era of Online Learning _____ 138

Jennifer Glennie, Tony Mays

Academic Libraries & Others:
Hunting for the Overlooked in Online Learning
Fred Stielow, Ph.D., M.L.S.[1]

Higher education is ensconced in a communication revolution and redefinition. Despite a spate of relevant scholarship, an inherent fog continues to cloud understanding of online education. On the pedagogical beat, literature deconstructs primarily as transitions from established practice—albeit adapted for both asynchronous and synchronous settings. Methods for lectures and media inclusion remain featured along with calls for embellishing with new Internet applications. Measurement surfaces from the ether as a yet unstandardized force for addressing the chimera of educational evaluation, as well as proactive engagement to enhance the classroom. MOOCs rapidly rise in disturbing fashion to command the conversation, but remain in an unsure position. On the practical side, modes of delivery and intellectual property rear to prominence. Schools struggle to cope with textbook inflation and look to OER (open educational resource) substitutes.

As displayed in this issue of Internet Learning, I take personal delight in helping to stretch that impressive list of topics. In keeping with someone engaged by a fully online university, different and emergent types of educational institutions need to be increasingly taken into account. From my position on the U.S. Commission to UNESCO, globalization and cross-cultural values certainly must be considered. As a librarian and archivist, I feel especially compelled to surface almost unconscionable oversights. The most traditional of academic support units offer tailored subject knowledge and Web skills to assist with such looming issues as:

• Instruction in new research paradigms as tailored to individual disciplines.
• Ensuring a proper injection of peer-reviewed/professional literature.
• Reducing the costs for course materials and textbook dependency.
• Maintaining currency in the rapidly changing Web environment.

About this Issue

This issue of Internet Learning is divided into two sections. As suggested above, the first embraces academic libraries. It joins at a pivotal moment in the development of online education and prospects for library sustainability. The contributions offer a sample of current issues. Most come from a call to the pens of distance education librarians—practitioners long consigned to the fringes of the main campus library, but now with an increasingly pertinent narrative. The second provides a sampler of pieces with different global and institutional perspectives, but also surface as primary research and opinion pieces in preparation for hypothesis testing by future investigators.

Reinventing Libraries for Online Education

The section also was designed to provide counterpoint contemporaneous with the release of my Reinventing Libraries for Online Education by ALA Publishing. That book lends full scope to the preceding de-

---

[1] APUS VP/Dean of Libraries, Electronic Course Materials & ePress, U.S. Commission to UNESCO

bate. Its CRIS (Classroom/Research Information Services) approach argues for a reversion to Sorbonne's original model. This applied theory calls for the university library to place a premium on actively engaging and populating the classroom. Librarians assert their unquestioned Web and subject-specialist skills to work in concert with the faculty. They combine unique knowledge of licensed and all-important peer-reviewed literature out of the library with exceptional abilities to vet related resources, social networking, and methodological sources on the Open Web. The results enhance the quality and currency of classroom readings, provide trusted launching pads for student research, and lower costs for students.

Prelude to Academic Libraries

A bit of historical reminding may be in order for the start of this issue. Robert Sorbonne led the way in the mid-13th century. His lasting reforms created the faculty-driven institution. They also extended to the invention of a university library. That creation was a socialistic operation in support of a higher good. The library was designed to alleviate costs for students, as well as serve the academic community at large by sharing knowledge with qualified scholars. This model drifted somewhat in the aftermath of Guttenberg. It took renewed importance in the 19th century with the German "New University" and American land-grant movement. The modern university library emerged as a campus landmark—albeit with an enhance research mission in support of burgeoning bands of new PhDs and the purchase of their monographic and journal outputs.

Although easily overlooked, the modern research library led the way in automating information resources and developing contemporary forms of scholarly research. In the early 1980s, the OPAC (online public access catalog) first introduced many college students to computers. Citation analysis began to leave its mark as a metric. Libraries blazed related openings on the Internet. They followed in the 1990s with pioneering presences that remain as major treasure troves of trusted material on the World Wide Web.

The web itself is wreaking fundamental change in libraries with direct implications for online education. Today's facilities extend to a look and feel unlike anything in the past. Users are no longer tied to a chain of physical engagement—dedicated visits, catalog/stack searches, physical retrieval, and opening materials for reading. Travel and parking have become optional. Hours of operation have vanished and library walls disappear before a virtual interface. By the early 21st century, the automated catalog has meshed with newly digitized hordes of content. Search engines have replaced the reference desk. Patrons anticipate anytime and anywhere access to full text on devices from desktop computers to smart phones.

While altered, the web did not obviate the academic library. That institution continues as intermediary to impact and define scholarly practice. 21st-century academics now need to master the intricacies of library-accessed databases to engage their trade, but also to prepare their successors. Yet, such new skills appear largely underappreciated in the literature of online education. Oversight is doubly so for populating online courses. OER proponents and textbook aficionados have studiously avoided the obvious. How can one discuss upper-division and graduate level online courses without active recourse to peer-reviewed content? Why turn to commercial producers and electronic textbooks without exploring the full range of university services—and, not incidentally, looking to the financial wellbeing of one's students? Moreover, who is better informed on the university's holdings and more expert with the new medium than professional librarians? Kay Cunningham begins such investigations with "Current Issues with Copyright and Higher Education." Intellectual property issues and overlapping balance with handicapped accessibility have taken front stage with the Web. To me, academic libraries cannot escape engagement and have an expanded role to play for their university community.

The parallel redefining of roles in the Web Age is on display in the form of faculty partnerships and information literacy specializations. Discussion unfolds within two complimentary articles: Denise Landry-Hyde and Laureen P. Cantwell: "Virtually Yours: Online Embedded Librarianship in Higher Education"; and, Jeneen LaSee-Willemssen and Lisa Reed: "Continuous Improvement and Embedded Librarianship." Library treatments close with MOOCs. In 2013, such facilities appear to have goaded an awakening of mainstream academic libraries to the opportunities and challenges of online learning. Hence, Laureen P. Cantwell responds with " 'MOOL' in a MOOC: Opportunities for Librarianship in the Expanding Galaxy of Massive Open Online Course Design and Execution." That is followed by Michael Stephens' treatment on educational needs with "MOOCs for LIS Professional Development: Exploring New Roles in Transformative Learning Environments."

The Other

The second section holds a small potpourri of "Other" articles. These had been scheduled before the librarian topic elbowed its way into the production schedule, but ironically match the theme of overlooked prospects. For example, Marco Castillo suggests the importance and needed research agendas for two-year institutions with his "Efficiency, Economy, and Social Equity in Online Education at America's Community Colleges." Molinari goes even further out-of-the-box with "Mindful Meditation for Online Learning: Lighting the Fire by Dimming the Lights: Helping College Students Relax and Focus to Prepare for Online Learning."

Global perspectives steps forward in the final two essays. Australia's Jayanath Ananda offers "Curriculum Design for Flexible Delivery: An Assessment of e-Learning Approaches," which explores "tertiary educators" and the challenges of designing e-learning course for business. Finally, South Africa's Jennifer Glennie and Tony Mays proffer policy considerations and a long-term view for their country in "Rethinking Distance in an Era of Online Learning."

Current Issues with Copyright and Higher Education: Lawsuits, Legislation, and Looking Forward

Kay Cunningham

Electronic reserves, digitization, streaming videos, and first sale were the topics of recent copyright lawsuits: respectively, Cambridge University Press v. Mark P. Becker (2012), Authors Guild Inc. v. HathiTrust (2012), the Association for Information Media v. the Regents of the University of California (2011), and Kirtsaeng v. Wiley (2013). Outcomes related to libraries are discussed in this essay, along with such amendments to the Copyright Act as the Technology, Education and Copyright Harmonization Act (TEACH Act) and the Digital Millennium Copyright Act (DMCA) and the possibility of revisions.

Keywords: copyright, digitization, electronic reserves, fair use, first sale, education, lawsuits, libraries

Current Issues with Copyright and Higher Education: Lawsuits, Legislation, and Looking Forward

For years, academic librarians have counted the numbers of interlibrary loan articles by journal, and added and removed reserve articles by the score, in order to keep their libraries on the straight and narrow regarding fair use of copyrighted material. Librarians have explained that while faculty may be able to show a film in class, they cannot show the same film to the campus unless a public performance fee has been paid. On many campuses, librarians became the answerers of all things copyright—no matter how comfortable they felt in the role that came their way by default and has grown increasingly more complex within an online environment. Now, librarians arrange for login protocols for off-campus use of their electronic resources. They explain how to use direct linking in course management systems, and they wonder what can be posted, digitized, and streamed while avoiding copyright infringement.

Historically, copyright infringement cases were between two authors or lodged against commercial entities. The Georgia State, HathiTrust, and UCLA cases were different, however, as they were filed against educational, nonprofit institutions. The full case names are Cambridge University Press, et al., v. Mark P. Becker, et al.; Authors Guild Inc., et al., v. HathiTrust, et al.; and the Association for Information Media, et al., v. the Regents of the University of California, et al. Each was important for issues involving fair use, academic libraries, and higher education.

The outcomes of the Georgia State and HathiTrust cases—along with the dismissal of the suit against UCLA—amounted to stunning affirmations of the fair use principle and its importance for libraries and educational institutions. Add Supap Kirtsaeng, d/b/a Bluechristine99, v. John Wiley & Sons, Inc. to round out the major copyright cases of recent years that were important for libraries. Along with Kirtsaeng's application of the first-sale principle to imported works, these copyright infringement cases helped clarify what academic libraries and educators can do with copyrighted works in their collections, in electronic reserves and courseware, as digitization projects, to stream online, for keyword indexing, and to serve the visually impaired. Fair use resided at the core of the decisions.

Copyright is complex and likely to grow more so. The copyright activities of multimedia conglomerates may seem far removed from the academic arena, but their activities affect everyone involved with copyright in any manner. Copyright is pervasive; there is little it does not touch—or cannot be made to touch. Of all the intellectual property rights, it is the easiest to acquire. Consider this: virtually everything in the United States is copyrighted—at least everything in a fixed form created since 1978, excepting most government publications. Everyone is an author. Everyone has copyright in something, such as a six-year-old kid's drawing, a high-school term paper, and photographs from that trip to Pensacola. Furthermore, copyright lasts a very long time—the life of the author plus 70 years. In short, if that artistic six-year-old lives to be 99, the copyright on his refrigerator-mounted art will not expire for another 163 years. Except in parental eyes, most six-year-olds do not grow up to be the next Picasso. Regardless, his yet-to-be-born great-grandchildren can rest easy with the assurance that their rights to his efforts with the crayon will be protected.

As copyright grows more expansive in its coverage, it has also become the right of choice for corporate interests to pursue, defend, and litigate. Further, the nature of copyright is fluid; lawsuits and legislation will continue to take note of this. This article aims to provide an overview of recent legal decisions related to copyright and libraries—the Georgia State, HathiTrust, UCLA cases, and Kirtsaeng—as well as such additions to the Copyright Act as the Technology, Education and Copyright Harmonization Act (TEACH Act) and the Digital Millennium Copyright Act (DMCA) and the possibility of copyright reform. Due to the recent nature of these cases, most of the literature reviewed has been drawn from legal documents, news, and commentary. Moreover, as two of the cases may move to courts of appeal, be aware that situations described here may change at any time.

Lawsuits

Cambridge University Press, et al., v. Mark P. Becker, et al. (2012)

In April 2008, Cambridge University Press, Oxford University Press, and Sage Publications, with the support of the Association of American Publishers (AAP) and the Copyright Clearance Centers (CCC), brought suit against administrators at Georgia State University for copyright infringement over the posting of their copyrighted material in the school's electronic reserve system. Georgia State claimed the use was acceptable under fair use. The publishers objected to the use of electronic courseware and electronic library reserve systems, which involve scanning and online distribution of material. Indeed the AAP held that electronic reserves, by their very nature, were infringements of copyright law (McDermott, 2012). In addition, the publishers alleged that the administrators used electronic reserves at Georgia State to encourage faculty in the systematic infringement of their publications (Pike, 2010). The case was heard in the United States District Court, Northern District of Georgia, Atlanta Division, with Judge Orinda Evans presiding.

Although prior decisions touched on issues being litigated in the Georgia State case, those earlier cases had involved commercial entities (Pike, 2010), not nonprofit, educational ones. The publishers wanted to connect the concept of photocopied course packs to that of electronic reserves, claiming that both infringed in the same way (Smith, 2013a). While the production and selling of course packs are commercial activities, an electronic reserves system—indeed the concept of reserves—is purely educational; libraries do not profit from them. In the Georgia State case, every aspect of copying for electronic reserves was for educational use (Pike, 2010).

At stake in the Georgia State case was the definition of fair use in the digital environment. A decision for the publishers could have had severe consequences for the university, if not all universities. The publishers were not merely seeking damages; they also wanted a permanent injunction against Georgia State that would affect all copying done on campus and severely restrict what could be used in teaching (Pike, 2012; Smith, 2011). Requiring that Georgia State's administration keep extensive records, the proposed injunction would have given the publishers monitoring authority over not only Georgia State's electronic reserves, but over individual faculty member's decisions regarding documents used in the course management system as well (Albanese, 2012c; Smith, 2011). Furthermore, only 10% of any class readings could have been acquired without permissions being paid, and the Copyright Clearance Center was the only source mentioned for gaining those permissions. The possibility of such demands being granted was truly frightening to librarians and educators and was described as "disastrous," "a nightmare," (Smith, 2011) and "catastrophic" (What's at Stake?, 2011).

However, when a decision was handed down in 2012, Judge Evans essentially sided with Georgia State. While the judge found the university at fault in five specific instances, the remaining 94 claims were not considered infringements on the grounds of fair use. In her decision, described as "careful, even fastidious" (Smith, 2013a), Evans provided 350 pages of detailed analysis of the works under consideration. She evaluated the use of each work against the four factors of fair use: character of the use, which was nonprofit educational; nature of the work; amount of the work; and effect of the use on the market (Cambridge v. Becker, 2012). A sample of Judge Evans' reasoning follows:

> As to the fourth fair use factor, effect on the market, the Court first looks to whether Professor Whitten's use of A World of Babies affected the market for purchasing the book as a whole. Students would not pay $30.99 for the entire book (or $55.99 for the hardcover version) when only 23 pages were required reading for Professor Whitten's course. Neither would a professor require students to purchase the entire book in such an instance. Therefore, the court rejects any argument that the use of the excerpt from A World of Babies had a negative effect on the market for purchase of the book itself (Cambridge v. Becker, 2012).

In addition, she made assessments of the acceptable amount of material that could be used. Although the publishers had contended that each chapter should be treated as a whole, the judge was fairly specific regarding the amount that constituted fair use: 10% of a book with fewer than 10 chapters and one chapter out of a book with more than 10 chapters (Pike, 2012).

The decision was a setback to the plans of the publishers, who had hoped to use the Georgia State case "to lay the groundwork ... to stop or dramatically limit the practice of unlicensed e-reserves on college campuses" (Albanese, 2012c). The judge distinguished between cost savings springing from use of technology and cost savings through the avoidance of fees (Pike, 2010). Most surprising was Judge Evans' order that the publishers pay Georgia State's legal cost, "a sharp rebuke," according to Albanese (Albanese, 2012c).

Cambridge University Press, Oxford University Press, and Sage Publications Inc. have elected to appeal Judge Evans' ruling, disagreeing with her interpretations of fair use. They filed their appeal in January 2013, objecting to Evans' failure to equate course packs with e-reserves, her evaluation of the 99 alleged infringements on a case-by-case basis rather than evaluating the overall impact, and her failure to recognize how e-reserves harmed their market, and insisting that the Guidelines of the Copyright Act of 1976 be interpreted strictly (Smith, 2013a).

Despite what appears to be a sound affirmation of fair-use rights in higher education, the appeal of the Georgia State decision suggests the role of fair use in electronic reserves will continue to be debated for years. Kevin Smith delivers a hopeful estimation that the ruling will be upheld, considering the thoroughness of the judge's analysis and the weakness of the appeal (Smith, 2013a). Librarians should be reassured that the fair use of unlicensed material in e-reserves remains an acceptable practice (Albanese, 2012d).

Authors Guild Inc., et al., against HathiTrust, et al. (2012)

HathiTrust was an outgrowth of the Google Books Project, wherein academic libraries allowed Google to digitize books in their collections. Google provided participating libraries with copies of the digital book files, and these copies were then added to the HathiTrust collection. Pooling the collection among the libraries generated benefits, particularly a simultaneous search interface and the ability to share storage. In September 2011, the Authors Guild filed a suit in New York Southern District Court against HathiTrust and five academic libraries, Cornell University and the presidents of the universities of Michigan, California, Wisconsin, and Indiana, involved in the project (HathiTrust Digital Library, 2013). The initial scanning, duplication of files, and mirror storage at HathiTrust involved copying books and were the grounds for infringement (Authors Guild v. HathiTrust, 2012; Crews, 2011).

In addition, the Authors Guild took issue with HathiTrust's intention to include orphan works in the database. Orphan works are those works still under copyright for which copyright holders cannot be found. Orphan works are not commercially available and have little monetary value; this does not mean that they lack value for researchers. The Google Books Project ran afoul of orphan works in its scanning efforts, but the nonprofit institutions making up HathiTrust, in their Orphan Works Project, thought they could avoid Google's problems, considering that their use of scanned orphan works would be noncommercial and limited to on-campus usage (Pike, 2011). Ultimately, HathiTrust elected to suspend the Orphan Works Project, leading the court to drop orphan works from the suit.

The case was heard in United States District Court, Southern District of New York, with Judge Harold Baer Jr. presiding. His decision, handed down on October 10, 2012, was a victory for HathiTrust and the principles of fair use, particularly regarding what libraries are allowed to do under fair use: making copies for preservation, making copies for the visually impaired, retaining scans for text searching, building databases for data-mining. According to Baer, all fell within the limits of fair use (Authors Guild v. HathiTrust, 2012; Crews, 2012). Specifics of the decision included a clarification of whether an academic library had the right to make copies of works for use by the visually impaired, which had been unclear heretofore. Although there was no ruling on orphan works, the judge's decision that keyword indexing was not a violation will enable those works to be included in search engines. Using digital copies to create a keyword-searchable index was held to be "transformative enough to be a fair use, even … on a large scale" (Unlocking the Riches, 2013). Notably, the orphan works were not singled out regarding digitization; instead the ruling applied to all books regardless of status (Grimmelmann, 2012). Being able to search digital works serves scholarship, as does storage of digital works—even when entire works are being saved. The decision cleared the path for more data-mining projects, especially in the humanities (Unlocking the Riches, 2013).

The HathiTrust ruling is important, and not just for HathiTrust libraries. Judge Baer analyzes fair use in such a way that it will be helpful in evaluating future digital projects (Crews, 2012). James Grimmelmann says, "…this decision is a big deal," and it "could well become a landmark in copyright" (2012).

The Authors Guild filed their appeal against the decision on November 8, 2012. The Guild holds that Judge Baer's ruling was in error on the following points: that HathiTrust's Orphan Works Project was not subject to judicial scrutiny because it had been suspended, that HathiTrust's mass digitization project with Google constituted fair use, that the Guild lacked the statutory standing to bring the suit, and that HathiTrust's mass digitization was permissible under the section of the Copyright Law that deals with reproducing material for the blind and disabled (Albanese, 2012a).

The Association for Information Media and Equipment, et al., v. the Regents of the University of California, et al. (2011)

The California Board of Regents and the University of California at Los Angeles were sued by the Association for Information and Media Equipment (AIME) over their project involving the digital conversion of videos owned by UCLA in order to stream the videos for classroom use. The project began in 2005. UCLA initiated its film digitization project at a time when few streaming products were available. Those that were available were bound by overly complicated licensing requirements and limited in what they delivered. The actions that UCLA took seemed to be in line with the requirements of the Technology, Education, and Copyright Harmonization Act of 2002, otherwise known as the TEACH Act. The posted videos were password-protected on the university website, and copying and retention of the videos was blocked.

Fair-use practices in the physical classroom have been established over time and are understood relatively well. Distance education, however, has no classroom. The TEACH Act was Congress's attempt to bring the rights of the physical classroom to its online equivalent and to balance the prerogatives of the rights holders with exemptions for online and distance education classes that fall more closely in line with the those historically exercised in the traditional classroom. The TEACH Act describes specific actions an institution must take to be in compliance with the law. These requirements go beyond the work of the library and are related to the activities of institutional officers, technology offices, and academic instructors (Nelson, 2009). The TEACH Act includes the following requirements:

1. The institution must have a copyright policy.

2. Copyright notices must be provided to students regarding materials used in online courses.

3. Access to material must be controlled (that is, only students enrolled in a class can view material).

4. Unauthorized distribution of the material must be prevented.

5. There can be no storage of material on the system.

6. Material can only be displayed as part of a class session overseen by the instructor.

7. Material must be related to the content being taught.

8. Only governmental bodies or nonprofit and accredited educational institutions are eligible to claim rights under the TEACH Act (Nelson, 2009; TEACH Act, 2002).

In 2009, while the project was still ongoing, UCLA was approached by a vendor offering to sell streamed content. In the discussion, UCLA expressed interest in the product but mentioned their scanning practices. Shortly thereafter, they were approached by AIME regarding their alleged infringements (Dougherty, 2010). UCLA argued that the rights of the classroom extended to online classrooms. The case came before Judge Consuelo Marshall in California's Central District (AIME v. UCLA, 2011).

AIME v. UCLA (2011) was dismissed on two grounds: first, AIME lacked the legal standing to bring the suit, and second, defendants had immunity in their roles as state officials. Because of this, no particular judgment regarding fair use can be drawn from the suit (McDermott, 2012). Despite the lack of a decision, an important point worth mentioning is Judge Marshall's assertion that she saw no difference in market effect between streaming a film and showing it in a classroom (Smith, 2012a). Also notable is the fact that the dismissal only applied to the specific defendants of the case; and while there can be no refiling of charges against UCLA, other institutions could be sued should a plaintiff with acceptable legal standing choose to do so (Smith, 2012a).

Supap Kirtsaeng, d/b/a Bluechristine99, Petitioner v. John Wiley & Sons, Inc. (2013)

The Kirtsaeng case did not deal with fair use but with another of the limitations of copyright, the first-sale doctrine. Student Supap Kirtsaeng was sued by publisher John Wiley & Sons, Inc. for his practice of buying foreign editions of Wiley textbooks and reselling them in the United States. First-sale rights allow individuals or institutions that have legally purchased copyrighted material to dispose of material however they will, whether by selling it, giving it away, throwing it away, etc. Wiley objected because Kirstaeng sold imported editions of its works. These were less expensive editions designed for other markets. At the core of the argument was the interpretation of particular wording in the Copyright Act: "lawfully made under this title" (Copyright Act of 1976, 17 U.S.C.). Wiley argued, and lower courts agreed, that this meant the geographic area where the U.S. Copyright Act held sway and so, first sale did not apply to imported works. Found in violation of copyright by lower courts, Kirtsaeng appealed his case to the Supreme Court (Kirtsaeng v. Wiley, 2013). The case had the attention of the library community because of the troubling implications for libraries, among others, of that geographic interpretation:

> Libraries are arguably engaged in the distribution of copyrighted works whenever they acquire materials for the collections and permit patrons to check them out. Distributions are often a core function of libraries, and many works in library collections are made outside U.S. borders. In fact, everyday life in the U.S. is rich with foreign made works that could be hamstrung by the decisions of the lower courts: American novels outsourced for printing, foreign movies on DVDs, letters mailed home from Europe, software inside an iPod or mobile phone, semiconductor code on computer chips, and even the computer programs embedded in the workings of a Honda, Toyota, Volkswagen, or other imported car. Regardless of where the copyright work originated, the constraint applied if the specific copy had been produced outside American borders (Crews, 2013).

In its decision on March 19, 2013, the Supreme Court overturned the lower court ruling and held that first sale applies to copyrighted works produced outside of the United States. Justice Breyer listed even more items that could be implicated had they supported the lower court:

> ... millions and millions of dollars' worth of items with copyrighted indications of some kind in them that we import every year; libraries with 300 million books bought from foreign publishers that they might sell, resale, or use; museums that buy Picassos that now, under our last case, receive American protection as soon as that Picasso comes to the United States, and they can't display it without getting permission from the five heirs who are disputing ownership of the Picasso copyrights . . . (Before the Court, 2012).

With this far-reaching decision, libraries need not worry about the origins of material in their collections, nor need they limit purchasing decisions based on the where materials were physically manufactured. Note that libraries are only one of the beneficiaries of the decision; it affects the work of bookstores and museums as well as the activities of anyone who buys or sells copyrighted material. It truly has the potential to affect everyone (Crews, 2013).

Of the four legal cases presented before the courts, only Kirtsaeng v. Wiley (2013) has been settled. Even in relation to Kirtsaeng, failure in the courts may lead publishers to increase their reliance on licensing to control their publications or to lobby Congress to change laws related to international business and imports (Crews, 2013). Regarding the other lawsuits and their impact on libraries, the outcomes were positive, to varying degrees, regarding the posting of material on electronic reserves and course management systems, digitization, database building, copying for the blind and for preservation, and the online streaming of videos. Most importantly, these three instances in which academic libraries were accused of infringement were all defended and decided to be fair use (Smith, 2012a). The courts have recognized the importance of fair use in libraries and education. Commentator Kevin Smith celebrated "a pretty convincing victory in the Georgia State e-reserves case, a sweeping one in the HathiTrust case, and a tepid affirmation of fair use (probably!) in this streamed video case" (Smith, 2012a). Andrew Albanese wrote that the "fair use decision for the HathiTrust was emphatic" (Albanese, 2012b), and Karen Coyle said, "Fair use . . . has been reaffirmed, with some eloquence, as a necessary social compact to further the creation of new knowledge" (Unlocking the Riches, 2013). The judiciary continues to treat fair use as important. As of this writing, the judges of a federal appeals court had unanimously decreed that a lower court had to consider whether Google's scans were such before allowing class certification to a group of authors (DeSantis, 2013). Fair use, however, has long been a target of corporate interests and will continue to be so.

Legislation

A long-standing principle in United States law, fair use was articulated and codified with the Copyright Act of 1976, which, with its amendments, remains the current law of the land. Fair use in education is only one aspect of the principle. That aspect of fair use was under consideration in the Georgia State case. Although this aspect of fair use is the one most familiar to librarians, classroom teachers are not the only people who can take advantage of this limitation to copyright.

As Aufderheide and Jaszi explain in Reclaiming Fair Use, unlicensed access to copyrighted work encourages new creation by new creators, who "inevitably need to access culture as they add to it" (p. 17). For the public, there are two kinds of fair use: private, personal, and (pre-Internet) unmonitored use and reuse of material to make something else (Aufderheide & Jaszi, 2011). By and large, fair use has been taken for granted by the majority of its users; many are probably unaware of their rights in this matter. Individuals have a variety of rights: personal study and research—whether by taking notes or photocopying—quoting from a work, selling or gifting purchased books and recordings, reusing facts and ideas, and recording television shows to watch later. The growth of digital culture has fueled corporate attitudes against any free use of copyrighted products, fair or otherwise, hence licensing agreements of all sorts, digital rights management software, and more (Aufderheide & Jaszi, 2011).

Copyright law in the United States has always encouraged the creation of new works by providing monopolies of limited times to authors. Article I, Section 8 of the Constitution states, "Congress shall have Power . . . To promote the Progress of Science and useful Arts, by securing for limited Times to Authors and Inventors the exclusive Right to their respective Writings and Discoveries" (Copyright Act of 1976, 17 U.S.C.). The limited time was only 14 years originally, with an option to extend for another 14 years. Authors' interests were important, but the public interest was vital as well, hence the limitation. Unending monopolies would have failed to promote progress because science and the useful arts would have been locked down. The creation and growth of culture is a public good that requires encouragement.

Several problems exist with copyright law—problems that have been aggravated by technology and time. The Copyright Act of 1976 was an attempt to bring copyright in line with technological developments of its day, such as television, photocopiers, and recording devices. Reform was then driven by corporate interests, particularly those with large copyright holdings. Taking effect in 1978, the revised law granted longer protection for works and stronger penalties for infringement. Works were protected from the moment of their creation; there was a single longer term for all new works; renewal was no longer a necessity; registration was no longer required; the copyright notice was no longer required (Aufderheide & Jaszi, 2011). Some of these changes may have seemed innocuous, but among their long-term effects have been the creation of orphan works and all problems related to them (McDermott, 2012). After the law took effect, no effort was necessary to acquire copyright, unlike the trademark or patent process, both of which ask the entity hoping to benefit from the rights to do considerable work. Because of the efforts of educators and libraries, however, legislators recognized the need to protect fair use and incorporated it into the law (Aufderheide & Jaszi, 2011).

As copyright has expanded, it has come to be viewed as a property right, esteemed more and more for its economic value alone. Never mind public culture; property rights are absolute. From this perspective, limitations like fair use are akin to taxes or subsidies taken from the copyright holder (Boyle, 2008). Copyrighted properties also are inheritable. Terms can be so long that control over works will likely fall into the hands of grandchildren, who may not even have been alive when the works were created. A particular problem is that heirs may choose to suppress works for any reason, including the desire to protect a forebear's image in the case of controversial material, a dislike of the work, the belief that they are the experts regarding the family member, or the feeling that somehow they are being cheated by someone. Some art historians of the author's acquaintance have dealt with just such a situation. They became the latest in a line of scholars attempting to study the work of a deceased 20th century American architect to find themselves stymied by offspring hoarding the parent's papers in a garage. It is not a climate-controlled garage either.

Excessive terms were accompanied by excessive damages ranging from $750 to $150,000 per work infringed. Material is under copyright longer, requiring permissions and the creating fear of infringement for longer periods of time. The potential for damages frightens most people from taking any risks involving copyrighted material, even when the material could be used fairly. The number of people facing potential lawsuits is increasing as the number of copyrighted works increases.

Since 1976, there have been legislative attempts to adjust copyright law to the digital world. The aforementioned TEACH Act was one such patch, and the Digital Millennium Copyright Act of 1998 (DMCA) another. Where the TEACH Act was an effort to expand access through fair use, however, the intent of the DMCA was to limit access. The DMCA made tampering with digital rights management software illegal and criminalized the sale of circumvention technologies (McDermott, 2012). DMCA forbade the circumvention of such copyright protections as encryption or password protection and imposed limits on what can be done with a file once it has been accessed—"the digital equivalent of barbed wire" (Boyle, 2008, p.86). While the act of copying a file may be legal according to fair use, breaking through any digital rights management technology that prevents that copying is forbidden (McDermott, 2012).

Another 1998 amendment was the Sonny Bono Copyright Extension Act, which established the copyright terms of the life of the author plus seventy years, or ninety-five years for works for hire (Copyright Extension Act, 1998). Even this is a simplification. See Cornell's web-based chart, "Copyright Term and the Public Domain in the United States," for every possible iteration of terms (Cornell Copyright Information Center, 2013).

Protecting the interests of publishers has increased at the expense of the public domain and even many authors. The point should be made that those who fight the hardest against fair use often try to garner sympathy for their cause by claiming they are only protecting authors. Cambridge, Oxford, and Sage did just that in their appeal of the Georgia State decision (Howard, 2012). Copyright holders are often corporations. Many authors sign their rights away. Some, such as academic authors facing a publish-or-perish situation, do so knowingly, valuing publication in a journal and the potential to be cited more than a monopoly on their work. This is unfortunate as "much scholarly work, work created for a social benefit and usually with costs underwritten by taxpayers, is turned over gratis into the hands of commercial entities. And those entities have proven that they will not shrink from fundamental attacks on teaching and research in order to squeeze every penny they can from that work" (Smith, 2013a).

Authors engaged in creative endeavors also have fallen into untenable situations with publishers. A current situation finds the first publisher going out of business and selling the contracts to a second publisher. The second publisher rewrites the newly purchased contracts, reserving 90% of the net sales for itself and 10% for the authors. The catch is if too few of the bartered authors agree to the new contract, the second publisher will declare bankruptcy, thus locking all the authors' books into legal limbo and preventing the authors from reprinting, selling adaptation rights, or writing sequels to their works until the bankruptcy is resolved (Foglio & Foglio, 2013).

In addition, the whole work-for-hire concept is an issue emerging from the Copyright Act of 1976. Most works for hire are produced by employees in fulfillment of their employment. Other works for hire may be contracted works, provided the contractor and the employer agree that the work is for hire. Oxford University Press (one of the plaintiffs against Georgia State) has begun requiring that authors contributing to their Handbooks sign a work-for-hire agreement. All rights then defer to the publisher, with none at all for the person who actually put fingers to keyboard (Shaviro, 2012). Typically, colleges and universities have not claimed work-for-hire rights over the scholarly output of their faculties, and they seem unlikely to risk inciting a faculty revolt by making such claims (Smith, 2012b). But with online instruction as a potential moneymaker, who knows what cash-strapped educational institutions may decide to try. Just this year, a school board in Maryland attempted to "claim copyright on the original creations of students as well as teachers" at an elementary school (Sainer, 2013). The hypothetical six-year-old artist is no joke.

Examples of more traditional work for hire are evidenced in Marvel Comics' Avengers. As a group, the Avengers have appeared in comic books since 1963 with a rotating membership that expands and contracts according to the need of the story. Some of the characters pre-date the first appearance of the Avengers, a few by decades; many others have been added over the half a century of the Avengers' existence. Some of the characters also support stand-alone series, but any and all of the characters, series, and stories could interconnect at any time. Some creators have agitated against the work-for-hire status with the publishers, but the Avengers are a corporate property. The Marvel Comics Universe, with its editors, writers, artists, colorists, letterers, inkers, gofers, and fans, was a crowdsourced creation before people knew what crowdsourcing was. With recent film productions, add to that the work of performers, directors, special-effects artists, and filmmakers of all sorts. All of the pieces are works for hire. Who is responsible for the creation of the Avengers? Better to ask, who profits?

Looking Forward

What brings comic book superheroes into a discussion of copyright issues in higher education? The reason is that any copyright laws rewritten in the future will be written to protect the likes of the Avengers and their fellows. Librarians and educators should never forget that as important as fair use is for academics, it pales before the economic value of popular culture icons. Something like fair use is likely to be trampled to death in the rush to lock in continued exclusive rights to the world's mightiest heroes, unless someone is willing to stand up for it. Compared to the copyrighted and trademarked properties of Disney, Time Warner, and other media giants, even the products of the scholarly publishers that loom large in the academic world are rather small.

Fair use is already under assault. David Shulenberger considers the Georgia State case just such an example, "part of an undeclared war on academic fair use" (What's at Stake, 2011). The large media companies, with the most valuable copyrighted content, hold "that the very notion of private fair use disappears on the Internet" (Aufderheide & Jaszi, 2011, p.19). Expect the assaults to continue. The courts seem willing to rule for fair use, and as James Grimmelmann wrote regarding the HathiTrust decision, the year was "a very good one for universities putting copyrighted materials online for their students" (2012). However, the job of the courts is to apply the law as it exists. Laws can be changed.

Copyright law needs revision, but it needs wholesale revision, not just patchwork. The current law is not merely outdated. It has grown unbalanced, supporting certain kinds of rights while abridging others that are just as valid. The digital culture of reuse and remix has complicated matters. Take, for example, pinning, posting, liking, and sharing; in the pre-digital world, this sort of behavior caused no concern. On the open web, activities that had been private and personal have become public and could become actionable when copyrighted material is involved. There is a need to rein in "copyright laws to ensure that more of what we value doing with digital culture is legal and to expand rights to reuse and remix copyrighted works in non-commercial contexts" (Karaganis, 2013). Copyright is out of control; it does not need strengthening. As Barbara Fister says, "There is no lack of copyright. There is, in fact, far too much in the way of restrictions" (Unlocking the Riches, 2013).

Although recent attempts to address specific concepts such as orphan works failed to garner enough support for Congress to pass legislation (Albanese, 2013), there is some possibility for change in the future. Register of Copyrights Maria Pallante has urged a total revision of copyright law (Pallante, 2013a; Pallante, 2013b). One of her recommendations is a reduction in term, but she also calls for stronger enforcement (Masnick, 2013b). In addition to the Pallante's efforts, there have even been some sparks of bipartisan interest regarding copyright reform (Goodlatte, 2013).

Unfortunately, copyright-watchers fear that Pallante's interpretation of copyright too often overlooks the public good and hews too closely to that of corporate interests (Masnick, 2013b; Masnick, 2013c). She is not alone. Industry lawyers and lobbyists supply government officials with most of their information about copyright (Smith, 2013a). Legislators on both sides of the aisle are likewise inclined to lean toward industry. Recent Congressional hearings on copyright reform illustrate problems with legislators misunderstanding the Constitution's actual words about copyright and the promotion of progress, suggesting that technology is the enemy of copyright and emphasizing the needs of certain classes of copyright holders (Masnick, 2013a).

Laws designed to strengthen the rights of copyright holders have proceeded out of Congress without much excitement since the 1970s. That is, until the Stop Online Piracy Act caused millions of agitated voters to call their representatives in protest, bringing to an abrupt end any sort of legislation to strengthen copyright. Post-SOPA, legislators seemed hesitant to do much else, the fear of constituents having had its effect, at least in 2012 (Lee, 2013). Likewise, consumer resistance to digital rights management has affected corporate behavior, but "since so much of the pressure to limit personal fair use comes from business practice, the continued resistance of consumers to limiting their personal fair use will continue to be important" (Aufderheide & Jaszi, 2011, p.19).

Cambridge University Press v. Mark P. Becker, Authors Guild Inc. v. HathiTrust, AIME v. UCLA, and *Kirtsaeng v. Wiley* were not the first cases about copyright limitations and copyright infringement, and they will not be the last. Coming conflicts over access to copyrighted material are just as likely to revolve around licensing, trade, and technological monitoring. K. Matthew Dames actually takes a jaundiced view of the future of copyright itself. Setting the recent court wins against the ability of licenses to override copyright, the establishment of the Digital Millennium Copyright Act, the growth of global media conglomerates, and global standardization of U.S. copyright law by trade process, he views licensing and open access as the future battlegrounds, whether the battle comes in the courts or in Congress (2012).

Overall, what do these cases and laws mean for academic librarians? Regarding the cases, librarians can feel more at ease when it comes to creating copies for the visually impaired and for preservation as well as when posting material in courseware and electronic reserves, as long as the four elements of fair use have been applied.

The increasingly complicated copyright law has had greater impact on academic librarians. Because of it, librarians have defaulted to being the campus "de facto copyright expert[s]" (McDermott, 2012, p.11), whether trained as such or not. While some university libraries may be large enough to have a copyright librarian, most are too small for such specialization. Even in large libraries, most copyright management typically falls to the interlibrary loan staff or the reserves staff (Hansen, Cross, & Edwards, 2013). Sadly, unless they are specialists, many academic librarians can be far too passive when it comes to providing copyright information. Librarians comply with what the law requires by ensuring that signs are up and notices are affixed, and they may mount web pages that are typically a tedious collection of links and legalese. Every library need not duplicate such sites as the one belonging to the Columbia University Library Science/Information Services Copyright Advisory Office (http://copyright.columbia.edu/copyright/), to name a particularly useful resource for keeping up with news about copyright lawsuits and other issues. What a library should do is take into account the needs, degrees of understanding, and purposes of its users and develop their pages accordingly.

More aggressive educational efforts are needed—librarians need to learn more, and, possessed of knowledge, they need to provide more useful information to faculty and students. When faculty come to a library for an answer to a copyright question, the answer too often devolves into don't. And while don't may be the correct answer in many cases, there also may be legal options that librarians fail to explain due to either a lack of knowledge or a fear of infringement, residing as they do in what Aufderheide and Jaszi call a "culture of fear and doubt" (2011, p. 1).

It will become more necessary for librarians to explain infringement and fair use to faculty and students because both infringement and fair use are part of copyright. Being able to explain copyright law and its challenges is also important because copyright affects faculty, students, and library patrons alike, both in their use of copyrighted material and in their creation of copyrighted material. Not just users, they are makers and copyright holders themselves, and they need information to manage their work and activities in this digital world.

References

Albanese, A. (2012a, December 3). Appeal Filings Outline Authors Guild's Objections to HathiTrust Opinion. Publishers Weekly. Retrieved from http://www.publishersweekly.com/pw/by-topic/digital/copyright/article/54982-appeal-filings-outline-authors-guild-s-objections-to-hathi-trust-opinion.html

Albanese, A. (2012b, November 14). Authors Guild Appeals Loss in Book Scanning Case. Publishers Weekly. Retrieved from http://www.publishersweekly.com/pw/by-topic/digital/copyright/article/54748-authors-guild-appeals-loss-in-book-scanning-case.html

Albanese, A. (2012c, August 13). Final Order in GSU E-Reserves Case Is a Rebuke to Publishers. Publishers Weekly. Retrieved from http://www.publishersweekly.com/pw/by-topic/digital/copyright/article/53543-final-order-in-gsu-e-reserves-case-is-a-rebuke-to-publishers.html

Albanese, A. (2012d, June 24). What's the Impact of the GSU E-Reserve Decision? ALA Panel Says None...Yet. Publishers Weekly. Retrieved from http://www.publishersweekly.com/pw/by-topic/digital/copyright/article/52743-what-s-the-impact-of-the-gsu-e-reserve-decision-ala-panel-says-none-yet.html

Albanese, A. (2013, March 8). Orphan Works Legislation Appears Unlikely. Publishers Weekly. Retrieved from http://www.publishersweekly.com/pw/by-topic/digital/copyright/article/56265-following-copyright-office-inquiry-orphan-works-legislation-appears-unlikely.html

Association for Information Media & Equipment, et al., v. the Regents of the University of California, et al. (U.S. Dist. C.D. Cal. 2011). Retrieved from http://newsroom.ucla.edu/portal/ucla/document/UCLA_Streaming_Video_Ruling.pdf

Aufderheide, P., & Jaszi, P. (2011). Reclaiming Fair Use: How to Put Balance Back in Copyright. Chicago: University of Chicago Press.

Authors Guild Inc., et al., against Hathi-Trust, et al. 902 F. Supp 2d 445, (S.D. N.Y. 2012). Retrieved from https://www.eff.org/sites/default/files/HathiTrust%20decision%20copy%202.pdf

Before the Court in Kirtsaeng v. Wiley: The Justices Weigh in on Copyright Law. (2012). Supreme Court Debates, 15(9), 42-45. Retrieved from http://ezproxy.cbu.edu:9000/login?url=http://search.ebscohost.com/login.aspx?direct=true&db=aph&AN=83651251&site=ehost-live&scope=site

Boyle, J. (2008). The Public Domain: Enclosing the Commons of the Mind. New Haven & London: Yale University Press. Cambridge University Press, et al., v. Mark P. Becker, et al. 863 F. Supp. 2d 1190, (N.D. Ga. 2012). Retrieved from http://blogs.library.duke.edu/scholcomm/files/2012/08/Order-for-relief-GSU.pdf

Copyright Act of 1976, 17 U.S.C. Retrieved from http://www.copyright.gov/title17/ Cornell Copyright Information Center. (2013). Copyright Term and the Public Domain in the United States, 1 Janaury 2013. Retrieved March 8, 2013, from http://copyright.cornell.edu/resources/docs/copyrightterm.pdf

Crews, K. (2011). Authors, Copyright, and HathiTrust. Retrieved June 7, 2013, from http://copyright.columbia.edu/copyright/2011/09/13/authors-copyright-and-hathitrust/

Crews, K. (2012). Court Rules on Hathi-Trust and Fair Use. Retrieved June 2, 2013, from http://copyright.columbia.edu/copyright/2012/10/11/court-rules-on-hathitrust-and-fair-use/

Crews, K. (2013). The Kirtsaeng Decision: Copyright, Logic, and Libraries. Retrieved May 30, 2013, from http://copyright.columbia.edu/copyright/2012/10/11/court-rules-on-hathitrust-and-fair-use/

Dames, K. M. (2012). The Copyright Game Is Over. Information Today, 29(11), 24-24. Retrieved from http://search.ebscohost.com/login.aspx?direct=true&db=aph&AN=83776050&site=ehost-live&scope=site;

DeSantis, N. (2013, July 1). Court Blocks Authors' Class Certification in Google Book-Scanning Case [Web log post]. Message posted to http://chronicle.com/blogs/ticker/court-blocks-authors-class-certification-in-google-book-scanning-case/62407

Dougherty, W. C. (2010). The Copyright Quagmire. Journal of Academic Librarianship, 36(4), 351-353. doi:10.1016/j.acalib.2010.05.020

Foglio, P., & Foglio, K. (2013). Publish & Perish. Girl Genius Adventures: The Latest News from Phil & Kaja Foglio, 2013(April 4), 4/16/13. Retrieved from http://girlgeniusadventures.com/2013/04/04/publish-perish/

Goodlatte, B. (2013). Chairman Goodlatte Announces Comprehensive Review of Copyright Law Retrieved June 15, 2013, from http://judiciary.house.gov/news/2013/04242013_2.html

Grimmelmann, J. (2012, October 13). HathiTrust: A Landmark Copyright Ruling [Web log post]. Message posted to http://blogs.publishersweekly.com/blogs/PWxyz/2012/10/13/hathitrust-a-landmark-copyright-ruling/

Hansen, D. R., Cross, W. M., & Edwards, P. M. (2013). Copyright Policy and Practice in Electronic Reserves among ARL Libraries. College & Research Libraries, 74(1), 69-84. Retrieved from http://crl.acrl.org/content/74/1/69.full.pdf+html

HathiTrust Digital Library. (2013). Information about the Authors Guild Lawsuit. Retrieved June 20, 2013, from http://www.hathitrust.org/authors_guild_lawsuit_information

Howard, J. (2012, September 10). Publishers Will Appeal E-ReservesDecision that Favored Georgia State U [Web log post]. Message posted to http://chronicle.com/blogs/wiredcampus/publishers-will-appeal-e-reserves-decision-that-favored-georgia-state-u/39732

Karaganis, J. (2013). Copyright For the Internet Age. National Review, 65(3), 20-22. Retrieved from http://search.ebscohost.com/login.aspx?direct=true&db=aph&AN=85336633&site=ehost-live&scope=site

Lee, T. B. (2013, Janaury 7). Still smarting from SOPA, Congress to shy away from copyright in 2013 [Web log post]. Message posted to http://arstechnica.com/tech-policy/2013/01/still-smarting-from-sopa-congress-to-shy-away-from-copyright-in-2013/

Masnick, M. (2013a, May 17). A Framework for Copyright Reform [Web log post]. Message posted to http://www.techdirt.com/articles/20130516/15445423110/framework-copyright-reform.shtml

Masnick, M. (2013b, March 15). More Details On Copyright Office's Suggestions On Copyright Reform; Some Good, Some Bad [Web log post]. Message posted to http://www.techdirt.com/articles/20130315/14043322341/more-details-copyright-offices-suggestions-copyright-reform-some-good-some-bad.shtml

Masnick, M. (2013c, March 18). More Details On Copyright Register Maria Pallante's Call For Comprehensive, 'Forward-Thinking, But Flexible' Copyright Reform [Web log post]. Message posted to http://www.techdirt.com/articles/20130318/11114922368/more-details-copyright-register-maria-pallantes-call-comprehensive-forward-thinking-flexible-copyright-reform.shtml

McDermott, A. J. (2012). Copyright: Regulation Out of Line with Our Digital Reality? Information Technology & Libraries, 31(1), 7-20. Retrieved from http://search.ebscohost.com/login.aspx?direct=true&db=aph&AN=76373083&site=ehost-live&scope=site

Nelson, E. (2009). Copyright and Distance Education: The Impact of the Technology, Education, and Copyright Harmonization Act. AACE Journal, 17(2), 83-101. Retrieved from http://www.editlib.org/p/27053

Pallante, M. A. (2013a). The Next Great Copyright Act. Paper presented at the Twenty-Sixth Horace S. Manges Lecture, Columbia University, Columbia Law School. Retrieved from http://www.copyright.gov/docs/next_great_copyright_act.pdf

Pallante, M.A. (2013b). The Register's Call for Updates to U.S. Copyright Law: Subcommittee on Courts, Intellectual Property and the Internet, United States House of Representatives, 113th Congress, 1st Session. Retrieved from http://www.copyright.gov/regstat/2013/regstat03202013.html

Pike, G. H. (2010). Copyright: A Partial Victory for Georgia State. Information Today, 27(10), 1-14. Retrieved from http://ezproxy.cbu.edu:9000/login?url=http://search.ebscohost.com/login.aspx?direct=true&db=aph&AN=55014488&site=ehost-live&scope=site

Pike, G. H. (2011, September 12). Orphan Works Project to Scan Library Books for Online Database. Newsbreaks, Information Today. Retrieved from http://newsbreaks.infotoday.com/NewsBreaks/Orphan-Works-Project-to-Scan-Library-Books-for-Online-Database-77583.asp

Pike, G. H. (2012). The Verdict in the GSU Case. Information Today, 29(7), 10-10. Retrieved from http://ezproxy.cbu.edu:9000/login?url=http://search.ebscohost.com/login.aspx?direct=true&db=aph&AN=77596768&site=ehost-live&scope=site

Sainer, G. (2013, February 21). Prince George's County Schools' Copyright Conundrum [Web log post]. Message posted to http://watchdogwire.com/maryland/2013/02/21/prince-georges-county-schools-copyright-conundrum/

Shaviro, S. (2012, January 22). Work for Hire update [Web log post]. Message posted to http://www.shaviro.com/Blog/?p=1030

Smith, K. (2011, May 13). A nightmare scenario for higher education [Web log post]. Message posted to http://blogs.library.duke.edu/scholcomm/2011/05/13/a-nightmare-scenario-for-higher-education/

Smith, K. (2012a, November 26). Another fair use victory for libraries [Web log post]. Message posted to http://blogs.library.duke.edu/scholcomm/2012/11/26/another-fair-use-victory-for-libraries/

Smith, K. (2012b, January 25). Who do you work for, faculty author? [Web log post]. Message posted to http://blogs.library.duke.edu/scholcomm/2012/01/25/who-do-you-work-for-faculty-author/

Smith, K. (2013a, February 4). Law and politics in the GSU case [Web log post]. Message posted to http://blogs.library.duke.edu/scholcomm/2013/02/04/law-and-politics-in-the-gsu-case/

Smith, K. (2013b, May 29). Time for breakfast at the 11th Circuit [Web log post]. Message posted to http://blogs.library.duke.edu/scholcomm/2013/05/29/time-for-breakfast-at-the-11th-circuit/

Sonny Bono Copyright Term Extension Act, Pub, L. No. 105-298, (1998). Retrieved from http://thomas.loc.gov/cgi-bin/bdquery/z?d105:S505:

Supap Kirtsaeng, d/b/a Bluechristine99, Petitioner v. John Wiley & Sons, Inc., 133 S. Ct. 469 (2013). Retrieved from http://www.supremecourt.gov/opinions/12pdf/11-697_4g15.pdf

Technology, Education, and Copyright Harmonization, Pub. L. No. 107-273, (2002). Retrieved from http://thomas.loc.gov/cgi-bin/bdquery/z?d107:H.R.2215:

Unlocking the Riches of HathiTrust. (2013, January/February). American Libraries Magazine. Retrieved from http://www.americanlibrariesmagazine.org/article/unlocking-riches-hathitrust

What's at Stake in the Georgia State Copyright Case? - The Chronicle Review. (2011, May 30). Chronicle of Higher Education. Retrieved from http://chronicle.com/article/Whats-at-Stake-in-the-Georgia/127718/

Virtually Yours: Online Embedded Librarianship in Higher Education

Denise Landry-Hyde[1], Laureen P. Cantwell[2]

While embedded librarianship has been in existence within higher education settings for quite some time, the proliferation of online learning opportunities and e-courseware products has generated an increase in options for librarian engagement in higher education coursework and course platforms. In online settings, faculty members, students, and librarians can engage in new ways, with exciting technologies, and using innovative strategies. The literature review included here provides readers with a wealth of readings to increase their familiarity with this topic. This article discusses the process of "embedding" a librarian (individually and institutionally); best practices for the use of technology in embedded settings; the management, readiness assessment, marketing, promotion, and evaluation of embedded librarianship and its efforts; and the value of collaboration within this environment. Additionally, the authors share a variety of web-based tools suitable for embedded collaborations, broken into four categories: digital learning object repository tools, content management tools, remote storage and collaboration tools, and synchronous and asynchronous learning and engagement tools. A brief discussion on the future of embedded librarianship in higher education concludes this article.

Keywords: embedded librarianship; online learning; e-learning; distance learning; instructional technologies; higher education; open access; information literacy.

Virtually Yours: Online Embedded Librarianship in Higher Education

Increasingly, academic librarians are teaching and supporting online students who they will never see face-to-face. As a result, librarians must use technological tools to reach those students in meaningful ways and to create a presence virtually when face-to-face encounters are not possible. Use of web–based tools, including social media, enables librarians to embed in e-learning communities.

The focus of this paper is on librarians embedding online. There are different definitions of embeddedness—no one size fits all. Jezmynne Dene (2011) succinctly defines embedded librarianship as "an integral part to the whole based on the geological definition of an embedded element" (p. 225). David Shumaker's definition, as noted by Jenny Dale and Lynda Kellam (2012), also captures the essence stating, "Embedded librarianship involves the delivery of highly customized and highly valued information and knowledge services to a customer group with well-defined needs" (p. 30). The factors that define embedded

---

[1] Reference/Distributed Learning Librarian at Texas A&M University-Corpus Christi. Correspondence regarding this article should be directed to Denise at Denise.Hyde@tamucc.edu or (361) 825-2608.
[2] Instructional Services Librarian at the University of Memphis.

librarianship, according to Shumaker (2012), are relationship, shared goals, and customized, high-value contributions (p. 6). The differences between traditional and embedded librarianship are anticipatory, in the case of embedded librarianship, as opposed to responsive in traditional librarianship; a team of collaborators versus the individual customer; customized versus standardized; ongoing projects versus single transactions; and partnership versus service. In short, librarians are in the midst of a redefinition of their relationships with their communities and embedded librarianship is a name given to this change (Shumaker, 2012, p. 13).

Background and Literature Review

Collaborations between a librarian and a learning community are unique. The types of services provided are customized and based on the needs of the particular group. A community can be a class, an academic department or program, a student organization, and so on. In higher education, embedded librarianship seems to have originated with liaison librarians working with and supporting subject- or discipline-specific students and faculty (Dale & Kellam, 2012, p. 30). The term "embedded librarian" was borrowed from the "embedded journalist" idea that came into use during the invasion of Iraq (Dewey, 2004, p. 6). Embedded journalists are deployed with troops; their goal is to report on what they witness, not to take part in the events they observe. Embedded librarians, on the other hand, actively engage with their user communities. They teach information literacy skills, frequently geared to specific assignments (Dale & Kellam, 2012, p. 31) at the "need-to-know" time. Often, librarians are able to work with faculty in developing assignments or even create assignments themselves. Librarians who are embedded in course management systems (CMSs) actively participate in online classes. This can take a number of different forms, such as participating in discussion boards, providing LibGuides, instructional videos, assignments, and other digital learning objects for use in class. These materials can be linked to or embedded in the CMS.

Embedded librarianship also has roots in the healthcare field of the 1960s when librarians accompanied doctors and nurses on their hospital rounds (Shumaker, 2012, p. xiii). Medical librarians lead the way and have done outstanding work in this area. David Shumaker, author of The Embedded Librarian, Innovative Strategies for Taking Knowledge Where It's Needed, spent more than three years studying embedded librarianship programs on behalf of the Special Libraries Association, from which he received a grant to carry out his research. As Janice Lachance, CEO of the Special Libraries Association, states in the Foreword to Shumaker's book (2012), Shumaker makes a case for "a model of librarianship based on community, flexibility, accountability, relevance, and responsibility" (p. xiv). He visited a number of organizations with embedded librarianship programs, conducted interviews and focus groups with librarians and their user communities, and made his own observations.

Liaison librarians were frequently associated with specialized branch libraries. Margaret Feetham (2006) dated the origins of subject specialist librarians to the University College London in the early 1900s (p. 3-17). Within a few decades, these librarians were well-established in Great Britain and the United States. Rudasill (2010) noted that reference, instruction, and cataloging, in addition to collection development, were sometimes included in the duties of subject librarians (p. 83).

The literature indicates that the primary focus of embedded librarianship at colleges and universities is the instruction mission. In his book, Shumaker (2012) provides, in table format, an extensive inventory of the embedded information literacy instruction programs described in the English-language professional literature from 2000 to 2011 (p. 49-50). Full citations to those publications can be found in the Recommended Reading list on his blog (http://www.embeddedlibrarian.com).

Shank and Dewald (2003) talk about micro and macro embedded information literacy instruction (p. 38-43). As discussed by Shumaker (2012), micro involves collaboration between librarians and faculty that results in customized instruction for each course (p. 51). Macro involves the creation of a more or less standardized library web presence that can be linked to or embedded in any course.

Hemmig and Montet (2010) highlight that interactivity is critical for a successful embedded librarian presence in online teaching (p. 668). This includes interaction between librarians and online learning staff, between librarians and faculty, and, in particular, between librarians and online students.

For two-year community colleges, the teaching mission of the institutions is their focus. The primary contributions of librarians are in information literacy instruction. However, in institutions that grant bachelor's degrees as well as graduate and professional degrees, research and service are also expected. The literature indicates, though, that teaching is the primary focus for embedded librarians at these institutions, also. There is a huge diversity of embedded information literacy instruction in higher education (Shumaker, 2012, p. 48-49).

In some cases, librarians are full partners with subject faculty in that they create syllabi together, design research assignments that include the use of information literacy skills, share teaching responsibilities, and even collaborate in grading papers. In other cases, the librarian is more of an "addition" to the course, rather than a full partner. This might include teaching one or more sessions, attending classes, and setting up consultations with students to help in their research. In other instances, instruction is delivered through standardized, self-paced modules (Shumaker, 2012, p. 51).

Strategically, librarians can participate in university-level curriculum development teams and work with faculty to identify the most appropriate places in the curriculum in which to embed information literacy instruction.

Best Practices in Embedded Instruction Technology

Shumaker (2012) makes the critical recommendation that librarians should use the same technology that instructors and students are using for other course activities (p. 53). If librarians do not use these same technologies, it is less likely that students or faculty will utilize librarians' contributions. Course management systems, for example, are being used increasingly in blended and face-to-face instruction, as well as in distance learning. Librarians must have a presence in this venue in order to be most effective in information literacy instruction.

Management

Since embedded librarianship can quickly become a 24/7 proposition, it is essential that library management be supportive of staff involvement in embedded instruction and that librarians set parameters on when they will be available to students and faculty. It is important to recognize this from the very beginning. Staff may have to spend less time at the service point or in other activities so that more time can be allocated to a librarian's research and consultation commitments. Students in classes who have embedded librarians usually contact their "designated" or "assigned" librarian for assistance.

Collaboration with Faculty

Hoffman and Ramin (2010), in particular, recognized the need for active collaboration with faculty. Having a very clear understanding of the embedded librarian's role in the class is critical to its success. At Texas A&M University-Corpus Christi, the embedded librarian in select Nursing classes has a BlackBoard-based "Library Corner" discussion board to which she can post recommendations to students, as well as respond to their library and research-related questions. At the University of Memphis, librarians embedded in University College senior capstone courses have an "Ask the Librarian" discussion board. This posting area was initially placed at the bottom of the list of course discussion boards but, as of the Summer 2012-2013 session, was relocated to the top of that list so that students would not miss this valuable discussion board, which is otherwise organized chronologically for course assignments and weekly discussions.

Faculty members have substantial power to dictate the terms of librarian involvement in an online course. Thomsett-Scott and May (2009) note this fact in their article "How May We Help You? Online Education Faculty Tell Us What They Need from Libraries and Librarians." Useful library and librarian contributions to online courses are listed in Table 3 of the article (p. 118). The top three contributions students perceived were providing library resources, offering instruction on using databases and indexes, and (tied for third) offering information literacy development assistance and providing useful databases. Table 6 (p. 121) indicates common areas of student difficulty with information and resource use, as reported by surveyed faculty members. Overall, student lack of awareness as to what tools and resources should be utilized for their assignment was a significant, recurring, and telling concern on behalf of faculty members.

Additionally, Thomsett-Scott and May's surveying highlights several impacts upon students when they do not plan ahead or take assignments seriously (p. 121). Among these reported issues are ill-timed interlibrary loan (ILL) or distance student item delivery requests; lack of time to prepare, learn resources, and/or ask questions of their human resources. Surveying also illuminated the fact that, when faculty are unaware of or feel unable to effectively utilize critical library resources, their students are then at a disadvantage, as faculty may not be able to make appropriate or effective recommendations at the point-of-need. These critical library resources will include ILL, chat, one-on-one research consultations, library-developed online tutorials, and much more. Embedded librarians have key opportunities to view discussion boards, have their own virtual consultation space(s), and voice suggestions that take a certain amount of pressure and stress off the shoulders of instructors while not interfering with course content.

When faculty members express student skill weaknesses or their own areas of unfamiliarity with library services, ask for updates on holdings and research tools, and make inquiries as to how their online course environment might be improved for their students, librarians are presented with an opportunity to lend support and tailored services throughout an entire course or assignment. Without faculty voices in this discussion, librarians can only hope students will visit the libraries in person or virtually and that the student can express the kind of assistance they need if and when they do reach out to a librarian.

Readiness Assessment

Shumaker (2012) notes that assessments of readiness must be done for the librarian and also for the organization (p. 128-131). The two are not the same. Elements of the librarian's readiness include:

- having the necessary skill sets;
- knowledge of the subject area of users;
- understanding the political and organizational context; and
- motivation in establishing strong, collaborative, working relationships with user groups.

On the other hand, elements of organizational readiness include:

- support of executive champions,
- good mid-management relationships between the library manager and the user-group managers,
- enthusiastic library users respected among their peers and managers (these users can help light the spark for the program), and
- management culture that encourages innovation and experimentation and that supports delegation and autonomy at the middle and lower organizational levels (Shumaker, 2012, p. 128).

A statement from Shumaker (2012) rings true: "Innovation gets weighed down with reviews and approvals until it grinds to a halt" (p. 131). It is critical to have an organizational climate that encourages pilot projects and reasonable, well-thought-out risk taking in getting efforts such as this underway.

Marketing and Promotion

The importance of word-of-mouth publicity cannot be overstated. If a few members of the user group are receptive to the idea of embedded librarianship and appreciate what that service can offer, chances are those individuals will communicate successes to peers. Presenting at new employee orientations is another way to reach out to communities. Emphasize the benefits of the service to potential customers—the "What's in it for me?" principle (Shumaker, 2012, p. 167).

Specifically in regard to virtual librarianship and embedded work, the authors suggest reading Veal and Bennett's (2009) "The Virtual Library Liaison: A Case Study at an Online University," where several key elements of librarian involvement in the virtual classroom are addressed, including collaboration in the course development process, reference or research assistance transactions, course content review, and more. Not only are these important terms librarians can use when marketing opportunities and options to faculty, but these are also key phrases that faculty can use in word-of-mouth suggestions to other faculty members— particularly in cases where a faculty member has indicated a need for certain kinds of assistance or noted particular types of assignments. Another faculty member could easily suggest reaching out to and/or collaborating with a librarian to aid in their student outcomes and retention rates, and other course-related points of assessment. Tenure-track faculty might be especially interested in efficient and effective collaborations, to raise retention and enhance evaluations.

E-mailing instructors before each term reminding them that embedded librarians are available and can assist students in their research, teach information literacy skills, and help students in completing assignments may spark interest. Timing of the message is crucial. When faculty are working on syllabi and planning their courses is the time to remind them of embedded librarian services—not at the beginning of the semester when things are most hectic.

Delivery of Value-Added Services

According to Shumaker (2012), the definition of "value-added" is constantly changing, so librarians' work must change, as well. Management writers such as Thomas Friedman and Daniel Pink have voiced similar concepts, as quoted by Shumaker, "What can be automated, will be. What can be outsourced or 'offshored' will be" (p. 170).

Librarians must first understand the needs of their users, and then employ their specialized skills to meet those needs. In higher education, different models of information literacy instruction have been used from highly customized classes to online, self-paced tutorials. Librarians have served as team members on curriculum development committees and have been able to influence the incorporation of information literacy learning objectives and instruction into the most appropriate areas of the curriculum (Shumaker, 2012, p. 171). Librarians have also helped to establish data management plans in fulfillment of National Science Foundation (NSF) grant requirements. They have helped spread the word about open access publication and alternatives to traditional forms of scholarly communication.

In the medical world, Kacy Allgood, an embedded librarian with Indiana University's School of Medicine's Department of Emergency Medicine, provides information services to the Indianapolis Emergency Medical Services (EMS). Known as the "ambulance riding librarian" (http://www.ambulanceridinglibrarian.com/), Allgood exhibits the lengths to which librarians will go to support their communities of users, and her role highlights the resourcefulness and creativity institutions and organizations can employ for the benefit of their constituencies and stakeholders.

Another aspect of "value-added" efforts would benefit library science students. Faculty members of all disciplines should be cognizant of and perhaps sympathetic to the need for experience among students within graduate schools. Institutions using adjuncts and PhD candidates as course instructors, now legion, may find those groups of faculty members especially welcoming to library science students having (supervised or unsupervised) opportunities to instruct library sessions, especially at lower levels in the curriculum or in general education required courses. Lillard, Norwood, Wise, Brooks, and Kitts (2009) use this concept in their article "Embedded Librarians: MLS Students as Apprentice Librarians in Online Courses." Such opportunities provide the Master of Library Science (MLS) candidate with a number of marketable skills, including: critical "relationship management techniques" (p. 12-13), experience with apprentice, mentor/mentee, and/or team-based instruction, and real-world understanding of the real and user-created barriers to student-librarian contact in embedded settings. Additionally, MLS candidates gain valuable wisdom about what users feel would be useful to have and whether users use the requested service(s) enough to substantiate adequate return on investment.

Another strong point of the Lillard, Norwood, Wise, Brooks, and Kitts (2009) article is the fact that this program has been implemented several times, in several environments, at several institutions, with a variety of results. This holds importance for faculty and librarians because groups of students differ, and thus users differ, instructors (and their goals) differ, and pedagogy and technology change over time. Continuous experimentation and evaluation are key elements in developing, understanding, and tweaking an embedded program or relationship, and in predicting what will best set up an effort for success in the future.

Continuing Evaluation and Communication of Evaluation Results

Different measures may be used in evaluating programs: counts of activities, such as numbers of reference questions answered and numbers of documents delivered; anecdotes about the impact of services, and outcome and impact metrics. If information literacy can be shown to improve student academic performance by, for example, raising the caliber of references in research papers, that measure shows impact of the program. More and more emphasis is being placed on accountability in education generally, and in higher education particularly, so learning outcomes and impact metrics should be used. Course management systems keep track of the number of logins and the number of postings made by each student in a course. A university tracking system could be used to compare the academic performance of students enrolled in courses with embedded librarians with that of students who are not enrolled in such courses, as long as privacy concerns are taken into account (Shumaker, 2012, p. 189). Then, develop an action plan with expected outcomes and completion dates.

Evaluation results must also be communicated to stakeholders. All parties need to understand whether or not embedded librarian programs are effective. If not, steps should be taken to see how the program might be improved. Consistent communication must take place in order for this to happen.

Summary of Best Practices

Shumaker (2012) quotes R. A. Cooper, "'Every example of embedded librarianship relies on two key elements: relationships and relevance'" (p. 323). Additionally, Shumaker (2012) provides a strong overview of best practices from several authors, including:

Heider (2010):

- Get buy-in from stakeholders.
- Attend user-group meetings.
- Teach and serve as guest lecturers.
- Publish and present with faculty.

Cooper (2010):

- Read pertinent e-mail lists.
- Go where the action is—student union, offices, labs, studios, dorms, and so on.
- Be pro-active in response to the need for current information—provide news alerts, for example.

Dene (2011):

- Start small and work up. Try a pilot program.

- Talk about library resources and services at orientation sessions.
- Collaborate with other units, such as IT, the Writing Center, the Distance Education Office, and faculty development centers.
- Assess.

Miller (2011):

- Seek out conversations with user groups.
- Participate in department events (p. 60-61).

Web-Based Tools

A plethora of web-based tools exist which can be used to enhance the educational experience. There are so many tools available that selecting the right one to use in any given circumstance can be overwhelming. Many of these tools can be divided into categories: digital learning object repositories and tools, content management tools, tools for remote storage and collaboration, and synchronous and asynchronous/recordable learning environment tools.

Digital Learning Object Repositories and Tools

Educators do not have to reinvent the wheel. There are an increasing number of sites that provide videos, animated tutorials, podcasts, presentations, and many other digital learning objects which can be used freely for educational purposes as long as credit is given. The Multimedia Educational Resource for Learning and Online Teaching, also known as MERLOT (http://www.merlot.org/merlot/index.htm), developed by California State University, is an excellent site and one of the first of its kind. Rice University's Connexions (http://cnx.org/) is an open repository of educational materials. YouTube (http://www.youtube.com/) is, of course, a favorite source for videos and it even has an education channel (http://www.youtube.com/education) that includes course lectures from top teachers around the world, speeches, and inspirational videos. The newly-launched Digital Public Library of America, or DPLA (http://dp.la/), is a partner with HathiTrust Digital Library (http://www.hathitrust.org), itself "a partnership of major research universities and libraries working to ensure that the cultural record is preserved and accessible long into the future" (HathiTrust, 2013). It contains millions of books and thousands of periodicals, including public domain and copyrighted content from a variety of sources.

The Library of Congress American Memory Project (http://memory.loc.gov/ammem/ index.html) provides access to a wealth of historical material, including images and maps. There is a section for teachers and an "Ask a Librarian" service to get help from an expert. PBS LearningMedia (http:// www.pbslearningmedia.org/) is a clearinghouse for accessing video, audio, documents, images, and interactive teaching/learning games for educational use. OER Commons (http:// www.oercommons.org/), an open educational resource, is a non-profit organization providing openly-licensed educational resources. And the list goes on.

Content Management Tools

Wikis, blogs, journaling, discussion boards, and Google+ all offer ways to share content. Buffy Hamilton's curated "Embedded Librarianship" on Scoop.it! (http://

www.scoop.it/ t/embedded-librarianship) is a great site for sharing ways in which librarians are embedding among their user groups. She also has a useful presentation on SlideShare "Taking Embedded Librarianship to the Next Level: Action Steps and Practices" (http://www.slideshare.net/ALATechSource/ taking-embedded-librarianship-to-the-next-level). Hamilton made the presentation for the American Library Association's TechSource Workshop. Both are fine examples of content delivered via the Web. Wikis, such as Wikispaces Classroom (http:// www.wikispaces.com/), are particularly useful when collaboration is needed. All parties can contribute to these wiki sites. Wikispaces also has room for discussions. Google Drive (https://drive.google.com/), formerly Google Docs, also allows users to collaborate in creating documents. An example using WordPress (http://wordpress.org/), a blog tool, publishing platform, and CMS, is the Research Coordination Network for Climate, Energy, Environment, and Engagement in Semiarid Regions (or RCN CE3SAR, see http://sites.tdl.org/ southtexassustainability/), an NSF-funded South Texas sustainability project. It collects, presents, and distributes digital material related to or produced by RCN CE3SAR. This WordPress site is part of the Texas Digital Library (www.tdl.org), a state-wide repository. As part of the research team, a project librarian adds information to the project site.

Tools for Remote Storage and Collaboration

Natives and non-natives of the digital information age will view and understand remote storage differently. These two groups often intersect in classroom settings. Librarians can serve as dynamic collaborators in this environment with regard to problem solving, emerging technology awareness, and assisting students and instructors in accomplishing classroom goals while developing valuable technological literacies. As institutions of higher education, as well as schools at the primary and secondary levels, choose to turn away from popular content management systems such as Blackboard and Desire2Learn, the ways in which they host and provide course content to users will also need to shift.

One common intersection of problem solving and librarianship often emerges in course assignments, particularly where research and research resources come into play. Midler (2012) discusses a collaborative effort using Google Docs, where an instructor shared editing privileges for class assignment documents with Midler, a school librarian. The documents were posted on the class website, where students could then not only access their assignments but their assignments now included tailored instructions from a librarian. This is an innovative use of Google Docs in the sense that assignment collaborations between instructors and librarians are far less common than other collaborative uses of Google Docs. Beyond documents, Google Drive has a wealth of other tools useful for librarians, instructors, and students including a calendar function, a presentation creation tool, Google Sites (for free, easy web design), Google Vault (for archiving purposes), and Google Moderator (for crowdsourcing and idea submissions). The calendar function could be employed for office hours, librarian appointments, and appointment reminders, while Google Moderator could permit lecture customization, project/assignment brainstorming, and more. For more information on Google Docs and other Google Drive "apps" for education, interested readers can explore http://www.google.com/apps/intl/en-GB/edu/.

Dropbox (http://www.dropbox.com), similarly, is a remote storage tool allowing users to share folders and/or particular items with collaborators. Innovative uses of Dropbox, courtesy of a Lifehacker post from The How-to Geek (2010), include:

- the ability to encrypt files using TrueCrypt, (e.g., for course grade documents or other files needing security);
- using shared folders for team-based projects such as student group work, publication collaborators, and so on;
- making useful information—shortcuts, fact sheets, and even PDF e-books—mobile for the researcher(s) on the go; and
- employing Dropbox as the equivalent of your "My Documents" folder.

As a backup for file storage, or a convenient alternative to carrying a USB drive, students and faculty alike will find Dropbox and its mobile app useful for accessing important documents on the go. Readers who have an interest in the discussion of security, privacy, networked learning, and file encryption may want to read Menchaca's (2012) article in the Journal of Library Administration.

A particular boon of Dropbox storage is the ability to access previous versions of a file through the web interface, in case one needs to view a specific, non-current version of a file. This would serve student groups well, but also provides a powerful editing and storage platform for publishers working with an editor(s). This often occurs at a distance as edits are now commonly made to PDFs and sent electronically to publishers, reviewers, and compositors, and backup files and versions may prove critical during the course of such projects.

Other products are also enabling Dropbox enhancements. VLC (formerly standing for VideoLAN Client) and the use of file transfer protocols (or FTPs) also offers users options for remote desktop access and networked file transfers; OneNote offers a notebook sync with Dropbox to allow remote access to class notes and lectures. Dropbox alternatives worth investigating as productivity tools include Opera Unite, Weave, Cheddar, and TagMyDoc.

For those needing to provide remote storage, remote access, and networked learning to students and collaborators using a variety of information formats (e.g., text, audio, images, and video), Evernote and Edmodo can also provide a useful space to connect and engage. The higher education edition of the EDUCAUSE Horizon Report (Johnson, Adams Becker, Cummins, Estrada, Freeman, & Ludgate, 2013) envisions apps such as Edmodo and Evernote will become more heavily used in bring your own device (BYOD) and multi-device scenarios, especially where group work, note taking, and multiple formats are concerned.

Librarians can work with instructors to create projects for students within these productivity and remote storage tools that enhance student skills development, better prepare students for research and other course projects and expectations, and provide useful and dynamic assistance to students at a distance. Popular library "scavenger hunts" could be made more interactive and technology-friendly by compiling the strengths of these tools (especially Evernote and Edmodo) to enable students to capture and post examples of primary resources for in-class or discussion board conversation. Faculty may find they have a behind-the-scenes expert who can suggest friendly amendments to assignment language within Google Docs, other Google

Drive for Education apps, and Dropbox. This could enable students to better understand the task at hand, might encapsulate general frequently asked questions (FAQs) and assignment-specific content from the library's perspective, and should provide other useful insights into the assignment's description and constructions, such as developing information literacy learning outcomes.

Synchronous and Asynchronous/Recordable Learning Environment Tools

Instructors and librarians alike must communicate and assist students within synchronous and asynchronous course environments, as well as in blended or hybrid contexts where courses are not taught exclusively online or in-person. While Google Moderator (see the Tools for Remote Storage and Collaboration section above) provides strengths for the student, instructor, or librarian working on a presentation, additional products exist to assist in engaging students in their learning environment. Here are a few:

- Skype: free video and voice calls with anyone else on Skype; free voicemail service; low rates for calling worldwide mobile and landline numbers; fee-based group video calls, call forwarding, and text messaging; available for desktop, mobile, tablet, TV, and home phone use; file sharing and screen sharing capabilities; integration with Facebook contacts and chat. Diane Cordell (2012) discusses the distinct benefits of Skype in the educational environment, stating that "Skype allows for a rich diversity of interaction: between teacher and librarian, librarian and librarian, librarian and student, expert and student, or student and student. It is the perfect vehicle for creating conversations for learning as an embedded librarian" (p. 8). For more details about the free and fee-based features of Skype, see http://www.skype.com/features; for additional information on Skype and distance education, see http://education.skype.com/projects/1783-distance-learning-with-skype.

- Google+ Hangouts: Google+ comprises an individual's profile, circles, communities, photos, Hangouts, and mobile Google+; connects individuals across computers, devices, and operating systems; enables use of photos and "emoji" (akin to emoticons) in a Hangout to create a fun, visually engaging environment; free video calls with up to ten individuals/locations; the archived, YouTube-accessible "Hangouts On Air" recording of a Hangout, useful for webinars and collaborating (see Pamela Vaughan's HubSpot blog post here: http://blog.hubspot.com/blog/tabid/6307/bid/32751/Google-Launches-Hangouts-on-Air-to-the-Masses-What-Marketers-Need-to-Know.aspx); publicly accessible schedule for public viewing of a Hangout to support and/or enhance course content. Students watching a scheduled Hangout On Air featuring museum curators as part of a museum studies or art history course, or viewing a gene patenting discussion for a medical ethics course, would have an opportunity to interact with experts in relevant fields, engage with a global learning community, and gain insights into educational content delivery methods. See http://www.google.com/+/learnmore/hangouts for additional details.

- Pearson's Open Class: Create/manage courses; add/manage content; a social learning environment with user profiles, statuses, and networks; study group creation options; Google tool integration for document creation/sharing/editing; conversation and discussion enabled with Google Chat and Skype features for organic, collaborative engagement; use of Open Educational Resources (OER) through platforms like Ted-Ed, Khan Academy, YouTube EDU, and other resources using Creative Commons licensing. See http://www.openclass.com/open/home/what for more information, and see their blog (http://www.openclass.com/blog) for news and developments, such as the Open Course Library, complete 11-week courses featuring completely OER content.
- Cisco WebEx, Adobe Connect, Citrix GoToMeeting, and Blackboard Collaborate: offer synchronous and asynchronous options; WebEx, Connect, and Collaborate often involve institutional licenses, but individual licenses may be affordable; they often have fee structures and may have limited free use; Blackboard Collaborate is the platform of choice for the international Library 2.0, Global Education, and Global STEMx conferences for live and archived presentations; Adobe Connect is Flash based; these platforms may have features such as limits on number of attendees, screen sharing, document sharing, whiteboard capabilities, limits on numbers of simultaneously shared screens, recording, audio, and attendee chat features, and logo branding options. Overviews of these and other similar products to help you bring online-based learning to online learners can be found through articles at PC World (http://www.pcworld.com/article/239419/business_videoconferencing_showdown_meet_face_to_face.html), Adobe (http://www.getconnect.com/resources/ competitiveprod-compare/), Knecht and Reid's 2009 article "Modularizing Information Literacy Training via the Blackboard eCommunity" (see References), and the Elearning Experts WordPress blog (http://elearningexperts.wordpress.com/2012/07/05/ choosing-a-webinar-solution/ and http://elearningexperts.wordpress.com/2012/08/09/choosing-a-webinar-provider-part-2/). Those interested in bringing these tools into their online instruction should consult with their institution's IT department. Faculty may also wish to discuss content development with their librarian(s) to explore the creation of information literacy goals, learning outcomes, and remote (a)synchronous library sessions to best suit and benefit the students in an online learning environment.
- Massive Open Online Courses (or MOOCs): a currently popular style of online instruction, using many of the tools and resources developed for blended, online, and distance learning over the past several decades; popular platforms include Coursera, Udemy, Khan Academy, Udacity, and EdX; platforms may be for profit, not-for-profit, or institutionally-based; certificates have gained in popularity and the for-credit MOOC is under intense development at the corporate organization and institutional levels; primarily asynchronous learning through videos with embedded quiz elements, readings, quizzes, peer review assignments, and discussion boards; synchronous options include Google+, Twitter, and

Facebook connections with classmates and instructors (thus creating potential for "live tweeting" and Google+ Hangout discussions) as well as occasional coordinated gatherings using MeetUps (http://www.meetup.com). For more information on MOOCs and working with librarians in them, refer to these two documents created by EDUCAUSE: "7 Things You Should Know About MOOCs" (http://net.educause.edu/ir/library/pdf/ ELI7078.pdf) and "What Campus Leaders Need to Know About MOOCs" (http:// net.educause.edu/ir/library/pdf/PUB4005.pdf), as well as Cantwell's article "MOOL in a MOOC"—also featured in this issue of Internet Learning.

This list of tools is not exhaustive and there may be more exciting or better-suited options for your institution, your course, or your goals in particular. When working to engage students in the online environment, it is worth getting creative and interactive, and embracing technology; the digitally native students will appreciate the effort and those who are not digital natives may have an opportunity to experience the "new" styles, pedagogies, and means of education that have developed alongside the rest of the online world. In an early 2012 article in Library Journal, Ben Showers highlights the concept of "the academic library as a model of change management" in that it must adapt to new technologies, and serve ever-changing and -shifting communities (and the expectations of those patrons), while under ever-tightening budgets and engaging in activist conversations related to open access, open education, copyright, intellectual freedom, and freedom of speech. Libraries have often been on the forefront of developing and harnessing new methods of and for content delivery and creation, as with "crowdsourcing," digital archives, gamification, and more. Showers (2012) quotes a senior editor from The Atlantic who stated, "the library sees its users as collaborators in improving the collections the library already has." Showers (2012) continues, writing:

> Libraries and staff suffer from their perceived lack of value within the information supply chain and the continuing devaluing of librarianship as a profession—the same disintermediation and de-professionalization as other industries such as music, media, and publishing. Yet, libraries have been able to utilize their staff as passionate advocates for innovation and user needs, as well as realizing the potential of their location within their communities and public spaces.

Using these synchronous, asynchronous, storage and collaboration tools, as well as the digital learning object repository resources, and content management systems featured in this article should aid faculty in better understanding and innovating in the online learning environment. These resources should also enable faculty to feel confident in approaching their librarians and information technology professionals to pursue these technologies, options, and opportunities for creative and engaging content development and delivery. Sodt and Pederson Summey (2009) wrote on using Web 2.0 tools to enhance the interaction between libraries, librarians, and their patrons and, for those interested in approaching librarians regarding opportunities to embed in online and other course environments, their article may provide additional suggestions as to tools and strategies to embed successfully.

As Showers indicates, librarians are "passionate advocates for innovation and user needs" and, in the world of online education, there is still ample room for further development and deeper librarian engagement to better meet the needs of its faculty and students.

What Lies Ahead?

We are in the midst of the greatest upheaval in the way information is handled in our society since the age of Gutenberg. We have revolutionized the way we create, store, manage, distribute, and consume information. This change has come about because of the Internet and the Web. Libraries no longer have a monopoly on information. Digital information and communication is ubiquitous—in homes, offices, schools, dorms, everywhere. Librarians must be where their users are. The traditional modes of library service are insufficient. Librarians must stay abreast of rapidly changing technologies, and develop new ways of organizing and new management techniques. Most importantly, we must build new relationships with our information users. We must focus on the needs and priorities of those we serve and determine how we can best address those needs.

Several areas in which librarians can take an active role are in MOOCs, mobile learning, gaming, Google+ Hangouts, in establishing data management plans to satisfy NSF grant requirements, and in open access publication and curating institutional repositories. As Stephen Covey would say (1990), "We must begin with the end in mind." And in the words of Alan Kay (1989), "The best way to predict the future is to invent it" (p. 1). Great changes bring about great opportunities. We are in an information and knowledge-based global economy, so the information skills of librarians are at a premium. Shumaker (2012) states, "The dominant form of community and corporate behavior is teamwork –embedded librarians must not stand apart; they must place themselves into teams as 'integral parts to the whole'" (p. 197). The interpersonal, institutional, and technological resources and tools discussed in this article hopefully encourage faculty to assist librarians in becoming part of the course team, as a mediator and an advocate for both faculty standards and expectations and for student needs and concerns.

References

Ball, S. J. (2013). What do war and embedded librarianship have in common? AALL Spectrum Online, 17(7). Retrieved from http://www.aallnet.org/main-menu/Publications/spectrum/ Spectrum-Online/war-and-embedded-librarianship.html

Bartnik, L., Farmer, K., Ireland, A., Murray, L., & Robinson, J. (2010). We will be assimilated: Five experiences in embedded librarianship. Public Services Quarterly, 6, 150-164. doi:10.1080/15228959.2010.498772

Carlson, J., & Kneale, R. (2011). Embedded librarianship in the research context: Navigating new waters. College & Research Libraries News, 72(3), 167-70.

Cooper, R. A. (2010). Architects in the mist: Embedding the librarian in a culture of design. Public Services Quarterly, 6, 323-329.

Cordell, D. (2012). Skype and the embedded librarian. Library Technology Reports, 48(2), 8-11.

Covey, S. (1990). The 7 habits of highly effective people. New York: Free Press.

Covone, N., & Lamm, M. (2010). Just be there: Campus, department, classroom…

and kitchen? Public Services Quarterly, 6, 198-207. doi:10.1080/15228959.2010.498768

Dale, J., & Kellam, L. (2012). The incredible embeddable librarian. Library Media Connection, 30(4), 30-31, 51.

Dene, J. (2011). Embedded librarianship at the Claremont colleges. In C. Kvenild & K. Calkins (Eds.) Embedded librarians: Moving beyond the one-shot instruction (219-228). Chicago: Association of College & Research Libraries.

Dewey, B. (2004). The embedded librarian: Strategic campus collaborations. Resource Sharing & Information Networks, 17(1/2), 5-17.

Drewes, K., & Hoffman, N. (2010). Academic embedded librarianship: An introduction. Public Services Quarterly, 6(2/3), 75-82. doi:10.1080/15228959.2010.498773

EDUCAUSE. (2012). What Campus Leaders Need to Know About MOOCs. Retrieved from http://net.educause.edu/ir/library/pdf/PUB4005.pdf

EDUCAUSE Learning Initiative. (2011). 7 Things You Should Know About MOOCs. Retrieved from http://net.educause.edu/ir/library/pdf/ELI7078.pdf

Edwards, M., Kumar, S., & Ochoa, M. (2010). Assessing the value of embedded librarians in an online graduate educational technology course. Public Services Quarterly, 6, 271-291. doi:10.1080/15228959.2010.497447

Feetham, M. (2006). The subject specialist in higher education—A review of the literature. In P. Dale, M. Holland, & M. Matthews (Eds.) Subject librarians: Engaging with the learning and teaching environment (3-17). Burlington, VT: Ashgate.

Freiburger, G., & Kramer, S. (2009). Embedded librarians: One library's model for decentralized service. Journal of the Medical Library Association, 97(2), 139-142. doi:10.3163/1536-5050.97.2.013

Hamilton, B. J. (2012). Case profile: Ellen Hampton Filgo. Library Technology Reports, 48(2), 16-20.

Hamilton, B. J. (2012). Conclusion: Best tools and practices. Library Technology Reports, 48(2), 27-54.

HathiTrust. (2013). HathiTrust Digital Library. Retrieved http://www.hathitrust.org/.

Haycock, L., & Howe, A. (2011). Collaborating with library course pages and Facebook: Exploring new opportunities. Collaborative Librarianship, 3(3), 157-162.

Heider, K. L. (2010). Ten tips for implementing a successful embedded librarian program. Public Services Quarterly, 6, 110-121.

Hemmig, W., & Montet, M. (2010). The 'just for me' virtual library: Enhancing an embedded eBrarian program. Journal of Library Administration, 50(5/6), 657-669. doi:10.1080/01930826.2010.488943

Hicks, A., & Sinkinson, C. (2011). Situated questions and answers responding to library users with QR codes. Reference & User Services Quarterly, 51(1), 60-69.

Hoffman, S. (2011). Embedded academic librarian experiences in online courses: Roles, faculty collaboration, and opinion.

Library Management, 32(6/7), 444-456. doi:10.1108/01435121111158583

Hoffman, S., & Ramin, L. (2010). Best practices for librarians embedded in online courses. Public Services Quarterly, 6(2/3), 292-305. doi:10.1080/15228959.2010.497743

The How-to Geek. (2010, April 29). The cleverest ways to use Dropbox that you're not using. Lifehacker. Retrieved from http://lifehacker.com/5527055/ the-cleverest-ways-to-use-dropbox-that-youre-not-using

Johnson, L., Adams Becker, S., Cummins, M., Estrada, V., Freeman, A., & Ludgate, H. (2013). NMC horizon report: 2013 higher education edition. Austin, Texas: The New Media Consortium. Retrieved from http://net.educause.edu/ir/library/pdf/HR2013.pdf.

Kay, A. C. (1989). "Predicting the Future." Stanford Engineering, 1, 1-6. http://www.ecotopia.com/webpress/futures.htm. Originally presented as an Address before the 20th Annual Meeting of the Stanford Computer Forum.

Kesselman, M. A., & Watstein, S. B. (2009). Creating opportunities: Embedded librarians. Journal of Library Administration, 49, 383-400. doi:10.1080/01930820902832538

Knecht, M., & Reid, K. (2009). Modularizing Information Literacy Training via the Blackboard eCommunity. Journal of Library Administration, 49(1-2), 1-9, doi:10.1080/01930820802310502

Lillard, L. L., Norwood, S., Wise, K., Brooks, J., & Kitts, R. (2009). Embedded Librarians: MLS Students as Apprentice Librarians in Online Courses. Journal of Library Administration, 49(1-2), 11-22. doi:10.1080/01930820802310544

Matos, M. A., Matsuoka-Motley, N., & Mayer, W. (2010). The embedded librarian online or face-to-face: American University's experiences. Public Services Quarterly, 6, 130-139. doi:10.1080/15228959.2010.497907

Menchaca, F. (2012). The future is in doubt: Librarians, publishers, and networked learning in the 21st century. Journal of Library Administration, 52(5), 396-410. doi:10.1080/01930826.2012.700804

Midler, Z. (2012). Case profile: Zoe Midler and Google Docs. Library Technology Reports, 48(2), 12-15.

Miller, C. (2011). Embedded and embodied: Dance librarianship within the academic department. In C. Kvenild & K. Calkins (Eds.) Embedded librarianship: Moving beyond one-shot instruction (47-63). Chicago: Association of College and Research Libraries.

Montgomery, S. E. (2010). Online webinars! Interactive learning where our users are: The future of embedded librarianship. Public Services Quarterly, 6(2/3), 306-311. doi:10.1080/15228959.2010.497467

Muir, G., & Heller-Ross, H. (2010). Is embedded librarianship right for your institution? Public Services Quarterly, 6(2/3), 92-109. doi:10.1080/15228959.2010.497464

Rudasill, L. M. (2010). Beyond subject specialization: The creation of embedded librarians. Public Services Quarterly, 6, 83-91. doi:10.1080/15228959.2010.494577

Rudin, P. (2008). No fixed address: The evolution of outreach library services on university campuses. The Reference Librarian, 49(1), 55-75. doi:10.1080/02763870802103761

Shank, J. D., & Bell, S. (2011). Blended librarianship: [Re]envisioning the role of librarian as educator in the digital information age. Reference & User Services Quarterly, 51(2), 105-110.

Shank, J. D., and N. H. Dewald. 2003. Establishing our presence in courseware:

Adding library services to the virtual classroom. ITAL: Information Technology and Libraries 22 (1): 38–43.

Showers, B. (2012, January 6). Backtalk: The constant innovator: The academic library as a model of change management. Library Journal Academic Newswire. Retrieved from http://lj.libraryjournal.com

Shumaker, D. (2009). Who let the librarians out? Embedded librarianship and the library manager. Reference & User Services Quarterly, 48(3), 239-242.

Shumaker, D. (2012). The embedded librarian: Innovative strategies for taking knowledge where it's needed. Medford, NJ.: Information Today, Inc.

Sodt, J. M., & Pedersen Summey, T. (2009). Beyond the Library's Walls: Using Library 2.0 Tools to Reach Out to All Users. Journal of Library Administration, 49(1-2), 97-109. doi:10.1080/01930820802312854

Thomas, E. A., Bird, N., & Moniz Jr., R. J. (2012). Informationists in a small university library. Reference & User Services Quarterly, 51(3), 223-225.

Thomsett-Scott, B. & May, F. (2009). How may we help you? Online education faculty tell us what they need from libraries and librarians. Journal of Library Administration, 49(1-2), 111-135. doi:10.1080/01930820802312888

Tumbleson, B. E., & Burke, J. J. (2010). Embedded librarianship is job one: Building on instructional synergies. Public Services Quarterly, 6(2/3), 225-236. doi:10.1080/15228959.2010.497457

Tumbleson, B. E., & Burke, J. J. (2010). When life hands you lemons: Overcoming obstacles to expand services in an embedded librarian program. Journal of Library Administration, 50, 972-988. doi:10.1080/01930826.2010.489002

Veal, R., & Bennett, E. (2009). The virtual library liaison: A case study at an online university. Journal of Library Administration, 49(1/2), 161-170. doi:10.1080/01930820802312938

York, A. C., & Vance, J. M. (2009). Taking library instruction into the online classroom: Best practices for embedded librarians. Journal of Library Administration, 49, 197-209. doi:10.1080/01930820802312995

Continuous Improvement and Embedded Librarianship in Online Learning Environments: A Case Study

Jeneen LaSee-Willemssen and Lisa Reed[1]

This case study describes how a college business instructor and an academic librarian collaborated, using the tenants of Continuous Improvement (CI) and embedded librarianship, to help improve student writing and information literacy skills in an online course. The authors detail their personal experiences, the challenges they faced, and the practices they developed. Data related to the successful results of the collaboration are shared, as are sample materials used in the course: a screencast video, email, and discussion post.

Keywords: Continuous Improvement; embedded librarianship; online teaching and learning; business education; case study

Continuous Improvement (CI) strategies are well known in the manufacturing world. Drawing on the Japanese principle of kaizen, CI is a "process of continuous incremental improvement" with the end goal of more effectively providing a better product for the customer (Singh & Singh, 2013, p. 32). One of the main tenets of CI is to provide value to the customer.

When applied in the educational environment, this might mean providing not only content, but also the skills that surround the content (writing, reading, researching, citing, etc.). In addition, because content-area experts are frequently not trained in teaching these general education skills, partnering with general education staff in order to provide this learning is an optimal method of helping students, the customers, obtain their goals. Finally, in order to apply CI in an educational setting, instructors must be willing to learn from their mistakes and make constant improvements to their processes and methodologies (Sayer & Williams, 2007).

Librarian and Instructor Partnerships

One frequent type of partnership that has developed over time is that between librarians and instructors. Usually, the partnership develops in order to help students develop and strengthen information literacy skills so that they may become better consumers and users of information, and thus more informed future professionals. Partnering between instructor and librarian can take the form of one-shot-workshops, collaborative assignment development, and shared grading—just to name a few examples. A more recent method of partnering, embedded librarianship, where the librarian strives to be "there with the user at the point of need, rather than waiting passively… [in] the library," is growing in popularity in higher education (Smith & Sutton, 2010, p.1).

---

[1] Rasmussen College

Embedded Librarianship

The practice of embedding in a brick and mortar setting can prove difficult because both instructional partners must have time to meet and plan, and the content instructor must substitute some content time for general education skills. Embedding in an online, asynchronous environment, however, removes many of the obstacles found in a synchronous setting. CI principles used in an embedded librarianship partnership can produce excellent results. Online embedding can help provide students, instructors, and librarians with an optimal learning environment: instructors can teach subject matter content, librarians can share information literacy skills, students can be successful learners, and content can be adjusted and changed continuously to meet the needs of all involved.

In this article, the authors seek to share the process of learning to partner and embed, using CI principles. We are very aware that we are describing a work in progress. We continue to learn from our efforts, our mistakes, and most of all from our students. The goal of this process is to provide the very best student experience possible in an environment of constant change.

Case Study

The Business Instructor's Perspective: Lisa Reed

I am a latecomer to the field of education. Previously, I had spent 21 years in the world of manufacturing management and had provided extensive training for employees both in formal classroom settings and in informal coaching environments. Additionally, I am a parent with all the training and coaching opportunities this particular role involves. As someone who had recently embarked on a second career on the shady side of 50, I was terrified that I might not be able to adjust to the challenges a career in education might demand.

I resolved that determination and extensive preparation would compensate for the actual teaching experience I lacked. I told myself I was prepared to thoughtfully and patiently lead students through their business course material. I would understand but be firm with those students who fell behind or lacked the proper motivation to succeed in college. I would be flexible with my schedule to make myself available whenever a student needed to contact me. I spent long hours agonizing over lesson plans and homework assignments, obsessing over which case studies would be most relevant to my students.

I eagerly anticipated reading the submissions for that first written assignment. This assignment asked students to share why they had chosen to study business and what career they hoped to pursue after graduation. The goal of this assignment was for me to get to know my students and for the students to reflect on their career choices. As I read the initial submissions from my students, there were several that contained statements like the following: "i [sic] want to study business because i [sic] need a job."

My preconceived notions died with a barely audible whimper. How could I teach business to students who were not willing or prepared to write at the level I was expecting? Were my standards too high? Was I not being clear in my instructions? I told myself this might have been a unique group of students, and that I would double my efforts with this group. Surely in the next term I would have students who were ready for and understood the challenges of college. The next term a similar pattern repeated itself and I found that my entry-level college students were again struggling with academic-level writing.

To stave off panic, I conferred with my colleagues. They had similar experiences. What was going on? I asked the librarian to help me with some research. We discovered that issues with writing were not unique to my students. In fact, articles bemoaning the poor writing skills of college graduates, much less new college students, were rampant. A research study by the College Board and the National Commission on Writing (2004) indicated that even though writing is considered an essential skill when hiring and promoting employees, businesses are spending "as much as $3.1 billion annually to remediate their employees' writing deficiencies" (p.4). Further, Quible and Griffin (2007) pointed to changes in the teaching of writing at the high school level due to high-stakes testing as possible parts of the problem. Similarly, the National Center for Education Statistics (2012) noted that in tests of writing skills, 74% of high school seniors were found to be less than proficient writers. Various other research studies unveiled additional contributing factors that were impacting the writing skills of students:

- An increasing number of college students are nontraditional and coming from a work environment rather than straight out of high school. This is not a new trend. The National Center for Education Statistics indicates that 37% of college students are enrolled part time, 32% are working full time, and 38% are over the age of 25 (Hess, 2011). For these students, writing a paper was a thing of the past; several years may have passed since they wrote their last academic paper.

- The world of social media is now ever present. The writing skills needed to post to social media technologies are far different than the skills required for crafting a persuasive argument or effective essay. While texting may or may not destroy the writing skills of the nation (Crystal, 2008), my students were including text such as "gr8" and "imho" in their papers.

- Many students are taking their first college courses online and not residentially. While Rasmussen College provides an abundance of support resources for our online students, those resources might be in a new and unfamiliar online format for students, and they might not take advantage of them.

It has been noted that when people are faced with difficult situations they revert back to their original training and background. A doctor will naturally speak of diagnosing the problem, the engineer will consider how to analyze the situation, and an information technology specialist might be most comfortable creating a flow chart to address an issue. My background includes many hours spent working on Continuous Improvement projects. So it is probably no surprise that in an act of desperation I chose to apply some CI concepts to this situation.

The first and most important tenet of CI is to provide value to your customer (Sayer & Williams, 2007). In this case, my customers were my students, and the value, or outcome, they were seeking was a college education. Professionals who work with CI will tell you that you do not get to select your customer, you have to adjust your product or service to provide value to your customer. Therefore, in addition to teaching business concepts to students, it is essential to provide instruction on how to write a paper. Similarly, while we might be more experienced with providing assistance to students in a face-to-face residential class, our students were frequently choosing the online platform for their classes. Hence, the task became how to teach business and writing to new college students in an online environment.

Another important tenet of CI is to consider input of all involved stakeholders (Sayer & Williams, 2007). This turned out to be a huge benefit for me because it encouraged me to continue to share my challenges with our campus librarian. She had seen this scenario play itself out in many areas beyond the school of business. As the campus librarian, she had heard students share their frustration with a process that required them to learn their subject course material, learn how to write a paper, and learn how to navigate online classes and resources simultaneously.

The Librarian's Perspective: Jeneen LaSee-Willemssen

Lisa's plight was not new to me at all—in fact, I could list a variety of skills in which students needed help. As a librarian, I work with students on a wide range of issues: computer use, course software navigation, Internet navigation, writing skills, editing skills, the ability to find and use quality information, and citing skills. The aforementioned skills are collectively known as information literacy.

Much of my time is spent helping students minimize information literacy gaps—either one-on-one or in workshops and webinars. Because not all students are required to attend workshops, I am not able to co-teach in all classes, and not all students are inclined to come in for one-on-one help, my information literacy instruction reaches only a limited number of students and only at certain points in their education. Thus, there is a lack of consistency and completeness to the information literacy curriculum provided by instructional librarians without a required class.

As an example, early in our partnership, Lisa's Introduction to Business courses were taught on campus rather than online, and we worked together to ensure that I regularly presented a variety of information literacy topics to students in the classroom. Topics included how to use specific resources for research, develop a thesis statement, and cite sources according to the Publication Manual of the American Psychological Association (APA). The sessions were helpful to students, but this format required Lisa to take time away from her business content to allow time for the information literacy content, that we both be in the class at the same time, and that the students had to wait until after class to practice what I presented. In short, there was room for improvement.

When Lisa's courses moved online, the transfer presented an incredible opportunity. We realized that I could become a member of the course in the mode of "lurking librarian," an "observer who monitors course discussion and initiates communication in response to perceived needs" (York and Vance as cited by Smith and Sutton, 2010, p. 6). As lurking librarian, I could share more content than I had previously, but without taking away from Lisa's business content. In addition, because the course was asynchronous (not in real time), Lisa and I did not need to match schedules; therefore I could post guidance and feedback in the course based on my schedule availability. Finally, the content I had been providing in one or two workshops in the past could now be spread out throughout the whole course and presented exactly when the students needed it. It was a win-win-win situation.

We began our adventure by enrolling me as a teaching assistant in Lisa's online Introduction to Business course. Lisa introduced me to the whole class, and together we explained what I would be doing: (1) perusing the assignments and readings, (2) reading student discussion posts, and (3) providing advice and guidance to individuals as teachable moments presented themselves. Once introduced, I logged in to the course every Monday and Thursday and emailed students with suggestions and advice as needed, based on what I was reading in their discussion posts. Lisa and I agreed that I would limit my comments to information literacy-related areas and skills and that she would address content. As we grew more comfortable with the collaboration, I also began proactively presenting information to the class as a whole via class announcements and discussion posts. For example, if the students needed to find unemployment statistics related to their state or county for a given module, the day the module opened I might introduce them all to the Bureau of Labor Statistics website and provide an explanation of not only how to best search it but also how to cite it using APA style. If students used "txt" language in their discussion posts, I might guide them away from that. See Figures 1, 2, and 3 for illustrations of content provided to all students.

Figure 1. Lurking Librarian Video for Module 3 Written Assignment

Lisa and I also worked towards laddering the way my content was introduced and assessed. We used CI principles in my instruction methodology. For example, I introduced APA style at the beginning of the course, but only had students learn and use certain components of it early on. In this way, mastery of APA style was not expected until the end of the course, and students had a safe environment in which to practice their new skills. Lisa graded the citation aspects of student papers accordingly.

During the first several rounds of embedding I was not sure if I was having a substantial impact. I wanted to help students become better consumers and users of information. I could see that some students were taking my advice, using the resources I had recommended and trying to cite the way I had modeled. Few, however, actually chose to contact me or ask me questions directly; and I could only see the discussion posts, not the papers. Lisa, however, reassured me that the presence of the lurking librarian was making a positive impact in student papers as well as discussion posts. The positive impact combined with lack of student interaction with me, the librarian, matches research by Tumbleson and Burke (2010), who note that even with students who found embedded librarians in their online courses helpful, only 27% reached out to that librarian with questions or for advice.

Results

After several quarters of embedding and lurking, an opportunity presented itself to prove that the initiatives were working. In the fall quarter of 2012, Lisa had two online sections of Introduction to Business rather than one. Jeneen lurked in one, and the other section became the control group. The class the authors part-

Figure 2. Sample Email for Module 6 Assignment

> Email
>
> In your week 6 written assignment, you need to research a software or hardware that facilitates or promotes team collaboration.
>
> 1. Make sure to cite the source of your information on the software/hardware that you pick!
>
> 2. Think about using Rasmussen College Library's subscription to Faulkner's Database for finding information about team work software. Tip: Once in Faulkner's, click on *Converging Communications* and then on *Conferencing* for a whole list of product profiles, marketplace reports, and tutorials. The Product Profiles will probably be most useful for this assignment.
>
> If you use Faulkner's resources, and have trouble citing, let me or your librarian know! We will try to help you out.

Figure 3. Discussion Post Prompt for Module 9 Assignment

> Discussion Post
>
> This week's discussion prompt will probably only have you citing your textbook. However, if you are curious about market segmentation and want to take it a step further, you might want to visit a source that was highlighted earlier in the quarter: **Best Customers: The Demographics of Consumer Demand**.
>
> If you live close to a campus, many of Rasmussen's libraries own a print copy. They also have an online copy via their eBooks via EBSCO subscription. You can link directly to the book at:
> http://ezproxy.rasmussen.edu/login?url=http://search.ebscohost.com/login.aspx?direct=true&db=nlebk&AN=345748&site=ehost-live
>
> Why is **Best Customers** so cool? You can search by product or service (everything from Apples and Appliances to spending on travel) and find out who is the most common buyer for that product/service: by age, by education, by geography, by income, by household type, and by race. It is fascinating.
>
> If you use Best Customers, note that you are getting this one from the database eBooks via EBSCO. If creating the reference is confusing, ask your librarian and/or visit http://rasmussen.libanswers.com/a.php?qid=128317 for more information on how to create a reference for an e-book.

nered in was weaker academically. These students had more difficulties writing and researching while the control group seemed better prepared. This assessment was made in part because the control group was writing more substantial posts and taking initial attempts to cite sources. By the end of the quarter, however, the section with a lurking librarian had become more successful researchers and writers than the control group. In specific, the students in the lurking group were integrating quality sources such as Bureau of Labors Statistics web pages into their writing, while students in the control group were still frequently picking sources that were lacking in authority if they were finding backup sources at all. The lurking group had started to understand the idea of backing up their points with outside evidence, while the control group still wanted to cite random concepts or to simply use personal experiences as substantiation. Finally, the lurking group students were starting to grasp the logic and details of APA formatting, while the control group students were still struggling with formatting issues like matching in-text citations to reference items. These results match what is available in the literature. For example, Tumbleson and Burke (2010) point out that "sixty-seven percent [of students who had taken an online course with an embedded librarian] agreed or strongly agreed that it was helpful" (p. 979).

Enamored by our success, we gathered the information Jeneen had provided to the students and created a file of announcements, discussion post starters, and course emails that could be reused in other sections of the same course, with or without an actual lurking librarian. The file, a Word document, was structured chronologically to match the course. Each type of information was identified by a header: email, announcement, discussion post, etc.

One could simply open the file and copy and paste the content into the appropriate module of the online course and upload it. The content was utilized with and without a lurking librarian in the following quarters with mixed success. Most quarters the lurking librarian content seemed to prove helpful to the students because, unlike past quarters, students would use quality resources, integrate sources into their writing, and attempt citing in APA style.

CI principles came into play again during the winter quarter of 2013. Lisa had one section of Introduction to Business in which a handful of students seemed to resent the fact that they were being asked to do things they felt were outside of the content of the course, namely to write clearly, provide researched backup to their statements, and cite their sources in their discussion posts. They seemed to feel that discussion board writing was much more casual than we did. At first, we worried that we were failing these students. Why couldn't they understand how important clear, persuasive writing with basic documentation was? We decided that that even though some of these students were expressing frustration at being assessed on their writing and citing, that that very frustration indicated a developing awareness of the importance of professional communication. That developing awareness is something we can continue working with.

Current and Future Endeavors

We are moving forward in three veins. First, we are sharing the wealth of information. Jeneen shared her file of cumulated discussion posts, emails, video links, and announcements she had used not only with Lisa, but also with the Rasmussen College librarian team so they could lurk with their own Introduction to Business instructors. It is our hope that this file will also be distributed to other business instructors, so that they may use the content.

Second, we aim to leverage our own success by continuing to apply CI concepts, specifically implementing stable processes and minimizing their variability so we can manage by exception. Accordingly, we hope to edit, modify, and use Jeneen's file of lurking librarian content to supplement future online Introduction to Business courses. One adjustment we will make in the near future is to address the frustration exhibited by some of the students in our winter 2013 section of Introduction to Business. We will be editing the lurking librarian content to help make it more obvious to the students that the writing, research, and citing skills we are sharing are essential to their development as future professionals and that assessment in this area now is to their benefit. Using this newly edited content will also allow us to spend more time focusing on providing individual feedback and support to students who need more help than already provided.

Finally, we couldn't help but notice that much of the lurking librarian material, lessons in formatting and structuring academic papers, searching databases, selecting quality resources, and citing sources, was general in nature. All of these instructional materials could be introduced into any introductory online course with relatively minor adjustments to fit specific assignments and/or disciplinary differences. Thus, it is our hope that other instructors and librarians will seek opportunities to collaborate and partner with one another, use the embedded librarian idea, implement CI concepts to keep improving, and share the results with world.

References

College Board, & National Commission on Writing. (2004, September). Writing a ticket to work...or a ticket out: A survey of business leaders. Retrieved from http://www.collegeboard.com/prod_downloads/writingcom/writing-ticket-to-work.pdf

Crystal, D. (2008). Txtng: The Gr8 Db8. Oxford: Oxford University Press.

Hess, F. (2011, September 28). Old school: College's most important trend is the rise of the adult student. The Atlantic. Retrieved from http://www.theatlantic.com/business/archive/2011/09/old-school-colleges-most-important-trend-is-the-rise-of-the-adult-student/245823/

National Center for Education Statistics. (2012, September). The nation's report card: Writing 2011: Executive summary. Retrieved from http://nces.ed.gov/nationsreportcard/pubs/main2011/2012470.asp

Quible, Z. K., & Griffin, F. (2007). Are writing deficiencies creating a lost generation of business writers? Journal of Education for Business, 83(1), 32-36. Retrieved from http://www.taylorandfrancisgroup.com/

Sayer, N., & Williams, B. (2007). Lean for dummies. Hoboken, NJ: Wiley.

Singh, J., & Singh, H. (2013). Continuous improvement strategies: An overview. IUP Journal of Operations Management, 12(1), 32-57. Retrieved from http://www.iupindia.in/

Smith, S. S., & Sutton, L. (2010). The embedded academic librarian. [White paper]. Retrieved from WakeSpace website: http://hdl.handle.net/10339/37676

Tumbleson, B. E., & Burke, J. J. (2010). When life hands you lemons: Overcoming obstacles to expand services in an embedded librarian program. Journal of Library Administration, 50(7/8), 972-988. doi:10.1080/01930826.2010.489002

York, A. C., & Vance, J. M. (2009). Taking library instruction into the online classroom: Best practices for embedded librarians. Journal of Library Administration, 49(1/2), 197-209. doi:10.1080/01930820802312995

"MOOL" in a MOOC: Opportunities for Librarianship in the Expanding Galaxy of Massive Open Online Course Design and Execution

Laureen P. Cantwell[1]

The discussion around, and analysis of, massive open online courses (or MOOCs) continues to grow and develop. Educators unfamiliar with MOOCs, their hosts, structures, benefits, and challenges will find this article helpful for gaining understanding of this on-trend form of distance learning and course delivery. Furthermore, the author proposes that the potential for librarianship within MOOCs should also be considered. Much of the relevant literature from the fields of education, librarianship, information science, and academia at large, reviewed here, have not delved too deeply into the concept of librarianship within this setting (yet). In an effort to discover MOOC faculty opinions, challenges, and incentives for MOOC creation and participation, as well as their thoughts on librarians in MOOCs, the author developed a survey. This survey aimed to assess: (1) the costs and benefits experienced by faculty teaching MOOCs; (2) perceived/anticipated student and learning environment successfulness within MOOCs; and (3) the extent faculty engage with their institution's librarians. Additionally, the survey approached MOOC faculty regarding whether they envision a future for librarians within MOOCs and what that future might look like. This article closes with discussion on survey findings, suggestions for future research, hypotheses regarding the future of MOOCs, and opportunities for a "MOOL" in a MOOC.

Keywords: MOOCs; massive open online courses; nontraditional education programs; open source education programs; online learning; distance learning; information literacy; media literacy; instructional technologies; higher education; e-learning; librarianship; copyright; open access.

Within the last two years or so, the landscape of education and of instruction delivery has shifted. While this shift has not been entirely new—online instruction and distance education have been around for decades—it has generated substantial buzz in terms of openness, access and accessibility, affordability, successfulness, and complications. Broad and affordable, yet complicated and contentious, the emergence of the massive open online course, or MOOC, serves as the origin of this transition.

The EDUCAUSE Library (2013) defines the MOOC very simply as "a model for delivering learning content online to any person who wants to take a course, with no limits on attendance." Though this brief explanation may not come across as groundbreaking, the MOOC environment, and the

---

[1] Instructional Services Librarian at the University of Memphis. For questions, comments, or other follow-up regarding this article, please contact her at lcntwell@memphis.edu or 901-678-8209.

benefits and opportunities it presents, offers a unique new look at how we approach education in general, distance learning, and distance instruction and content delivery. (See Figures 1 and 2 at the end of this article for two multimedia presentations. Figure 1 is an MP4 of a presentation by the author called "What Teachers Can Learn as Students in MOOCs," delivered at the Global Education Conference in November 2012. Figure 2 is a Prezi entitled "MOOCs: What Are They and How Do They Work?" created July 2013 by the author for this publication.)

Literature on teaching and learning, as well as about librarianship, abounds—yet the fields do not always comingle in their discussions as much as they could. A literature review opens up this education and librarianship discussion with the intention to lead into establishing the connections between these fields. Then, current literature on MOOCs will provide background on the MOOC environment and the idea of "place" in the online atmosphere, followed by the MOOC as a consumer and provider of access, content, and resources. Lastly, the literature review addresses prognostications for the future of MOOCs and the engagement (and potential for engagement) with librarians.

A survey was conducted to explore MOOC faculty feelings, impressions, and realities with regard to delivering instruction and content in this setting. The study purpose, demographics, methods, results, and lessons learned are detailed, followed by a discussion of the survey and its results. The underlying hope for the survey was to create reflection upon MOOC faculty as to their expectations, their observations, their experience of costs and benefits, and their understanding of the twenty-first century academic library and the skillsets of its librarians.

Relevant literature, survey responses, and additional resources from the field of librarianship led to the vision of a "MOOL" in a MOOC—that is, the concept of massive open online librarianship, or (with less jargon) acting as a librarian and/or providing library resources in the MOOC setting. Resource creation, course content design and delivery, and issues of copyright and access constitute the three major foci of this section. In the final section, the author recommends several areas for future research, including the impact of the MOOC on copyright issues and access shifts on the side of publishers.

Review of Relevant Literature

Teaching and Learning: A Few Highlights

At the heart of the MOOC lies the debate about whether such a course is or can be an effective means of instruction delivery, on the behalf of its faculty members, and of education, on behalf of those enrolled. College and university faculty and administrators, as well as government and other organizations, have placed importance upon the study of data gathering about the experience of teaching and learning. A substantial study, conducted by Lawrence M. Aleamoni (1999), addresses student ratings (and the myths surrounding their course and instruction evaluations) and research-supported facts with supporting evidence spanning from 1924 to 1998. Critically, these myths highlight the disconnect between faculty and administrator flippancy regarding student opinions (e.g. "it's a popularity contest," students are immature/inexperienced/capricious, students need hindsight to evaluate "accurately," majors versus nonmajors significance, course grade versus course rating correlation suspicions, and so on) and faculty opinions of the usefulness and validity of student evaluations (e.g., unreliable; invalid; impacts of class size; faculty–student gender impacts; class time impacts; requirement versus elective; course level impacts; instructor rank; existence of rating rubric differences by discipline). The final myth, especially important here, speaks to whether student ratings can be meaningfully applied toward improving instruction—Aleamoni indicates that, by consulting with students, instructors can indeed improve their instruction, and their ratings.

Following Aleamoni's discussion, Scarboro (2012) conducted a survey of more than 13,000 students in Istanbul, seeking information on how to improve pedagogy and how to promote student learning while also providing an actual learning task for students in his undergraduate Sociology research methods course. Their primary question ("What do university students perceive as the teaching strategies, environments, and tools that promote their learning?") takes Aleamoni's work a step further, beyond student evaluation-related evidence. Scarboro writes, "We were further interested to discover if gender, student residence (at home, in a dormitory, or in an apartment), academic achievement, discipline of study, national or international student status, year in school, and other factors shaped student preferences for teaching and learning approaches" and includes the English version of the questionnaire in the article's appendices (p. 52). Of Scarboro's conclusions, we find that students "perceive their faculty as very important in their success as learners," and that faculty research interests and activities enhance student learning (p. 55). In the world of MOOCs, we can apply the favorable student perceptions of peer-to-peer information sharing (e.g., they much prefer study groups to group assignments) and an internationally diverse environment, as well as the use of modern technological aids. Further supporting Aleamoni's research, Scarboro also finds that faculty rank "seems unrelated to student learning," and that gender and national origin did not seem to have an impact either whereas factors like reliability, the use of technology, and engagement in their field or discipline to be of far greater interest to students and have an impact upon their learning.

The world of blended learning continues to shapeshift, as described in Wang, Shen, Novak, and Pan's (2009) article on mobile learning, or m-learning. Where both "individual flexible learning" and "extended classrooms" have become more popular, students can transform from passive learners in traditional classroom environments into engaged learners who are behaviorally, intellectually, and emotionally involved in their learning task (p. 674). But mobile learning and technologies integrated into course delivery are only part of the battle to demonstrate value in education, though they certainly seem like dazzling components for driving student participation. Additional current and recent discussions of value include those about: integrating competencies into the undergraduate curriculum (Scaramozzino, 2010), faculty members and administrators engaging with students in new contexts and environments (Haden, 2013), the concept of quality control in higher education settings (Hazelkorn, 2013), freshman research skills and overconfidence (Gustavson & Nall, 2011), accomplishing library services and education in transnational educational settings (Green, 2013; Mangan, 2011), and the need to reinvent teaching while monitoring costs and/or suffering budget cuts (New, 2013; Rivard, 2013).

Reflecting on these topics and the world of MOOCs, many MOOCs and their hosts (e.g., Coursera) integrate learning outcomes, instructional technology, and pre- and post-course evaluations, and highlight faculty expertise and research interests in a new environment. These features often exist automatically in the very design and presentation of the MOOC. Other elements, like student research and critical thinking skills (as well as cost monitoring), are not so simply accomplished in this environment. There are issues, such as publisher and database restrictions and embargoes, as well as faculty human resource or human capital costs (e.g., course releases or graduate assistant(s) usage), institutional funding and/or grant funding, technology costs, and opportunity costs (e.g., What are faculty not doing so that they may take on MOOC-related responsibilities?). The survey conducted for this article aims to better understand these aspects of MOOC instruction and delivery, as well as the relationships institutions have or are cultivating with their MOOC instructors. These articles and the concepts detailed here set the stage for moving into the literature regarding librarianship and librarian engagement with online instruction and learning.

Librarians in Online Instruction and Learning

One finding from the Scarboro article suggests that when students deem university library collections insufficient, they perceive libraries to be a detriment to their learning (p. 57). He states, "strong libraries and helpful librarians, ease of access to electronic journals, strong computer laboratories and well-equipped science laboratories were all seen as vital to their learning" (p. 60). But what defines a "helpful" librarian in the twenty-first century academic environment and to the Millennial-generation student? Frank, Raschke, Wood, and Yang (2001) believe one of the critical components of academic library success lies in the role of librarian as information consultant—an individual who "cultivates active partnerships with students and scholars, collaborating on the design of meaningful learning experiences for students and providing relevant value-added information […] Delivering the right information to the right people at the right time underscored the value of librarians and libraries" (p. 90). They believe that in embracing the concept and opportunity of librarian-as-information-consultant, the relationship is more about collaboration than mere cooperation, where goals are defined together and, hopefully, achieved together (p. 92).

While subject specialization has been a part of librarianship in the United States and Great Britain since just after World War II, the concept of "embedded librarianship" has altered not so much what librarians do as it has how librarians provide what they do to their patrons and users (Rudasill, 2010). The concept of "holistic" or "comprehensive" librarianship entails: reference service and instruction (oftentimes now termed "research and instructional services"), collection development (e.g., purchasing, weeding, recommending, and usage tracking), and at times even cataloging work for a specific subject area. This may be the traditional understanding of the job of an academic librarian, and yet librarianship has also changed with the tremendous leaps of technology that we have seen in the new millennium.

Numerous job functions have been added and these are, in a sense, part of what may fall under "other duties as assigned" in a librarian's job description (Rudasill, 2010). The work of an embedded librarian may fall into this area. These "other duties" unfortunately mask (internally and externally) the closeness, the liveliness, and the enterprising nature of being "embedded." Rudasill writes, "Embeddedness implies that the librarian is sharing in the life of the department or program, understanding the dynamics of relationships between individuals within the department as well as relationships between departments or departments and higher administrators" (p. 84). Included here may be outreach to teachers outside the college/university, teaching credit-bearing courses, department meeting attendance, grant writing collaborations, being on-site (physically or remotely) to better cover for users' points of need, and much more (Rudasill, 2010; Rudin, 2008; Cordell, 2012). Covone and Lamm (2010) note that, "Embracing a proactive approach to library service is necessary in order to be successful and relevant in the academic environment" and they urge librarians to become a part of the "global campus environment" (p. 198-199).

Why is embedded librarianship a developing new realm of the work of librarians? Rudasill (2010) found four common factors at the helm: innovation, access, budgets, and pedagogy (p. 85). Rudasill also notes that opportunities for embedding librarians are limited, regardless of how exciting they can be as drivers of change; the library, as a place, must still be provided for and it may not be necessary or even possible to embed a librarian in every department or course at an institution. Rudasill is not alone in stressing the importance of new forms of librarianship. In an article about embedded librarianship, Hoffman (2011) highlights a concern from a 2003 article by John Shank and Nancy Dewald, where the authors felt "librarians should become involved in distance education at the course level or they would 'risk being bypassed by technology and losing relevance to students and faculty'" (p. 445).

Despite Rudasill's wide-ranging concept of embedded librarianship, perhaps one of the most efficient and popular environments for embedded librarianship is the online course environment. This particular environment enables librarians to serve a community that often does not have easy in-person access to librarians and just as often does not understand the nature and nuances of their access to library resources. Librarians can be "intense[ly] integrat[ed]" into the course, where the best implementations of this effort include transformative information literacy components (Lloyd, 2004) and "multiple opportunities for rich interactions with the librarian" (Edwards, Kumar, & Ochoa, 2010). Because online courses are not traditional learning environments and librarians do not always have the extensive history of providing assistance in that setting (Piper & Tag, 2011, p. 320-321), these courses in particular require the librarian to be flexible and innovative. Edwards, Kumar, and Ochoa's (2010) article includes a section on "Embedded Librarians in Online Courses" which highlights much of the relevant literature and discussion of a variety of implementations (p. 277-278). Furthermore, Wang, Shen, Novak, and Pan (2009) assert that "distance learning with no interactivity reinforced the negative effects of passive nonparticipatory learning" (p. 675). While Lai, Chang, Li, Fan, and Wu (2013) focus on outdoor education in their article for the British Journal of Educational Technology, several of their points apply to instruction taking place outside of traditional classroom environments, in general: the teaching and learning that occurs outside the classroom facility has different values and qualities which must be considered; teachers must consistently explore ways to create dynamic content for that atmosphere, including "meaningful contextual experiences"; and that the experiences of this environment should "complement and expand classroom instruction" (p. E57). As such, it is then critical that librarians and faculty in the online course environment work to create dynamic content to engage and support students. Librarians and faculty may need to seek out professional development within and beyond their institution to develop the skills and know-how regarding online content delivery options.

The librarianship workforce has grown to not only include embedded librarians but also "blended librarians." Like embedded librarians, these librarians also have much in common with "traditional" librarians (reference, instruction, collection development), but "blended" librarians also take on instructional design responsibilities and have a wealth of knowledge, training, and affection for instructional technology. These librarians are, at least in part, sought out as a result of the challenges and opportunities technology has brought to the ways libraries handle the storage, collection, spread, and use of information and resources. Shank (2006) includes tables of frequently required qualifications (p. 519) and frequently desired qualifications (p. 520), as well as primary responsibilities (p. 521), in the role of an instructional design librarian that may help the reader better understand the demands of such a position. Top requirements include web/multimedia application experience (e.g., Adobe), communication and interpersonal skills, and organizational skills; top desired qualifications include project management experience, completed coursework in instructional design and technology, and online courseware experience; and top responsibilities include creating online tools and resources (e.g., modules, tutorials, or guides), current and emerging technological skills and experience, and library instruction (p. 519-521). And we may find that further "blending" occurs, where instructional designers may not (yet) be present at an academic library but where librarians have the technological and pedagogical skills to serve, in a limited fashion, in the kind of "blended librarian" role Shank describes. Additionally, Shank and Bell (2011) declare that "[b]lended librarianship is intentionally not library centric [...] but, rather, it is librarian centric (i.e., focused on people's skill, knowledge they have to offer, and relationships they build)" (p. 106). It is, therefore, the integration of the librarian, more than only the library, that should make for the most engaging, dynamic, and critical resource in the collaboration between a course and a library—the human resources driving toward student success within both environments, the course and the library, are its most powerful components.

As Pritchard (2010) writes, embedded librarians begin engaging in elements of instructional design alongside the faculty member(s) of a particular course, serving as a collaborator in the entire course process rather than in a session or two of the course, or just in the content management system (CMS) element (e.g., Blackboard or Desire2Learn). Pritchard lists attitude, visibility, and professional expertise as the most important factors in establishing this kind of team-teaching effort with a faculty member (p. 387-388). Montgomery (2010) writes, "Social networking tools provide [college students] with an interactive online experience. Academic libraries and librarians need to provide the same experience" (p. 307). Instructional webcasts (e.g., YouTube videos), Facebook pages for academic libraries, Skype interactions, and other virtual services aimed at increasing library/librarian visibility to students and online-based professional expertise for librarians all echo and heighten the presence of courses and other institutional services in similar formats. Embedded librarianship has become well-known enough that best practices have been researched and delineated, such as those found by York and Vance (2009), and these will likely grow and change over time as the role of librarians engaged with instruction and technology continues to evolve and as faculty awareness and appreciation for what librarians can contribute to their course, and to student success, continues to grow.

Gustavson and Nall (2011) highlight one such example where faculty members often bemoan the lack of "real" research skills in their students, often specifically with regard to a major or discipline. Librarians are uniquely poised to monitor, make suggestions to, and consult with students and to remedy deficient skills. (Pickard and Logan (2013) also elaborate on student understanding (or lack thereof) regarding the research process and the library.) Librarians do this, most critically, without altering or stepping on course content and without taking time away from course content instruction by the faculty member, but they work alongside the instructor to drive student engagement in research and learning and change or update the way students view the library as a resource (Kuh & Gonyea, 2003). Roff (2011) calls attention to the comingling of librarianship training with museum studies training, such that librarians may be able to use their knowledge of information literacy in combination with their understanding of exhibitions (scripting, press releases, and so on) in order to deliver an information literacy course with historical, and visual, primary source materials. Montiel-Overall and Grimes (2013) point to AASL's Standards for the 21st Century Learner Guidelines (specifically pages 13, 20, and 25), stating that librarians must be sure to target their information literacy instruction toward essential twenty-first century learning skills, to collaborate with members of the learning community (not necessarily limited to faculty and/or students), and to implement inquiry-based learning approaches regarding the information search process (p. 41).

Mackey and Jacobson (2011) broaden the concept of information literacy involving a variety of formats into the concept of "metaliteracies"—the "overarching, self-referential, and comprehensive framework that informs other literacy types"—which "provides an integrated and all-inclusive core for engaging with individuals and ideas in digital information environments" (p. 70). These authors argue that an information literate individual "[applies] information knowledge gained from a wide range of verbal, print, media, and online sources and continuously [refines] skills over time. This constitutes a practice of critical engagement with one's world as active and participatory learners" (p. 70). With these quotes in mind, one can readily see overlap between the MOOC's opportunity to provide global learning environments and the kindred opportunity for librarians to investigate and incorporate metaliteracies into the MOOC curriculum in collaboration with MOOC faculty.

While not specifically focused on librarianship, Hopper (2012) takes a valuable approach to the concept and growing field of instructional design, creating a conversation between an institution's instructional designer ("Dave") and Buddha (aka "Sid"), who is about to teach "PHIL5001—Special Topic—Toward Nothing." Those reading the article should note the instructional designer (who could be a librarian or could be a faculty member in another department entirely) sees his role as that of a consultant—assessing faculty needs, informing them of standards and regulations, offering solutions, recommendations, and assistance. Essentially, the instructional designer focuses on making the most of the online environment for the students while adhering to faculty desires, skills, and plans.

Librarians take their role in the development of lifelong learners and the information literate very seriously. Educators curious about working with librarians in online or other settings for instruction, embedded collaborations, and creating meaningful student–librarian interactions may benefit from exploring the freely accessible "Analyzing Your Instructional Environment: A Workbook" (IS Management & Leadership Committee, 2010). Whether approached individually or with a librarian, this resource should provide a wealth of concepts and ideas for future discussion and, perhaps, implementation.

MOOCs, Their Future, and Librarianship

Little scholarly research regarding the future of MOOCs with direct reference to librarians and libraries exists, and with good reason. MOOCs are new enough that research into MOOCs and their needs in order to achieve success (for a variety of definitions of success) are still very much in an emergent stage. Institutions engaging in discussion, planning, development, and augmentation of their MOOCs will conduct and participate in research pertaining to those aspects of MOOCs. As the prevalence of institutionally hosted platforms and credit-bearing MOOCs continues to grow and transform, that will also serve as a burgeoning area of MOOC research. MOOCs also have, and will continue to have, an impact on the world of copyright clearance, open access, and creative commons licensing. While some up-to-the-minute conversations on those topics are shared in the "Survey Comments, Feedback, and Lessons Learned," "Further Survey Discussion: A Vision of 'MOOLing' in a MOOC," and "Future Research" sections below, these are only conversations and only time will tell where MOOCs and the scholarly research around them will go.

But researchers will not hunger for inspiration. The "literature" in Appendix A consists of a mix of more popular items (blog, non-scholarly journal, and Chronicle of Higher Education articles), multimedia resources to explore, and several scholarly publications. These inclusions will demonstrate the wealth of ways in which librarians are involved in, engaged with, and ready to assist MOOCs.

The survey conducted in preparation for this article also seeks to illuminate areas of real and potential involvement of libraries and librarians with MOOCs. Later sections continue this discussion using survey findings related to the future of MOOCs and where librarians may fit within that scope.

Survey of Coursera MOOC Instructors

Purpose of the Study

In considering the potential for librarians in the instructional and educational environment of the massively open online course, we must also assess whether and to what extent faculty teaching MOOCs see a place for librarians in that atmosphere. With that in mind, the author decided that a survey of MOOC faculty could accomplish several goals, including the primary area of research interest: gauging MOOC faculty interest in and conceptualization of librarians in MOOCs. Additional goals of the survey as stated in the Institutional Review Board (IRB) form were:

• to discover variations in faculty status among MOOC faculty;

- whether MOOC faculty have established relationships with the library and/or librarians at their home institution;
- whether MOOC faculty attempt to incorporate information literacy outcomes into their MOOC through learning objectives or other means;
- whether librarians at the home institution of the MOOC faculty member have played a part in the MOOC course development process; and
- to gain insights regarding institutional (or other) incentives for MOOC faculty, which may illuminate both barriers to and opportunities for librarians in MOOCs.

This survey was not designed to be exhaustive, but to be exploratory. Data gained from responses shared a common level of importance with qualitative replies from survey participants.

Methods

As the author focused on MOOC faculty solely within the Coursera site (http://www.coursera.org), a Microsoft Access database was built containing information from each MOOC home page (all 367 of them, as of May 15, 2013) within Coursera, regardless of whether the course was complete, in-progress, or upcoming. This database contains a unique ID for each course title, course titles, the primary instructor's name and email address (gathered from web searching), course category/subject areas, course duration, course estimated workload (in hours), whether a "signature track" was available for that course (and, if so, at what cost), the home institution of the primary instructor of the MOOC, the location of the home institution (country), the language of the MOOC, the names of up to three additional instructors, and the total number of non-primary instructors for the MOOC. This database provided the author with an opportunity to understand the distribution of MOOC subject areas, engagement of international faculty members, extent of team-teaching used for MOOCs, and the average workload a Coursera MOOC student might anticipate doing in order to complete a MOOC. This resource also enabled the author to gauge the number of courses with "TBA" instructors, instructors outside of traditional higher education institutions, and potential survey participants who may or may not speak (fluent if any) English. Data from the Access database dates to May 15, 2013 and thus courses created in Coursera since then were not included in the survey.

After building the Access database and much internet searching to discover MOOC faculty email addresses, the author built a survey using Qualtrics through an institutional license. This software was chosen as it allows the survey designer to route participants based on responses, allows for a record of informed consent from participants, permits relatively quick and easy emailing of potential survey participants (for initial contact and reminders), and automates "thank you" messages to survey respondents. Questions in the survey were multiple choice, "choose all that apply," or written responses (most often used where the author sought elaboration or thoughts related to a particular question or response). The complete survey is available in its entirety in the appendix of this article. The author generated a report based on survey responses on July 7, 2013 for the purposes of this article. Any responses completed after that date will not be included in this article.

Access Database Demographics Information

Prior to and during the survey (see Question 7), several points of data were gathered or requested regarding survey participants, both real and potential. As described in the Methods section, the Access database created to support this research project can establish a number of valuable points of data. Tables 1–3 of the present article display the most prominent Coursera host institutions within the United States, the most prominent Coursera host countries outside the United States, and the distribution of Coursera courses by sole or primary subject area/category, respectively. Consider the following additional Coursera-specific MOOC details gleaned from the author's database:

• Five MOOCs listed would be taught in Chinese, eight in French, one in Italian, one in German, and 10 in Spanish—this group (25 courses, or 7%) would be surveyed, but participation levels may be low, depending on primary instructor's fluency in English.
• Nineteen courses (5%) were not hosted by traditional institutions of higher education (e.g., the American Museum of Natural History or Exploratorium).
• Institutions outside the United States host 101 MOOCs (28%) on Coursera—the Commonwealth Education Trust (United Kingdom), the University of Copenhagen (Denmark), and the University of Toronto (Canada) were each hosting eight MOOCs (2% each, or together hosting 6%–7% of the 367 MOOCs on Coursera).
• Of the 25 MOOC categories, or subject areas, used by the Coursera site, 194 (53%) were listed for more than one category—this may or may not indicate interdisciplinary collaboration between MOOC faculty.
• Sixty-seven (20%) of the 339 unique MOOC faculty members surveyed were female (Note: those listed as the primary instructor for multiple MOOCs on Coursera were not counted more than once).
• Fourteen courses (4%) anticipated student workload would be a minimum of 10 hours per week, 50 courses (14%) anticipated coursework would consume up to 10 hours per week, and 109 courses (30%) anticipated between 1 and 5 hours of coursework each week for students.
• Eleven MOOCs on Coursera had a Signature Track available for enrolled students (fees per Signature Track course ranged from $39.00–$79.00).

The details extrapolated from this database do not provide any conclusive information regarding MOOCs, but they do give readers an impression of what MOOC students have to choose from in terms of subject area and workload, broadly who is involved in MOOC hosting and instruction (countries, institutions, and individuals), and what options are being explored on the Coursera for-profit platform (e.g., course lengths, workloads, and free versus fee-based courses).

Survey Demographics

One additional piece of very valuable demographic information was gathered using the Qualtrics survey. Of those who responded, approximately 18% of those contacted (335 unique MOOC faculty members) completed the survey, though 80 individuals (24% of those contacted) began the survey. Questions 7 and 8 of the survey sought information as to the status, faculty and otherwise, of MOOC primary instructors on Coursera. A full 70% (61) of those responding to Question 7 indicated that they are tenured faculty at their home institutions; 11% indicated that they are adjuncts, instructors, or "other." Those who responded with a status of "Instructor/Adjunct/Non-tenure track" (11 respondents) were asked to elaborate on their status in Question 8. Two individuals elaborated that they are research faculty at an institution, rather than tenured or tenure-track faculty, and only occasionally teach. These two questions become important when considering the community of MOOC faculty on Coursera, what habits and responsibilities they may have at their home institution, and other survey findings from the Survey Discussion that follows.

Survey Comments, Feedback, and Lessons Learned

This survey was by no means "perfect" though it did accomplish at least two important goals of the author, one primary and another an underlying hope. The first goal, to approach MOOC faculty about their role in MOOCs, their engagement with their institution's library/libraries/librarians, and their thoughts on whether librarians have a place in MOOCs (and what that place might look like), was front and center within the survey. The underlying hope of the author, however, was to create a thought-provoking survey that would generate further discussion among MOOC faculty, among faculty in general, and among faculty and librarians about what roles we can all play in the MOOC setting and how those interested in supporting, rather than instructing, a MOOC might best be able to assist MOOC faculty.

After completing the survey, three faculty members approached the author for additional discussion on the topic as well as possible future collaboration. Five faculty members (three from survey participants and two from the fields of Instructional Design and Librarianship) and a director at the Copyright Clearance Center (CCC) have indicated interest in the survey results and exploring the data and subject matter further.

If this survey were to be repeated in the future, the author would apply several of the suggestions of and feedback from those contacted about the survey including, perhaps, different surveys entirely for those who have not yet taught, those who have finished teaching, and those who are currently in the midst of teaching their MOOC(s); stating a response deadline; including a brief description of "information literacy" (rather than a link to a definition); and strengthening the "permission to quote" section of the survey with clearer options that the respondent can select for how their responses may be handled in publication.

Survey Discussion: A Vision of "MOOLing" in a MOOC

The concept of a MOOL in a MOOC was foreign to some MOOC faculty on Coursera but, when loosely defined, was somewhat in use by or favorably imagined by many who responded to the Qualtrics survey. Several respondents made common suggestions or shared similar thoughts. Additionally, the author consulted with a director at the CCC (Tim Bowen), an Instructional Design and Technology faculty member at the University of Memphis (Dr. Trey Martindale), and an Instructional Design Librarian from Pennsylvania State University's Berks campus (John D. Shank) for further thoughts on MOOCs and MOOLs. Both survey results and valuable thoughts from those conversations are used in this section to discuss current uses and future opportunities and options for librarians interested in involvement with MOOCs.

While there may not be much that a MOOC faculty member may want a librarian to develop, it is still critical that faculty members are at least aware that librarians may very well be interested in engaging with their home institution's MOOCs. Additionally, faculty members also need to have some understanding of what their librarians may be able to contribute—they need not aim to incorporate every librarian strength, tool, resource, and ace-up-the-sleeve, but it is a lot easier to pick the proper tool in a toolbox if you know what they do.

Within the survey, Question 25 ("Have you ever had a librarian embedded into your courses at your institution?"), Question 28 ("Please describe the involvement of the library and/or librarians in your MOOC(s)"), and Question 31 ("Do you envision a future where librarians can/will be a part of the MOOC course environment?" and its "Please elaborate" follow-up prompt, Question 32) were particularly informative with regard to perceived usefulness of librarians in a variety of settings, as well as how MOOC faculty are accustomed to using librarians at their home institution.

Despite the low number of responses for the survey, in terms of significance, the repetition of a number of comments, especially in the questions noted above, leads the author to believe that there are at least a few common understandings of the role librarians can serve and whether and how that may be applicable to the MOOC. These trends include librarians as resource creators, librarians as experts or support for course content design and delivery, and librarians as hubs for knowledge and negotiation of copyright and access.

Resource Creation

A number of survey responses to questions 31 and 32 indicated the need for close conversation with the librarians of their home institutions in order to hone in on the best ways in which librarians could become engaged in their MOOCs. Comments and perceptions were quite mixed: "I'm not sure what role an academic librarian could play in a course where the students aren't affiliated with the institution," "Most of the functions of a librarian can now be automated," "On line education is in a state of a rapid evolution. Who knows what will happen...," "Not easy to see what they can do that they don't already do for regular courses," and "Librarians could be key players in a connectivist MOOC."

Overall, MOOC faculty indicated the most interest in librarians serving as experts in managing digital assets, suggesting additional readings to students, citing sources, discovering and using information, and evaluating resources. Question 28, which asks respondents to elaborate on how librarians are involved in their MOOC, received a few comments that indicate to the author that some MOOC faculty are already harnessing these identified skills of librarians for their MOOC. Responses included: "I asked a librarian to film two videos about how to locate information and do online research and the difference [between] peer reviewed and popular literature," "locating open access material," "establishing learning outcomes," and "We incorporated materials developed by our librarians for research assistance, evaluating sources, other tasks. I think all were re-purposed from previously prepared library skills teaching materials." These comments suggest that, even in small ways, librarian skills and resources can be mounted into

MOOCs to provide additional support, content, and learning objects for the global MOOC community.

Librarians—especially those engaged in digital preservation, instruction, emerging technologies, and instructional design—enjoy working with and showcasing technology and resources. Some MOOC faculty are very aware of these skills and interests and have started taking advantage of them; other faculty have not yet had sufficient discussion at the local or institutional level to know what collaborative opportunities may best suit their MOOC. Additionally, other MOOC faculty are aware of the fact that their particular MOOC—often in the sciences—may not be suited to this kind of partnership. As with on-campus collaborations, librarians engaged in resource creation (and/or even some MOOC instruction through videos) for use in a course must fit the course, its needs, and its population.

Course Content Design and Delivery

MOOC faculty often spend significant amounts of time adapting content to and creating content for the MOOC setting (see questions 18–21). Responses to the author's inquiry as to the amount of time spent adapting their course to the MOOC platform ranged from estimates given in hours, days, weeks, months, and even years. Faculty hour estimates ranged from a lower end of 30–60 hours to a high end approximating thousands of hours of effort. As many faculty indicated that teaching assistants, graduate assistants, student workers, and other forms of human resource capital had at times been made available to them, often perceived as a form of incentive (survey questions 10 and 11), the high estimates for adaptation time will likely be due to MOOC faculty factoring in the effort per person involved in mounting and/or adapting their course. The estimates here are not necessarily given at the individual level, yet they are no less telling.

With regard to Question 25 in particular, of the 14 respondents (23%) stating that they had used embedded librarians before at their home institution, there were no stated disadvantages of that collaboration when they responded to the follow-up (Question 26). Two respondents commented "all advantages" and "no disadvantages" explicitly in their reply. This would indicate to the author that, at least for these 14 MOOC faculty, the concept of an institutionally embedded librarian of some sort would be favorably received in the MOOC setting. Coincidentally, 14 respondents also indicated that they had involved librarians from their institution in their MOOC (Question 27). While it is not clear that these responses come from the same 14 faculty members, it could indicate that those more accustomed to collaborating with librarians at their institution may be more open to collaborating with librarians in their MOOC.

Copyright and Access

Librarians frequently engage in discussions about and in activities involving copyright, open access, fair use, creative commons, and many other terms and arguments regarding these concepts. They may be the institutional liaison to the CCC; they may be instructing students on plagiarism and fair use; and they may be discussing the frustrations with and/or importance of obtaining copyright clearance, or what open access is, or many other nuances of the publishing world as it relates to education. Librarians are, therefore, part of the voice regarding copyright and access.

Furthermore, librarians are part of the actions involved in copyright adherence and advising. They often arrange for electronic and print reserve items, may administer or post cleared PDFs to an institutional CMS (e.g. Blackboard), may assist student and faculty members with printing or scanning at the libraries, and may instruct users on how to access e-books (and e-book limitations and copyright stipulations). Given the wealth of direct and indirect copyright-related activities in which librarians engage, it seems a natural fit that faculty instructing MOOCs would approach librarians about course content concerns, issues, availability, and negotiation. Furthermore, as the MOOC grows in a credit-bearing direction, librarians will be an important institutional resource.

At the American Library Association 2013 Annual Conference (June 27–July 1, 2013), the CCC hosted a Product Advisory Session for College and University Librarians (June 28, 2013). The first item on the agenda was "MOOCs Licensing" and was led by Tim Bowen, the Director of Academic Products and Services at CCC. In Spring 2013, the CCC piloted a partnership with the Stanford Intellectual Property Exchange (SIPX) with a Stanford course offered on Coursera. The goal was to create the equivalent of a "course pack" where, if they wanted to, students enrolled in that MOOC could pay to have access to course materials—as one-offs, if there were only certain items or sections in which they were interested, or the option to purchase it all—and if they did not, would still have access to all the lectures, quizzes, and so forth. Bowen stated that roughly 4,000 students "completed" the MOOC, and approximately 1,200–1,300 of them purchased the "course packs" at $98 for the full array of content.

This meeting engaged librarians in discussion as to whether we felt this would be a viable option moving forward and whether we had additional ideas or concerns about this plan—which they hope to unveil in the next few months. Librarians have long had a strong voice in the argument for information access and freedom of speech, and now librarians are clearly seen as an important community to consult in the confluent discussion of copyright, access, and open education. Yet, the open access movement will provide compelling opportunities for MOOC content in the sciences in particular as major industrialized countries, like the United States and the United Kingdom, pursue making publicly funded research freely accessible to the public (Rushby, 2012). The medicine, technology, and science subject areas account for approximately 50% of the MOOCs available through Coursera (see Table 3) and increased use of scholarship from open access avenues should be expected.

Additional Feedback on Librarians and MOOCs

Only 13 respondents (22%) felt they would take advantage of a Coursera-provided librarian if one was to be offered to them for use in their course (Question 33); the majority of respondents here (29, or 48%) answered "maybe." Based on participant responses in the follow-up prompt (Question 34) and to questions 31 and 32 (discussed earlier), there are several reasons why faculty may be unsure. The degree to which a MOOC involves information literacy components and/or is "information-oriented" were noted variables. Several participants voiced wariness about Coursera providing such a resource. Comments related to that include: "I think a local contact is better," "I'd prefer to make one of our institution's librarians a partner in our course and deliver library services I have confidence in," and "Coursera is a for profit company. Frankly, their goals are entirely different than those of an instructor." That last remark indicates awareness on the part of MOOC faculty members that their goals and the goals of the platform may be somewhat at odds. Faculty interest in "local" collaborators and desire for "confidence" in their resources may further indicate that librarians do have a place in the future of the MOOC, especially where support for course design and content delivery are concerned.

Within Question 35, participant responses to this question indicated a few other areas librarians may want to delve into when vying to be part of MOOCs:

"Two-thirds of the academic work involves the on-line questions, which you did not ask about. [...] The issues are identifying suitable questions, deciding the format of the questions, entering questions, and testing questions. In my subject, and I think in most others, good questions, well formulated, are hard to find. I wonder if there might be a lot of expertise among the community of librarians that might be brought to bear."

"MOOCs could certainly benefit from knowledge management teams—several NGOs that are involved in continuing education frame this in the context of knowledge management, program learning and the like and an expanded definition of a 'librarian' certainly is valuable there"

"I just participated in a virtual panel on MOOCs, organized by the Association of College and Research Libraries (ACRL). It confirmed my opinion that librarians are way ahead of most academics when it comes to the transformative power of information technology."

"I believe that overall the issue of librarianship has so far received insufficient attention in the discussion on MOOCs. There is an unfounded belief that the brave new world of online learning relegates libraries to a secondary position. This is, in my view, wrong. Libraries remain indispensable and we have been extremely grateful for the support we have received from the Royal Library of Denmark."

These statements indicate several areas of collaboration that had not been recognized previously by the author—essentially, this is a wonderful thing, as the dialogue of collaboration should involve the sharing of ideas. The survey was intended to generate discussion, rather than establish firm answers, on the topic of librarians in MOOCs. The fact that a number of MOOC faculty did take the time to address their own fresh thoughts on potential collaboration between MOOC faculty and librarians does indicate at least some amount of success in developing additional conversation.

Future Research

Predictability: Library Use and MOOCbrarians

While the survey detailed in this article did aim to unveil elements of that information, the response rate (18% of all individuals surveyed) was not high enough that any clear conclusions could be drawn (Instructional Assessment Resources, 2011). Thus, no conclusions can be drawn with regard to a relationship between MOOC faculty use of their library for their non-MOOC courses and research and whether they feel there is a place for librarians within the MOOC environment. The author would suggest further research into whether MOOC faculty members who are regular users of their institutional libraries and librarians more or less predictably have an interest in bringing librarians into their MOOC environment. As institutionally run and credit bearing MOOCs become more and more popular and prevalent, the author expects that institutional libraries and their librarians will become more and more involved. Additionally, it may be easier to survey in that circumstance, institution by institution, rather than approaching all Coursera MOOC faculty, as was done here.

Additionally, the author predicts that, as humanities MOOCs continue to develop and become more popular (currently more MOOCs are offered for the physical, biological, and social sciences), the special collections and archives of institutional libraries and other relevant library collections, academic institution-based or not, will become more involved in MOOCs as well. Future research could be conducted regarding whether this relationship develops, as predicted here, or not.

Copyright and Access Regulation Shifts

Given the fact that the CCC approached the largest conference of librarians in the United States (ALA Annual, 2013) for advice and opinions on copyright, access, and the directions the CCC is planning to head regarding MOOCs, this will not be the end of the discussion but is merely a tributary new channel in the flow of conversation between copyright providers and copyright navigators. If the CCC and SIPX follow through on expanding their pilot with Stanford and Coursera from Spring 2013, and offer that option to all MOOCs, research into the impacts of that relationship and that option will be important.

Future research regarding the impacts of these partnerships will be most important in terms of: (1) the completion rate of these courses, (2) how MOOC faculty respond to these fees, (3) how students respond to these fees, and (4) whether students and faculty work to circumvent or otherwise avoid these barriers to access (which may be financial, but which may also be impacted by international copyright regulations, faculty interest in/intention to provide open education, publisher agreements, and more). The OCLC conference at the University of Pennsylvania in March 2013 also raises the question of whether tuition translates to productivity, which the author believes raises a fair point—one with which educators will be familiar from more traditional instruction settings. No matter the type of institution, or the cost of your course, students will always span the spectrum .

The author urges faculty to continue placing a premium on providing open education regardless of financial or other resources. She also urges researchers, MOOC platforms, and host institutions to consider and analyze the international impacts of these regulations, the prohibitive and exclusionary nature of such fees for non-credit bearing work, and the good intentions of an open education resource and the opportunity for self-improvement in a world of people who may otherwise not have access to such options, let alone to courses taught by such "experts" as those teaching and supporting MOOCs and their development.

Survey questions 21, 22, 24, and 28 engaged participants in reflection on special permissions from publishers and/or vendors, obtaining those special permissions, how MOOC faculty use their home institution library (or libraries), and how librarians have been involved in MOOCs with survey participants thus far.

Delivery and Success of MOOC Learning Outcomes

Research on these topics has already commenced, but it will continue. Many different communities have an interest in the percentages of stick-with-it students and "dropouts," issues of plagiarism, accomplishments of MOOC learning outcomes, assessments and measurability, academic integrity, user privacy and authenticity, and the MOOC "honor code(s)," to name just a few areas of curiosity regarding the successfulness (or unsuccessfulness) of the MOOC. T. Hugh Crawford's article for CHE (2013) states that, "to MOOC or not to MOOC [is] not really the question. The real issues [is] how brick-and-mortar institutions could embrace MOOCs while continuing to build on the strengths of local, capital-intensive pedagogical practices—actual in-the-flesh pedagogy in a world of Coursera." And so, at the most basic level, the resources devoted to the delivery and success of any MOOC should supplement the attention an institution devotes to its paying customers, its students. The capital-intensive investments of human resources, programming, technology, and support systems at brick-and-mortar institutions should drive the ability to create, hone, and sustain global education efforts and achievements. Crawford does not encourage institutions to turn a blind eye to the opportunities beyond their doorstep, merely to keep in mind that home is where the heart is and there is much we can do, always, to better how we educate the students who pay us for the privilege.

Yet there may be ways to meet in the middle. For those looking to create institutional platforms (whether for-credit or free), whichever institutional faculty members have already used MOOCs hosted by for-profit entities (e.g., Coursera) will have the advantage of having experimented in these learning environments already. These faculty members will have delivered video lectures with embedded quizzes, created weekly (or bi-weekly) quizzes with honor codes, created mass assignments, used peer review options in this setting, and more. EDUCAUSE (2012) notes the MOOC business model opportunities that institutions may consider pursuing: data mining, the cross- or up-sell, advertising and course sponsorship, tuition-based models, and/or the spin off/licensed content model (p. 2). Slate's Will Oremus (2013) suggests that MOOCs should not act as a supplement to teachers and classrooms, but that "MOOC-style video lectures and online features [should be used] as course materials in actual, normal-size college classes" utilizing blended and flipped classroom strategies. Thus, there is not a complete transformation of the education delivery system after all, but instructors are just taking advantage of newer content delivery methods and bringing them back home to institutions. This may also be a useful way for MOOC-ing institutions to make better use of MOOC content for their on-ground or otherwise enrolled students paying for the enhanced version of a course—with library materials, guided research, and more traditional "perks."

If the MOOC is to live on, and the author believes it will do so in a variety of permutations, then we will need to continue developing ways to strengthen the level of engagement students have in the MOOC, the accountability and ethics of those taking the MOOC, and the technological elements within the MOOC (e.g., in-video quizzing, closed-captioning in non-English languages) especially as they relate to and increase the chances of students completing the course and the ability of adaptive instruction to increase skills development and knowledge retention. Research deeper into these features and how they support learning outcomes, knowledge building, information retention, and student engagement will be critical to the profitable development of MOOCs, as well as the experience of the non-paying student.

Librarians engaged in instructional design and information literacy, including media and technology literacies, will be looking out for research on MOOCs and (like the author of this article) conducting their own research (e.g., participating in MOOCs) to understand how learning outcomes and course competencies are achieved in this educational environment and, more generally, what it takes to run and support a MOOC. Especially by taking MOOCs hosted by their home institution, librarians will have the first-hand knowledge necessary to give strategic feedback and suggestions to MOOC faculty, and perhaps better understand specific scenarios in which they can contribute their skills as a librarian into the MOOC. The author suggests collaborative research between MOOC faculty and librarians to gauge the complexities, necessities, challenges, and benefits of collaborative work between MOOC faculty and "MOOCbrarians"—or "MOOLs in a MOOC."

Lastly, the author suggests that special collections, archival, and outreach librarians also keep an eye on these developments and the MOOCs that they may be able to support—whether at their home institution or not. Libraries will always seek ways to better demonstrate and highlight their value. Bringing 2,000–10,000 unique users to your digitized collections over the course of one MOOC (which might run as few as three weeks), from all over the globe, would be a coup, internally and institutionally, and statistics would not be terribly difficult to gather as well, with tracking support from a systems or information technology department. Sharon Weiner (2009), Dean of Library Services at the University of Massachusetts Dartmouth, notes "[t]here is a growing consensus that the library should be recognized as a partner with other entities in the university in supporting the institutional mission, resulting in increased integration of the library" (p. 4). If an institution chooses to offer MOOCs as a way to engage with the global learning community and increase access to their resources, including human (faculty) resources, then a shift has occurred in the institutional goals and priorities, and libraries must pursue (and be pursued regarding) opportunities for engagement with this community and their potential needs. Most specifically, scholarly communication models development, curricula development, and student learning integration are all areas where the libraries might engage in boundary spanning efforts within their institution (Weiner, 2009, p. 9).

Hypotheses?

What might the future hold for MOOCs? The author suggests a few hypotheses.

(1) Many students will still pursue the full extent of open education (free of barriers to entry), without the intent to seek certification or other credit for the course. These students will resist requests to pay for a MOOC or its contents and seek the access to opportunity rather than academic credit or otherwise attaining some sort of official achievement.

(2) We will find those who are willing to pay because they seek credit for completing the course—and those for whom such fees will continue to prevent their access to educational opportunities.

(3) There will be ramifications to the educational community, which has already begun transforming in response to the MOOC. For example, Harvard requires students take an introductory level economics MOOC with Brigham Young University, rather than taking the course with Harvard's own faculty. As the Tennessee Board of Regents begins a relationship with Coursera, it will be interesting to see the impact of MOOCs at the state consortium level (University of Tennessee Media Resources, 2013). Among those who could very likely suffer are community colleges and their faculty, where students may be able to replace for-credit courses there (often used for placement and transfer into four-year schools and programs) with the burgeoning for-credit MOOCs, thus offering the already-strained budgets of community colleges an opportunity to cut faculty numbers (and diminish the budget lines that accompany them).

(4) The educational sphere will need to work to create an open education system that stays open, perhaps still relying on venture capitalism but also perhaps finding venture capitalists that are more interested in the adventure and the benefits to humanity than in the capitalism. John Daniel (2012) states, "While the hype about MOOCs is presaging revolution in higher education has refocused on their scale, the real revolution is that universities with scarcity at the heart of their business models are embracing openness" (p. 1). Regarding the pursuit of MOOCs for financial gain, Ed Techie (2013) writes, "So what about MOOCs, you know, those free open courses? Is this the end of them? No, I don't think so, but maybe they can now become what we always wanted them to be, focused on access and experimentation, not hype and commercialism." Where Charles Rinehimer (2013) knows that, many times, the student with the spark is his motivator for "walk[ing] into class every day with a smile on [his] face and a sense of anticipation"— MOOC students with "the spark" deserve a chance to make a MOOC professor's day, and MOOC faculty deserve the opportunity to engage that spark.

Many in education who hope for the redefinition of "return on investment" will want that return to be a smarter, more curious global community with access to opportunities for personal betterment and achievement, regardless of whether they live on Long Island or on Micronesia. Such opportunities might require not a form of tender from students but a desire to learn and a willingness to try, and hands and minds that want to be part of such an adventure—to keep it growing and improving, yes, but also to keep it free.

References

Aleamoni, L. M. (1999). Student rating myths versus research facts from 1924 to 1998. Journal of Personnel Evaluation in Education, 13(2), 153-166. doi: 10.1007/BF00143282

Association of College and Research Libraries. Working Group on Intersections of Scholarly Communication and Information Literacy. (2013). Intersections of scholarly communication and information literacy: Creating strategic collaborations for a changing academic environment. Chicago, IL: Association of College and Research Libraries.

Booth, C. (2011). Reflective teaching, effective learning. Chicago, IL: American Library Association.

Chen, J. C. C. (2013, August). Opportunities and challenges of MOOCs: Perspectives from Asia. Paper presented at IFLA World Library and Information Congress, Singapore.

Cordell, D. (2012). Skype and the Embedded librarian." Library Technology Reports, 48(2), 8-11.

Covone, N., & Lamm, M. (2010). Just be there: Campus, department, classroom ... and kitchen?" Public Services Quarterly, 6, 198-207. doi:10.1080/15228959.2010.498768

Crawford, H. T. (2013, April 29). Rediscovering the material world." The Chronicle of Higher Education. Retrieved from http://chronicle.com

Daniel, J. (2012). Making sense of MOOCs: Musings in a maze of myth, paradox and possibility. Journal of Interactive Media in Education, 3. Retrieved from http://www-jime.open.ac.uk/jime/article/viewArticle/2012-18/html

Denlinger, K. (2013, May 10). ZSRx: The MOOC that wasn't a MOOC [Web log post]. Retrieved from http://cloud.lib.wfu.edu/blog/gazette/2013/05/10/zsrx-library-mooc/

Dill, E. (2012, August 14). MOOCs: Where are the librarians? [Web Log post]. Retrieved from http://hastac.org/blogs/elizabeth-dill/2012/08/14/moocs-where-are-librarians

EDUCAUSE. (2012). What campus leaders need to know about MOOCs. EDUCAUSE. Retrieved from http://net.educause.edu/ir/library/pdf/PUB4005.pdf

EDUCAUSE Learning Initiative. (2011). 7 things you should know about MOOCs. EDUCAUSE. Retrieved from http://net.educause.edu/ir/library/pdf/ELI7078.pdf

EDUCAUSE Learning Initiative. (2013). Initiatives: Content anchors. Retrieved from http://www.educause.edu/eli/programs/seeking-evidence-impact/content-anchors

EDUCAUSE Library. (2013). Massive Open Online Course (MOOC). Retrieved from www.educause.edu/library/massive-open-online-course-mooc

Edwards, M., Kumar, S., & Ochoa, M. (2010). Assessing the value of embedded librarians in an online graduate educational technology course. Public Services Quarterly, 6, 271-291. doi:10.1080/15228959.2010.497447

Essig, L. (2013, March 25). The conversation: It's MOOAs, not MOOCs, that will transform education [Web log post]. Retrieved from http://chronicle.com/blogs/conversation/2013/03/25/its-mooas-not-moocs-that-will-transform-higher-education/

Evans, B. (2013, March 23). OCLC research presents MOOCs and libraries: Massive opportunity or overwhelming challenge? [Web log post]. Retrieved from http://bclibsconf.wordpress.com/2013/03/23/oclc_moocs_and_libraries_2012_03_18/

Fischman, J. (2011, May 8). The digital campus 2011: The rise of teaching machines. The Chronicle of Higher Education. Retrieved from http://chronicle.com

Frank, D. G., Raschke, G. K., Wood, J., & Yang, J. Z.. (2001). Information consulting: The key to success in academic libraries. Journal of Academic Librarianship, 27(2), 90-96.

Green, H. (2013). Libraries across land and sea: Academic library aervices on international branch campuses. College & Research Libraries, 74(1), 9-23.

Gustavson, A., & Nall, H. C. (2011). Freshman overconfidence and library research skills: A troubling relationship? College & Undergraduate Libraries, 18(4), 291-306. doi:10.1080/10691316.2011.624953

Haden, P. C. (2013, May 13). People: It's no act: Athletic director tries out a new role. The Chronicle of Higher Education. Retrieved from http://chronicle.com

Hazelkorn, E. (2013, May 23). Has higher education lost control over quality? [Web log post]. Retrieved from http://chronicle.com/blogs/worldwise/has-higher-education-lost-control-over-quality/32321?cid=wb&utm_source=wb&utm_medium=en

Hoffman, S. (2011). Embedded academic librarian experiences in online courses: Roles, faculty collaboration, and opinion. Library Management, 32(6/7), 444-456. doi:10.1108/01435121111158583

Holdaway, X., & Hawtin, N. (2013, April 29). The digital campus 2013: Major players in the MOOC universe. The Chronicle of Higher Education. Retrieved from http://chronicle.com

Hopper, K. B. (2012). The Buddha's distance learning consult. British Journal of Educational Technology, 43(4), 534-539. doi:10.1111/j.1467-8535.2011.01227.x

Howard, J. (2011, May 8). The digital campus: Tomorrow's academic libraries: Maybe even some books. The Chronicle of Higher Education.Retrieved from http://chronicle.com

Instructional Assessment Resources. (2011). Assess teaching: Response rates. Retrieved from www.utexas.edu/academic/ctl/assessment/iar/teaching/gather/method/survey-Response.php

IS Management & Leadership Committee. (2010). Analyzing your instructional environment: A workbook. Chicago, IL: Association of College and Research Libraries Instruction Section & the American Library Association. Retrieved from http://www.ala.org/

Jones, L. D., P. Regan, & C. E. Mitra. (2011). Mainstreaming information literacy skills into a social enterprise environment. College & Undergraduate Libraries, 18(4), 391-398. doi:10.1080/10691316.2011.624947

Koller, D. (2012, August 1). What we're learning from online education [Video file]. TED Talks. Retrieved from http://www.ted.com/talks/daphne_koller_what_we_re_learning_from_online_education.html

Kolowich, S. (2013, April 23). Why some colleges are saying no to MOOC deals, at least for now. The Chronicle of Higher Education. Retrieved from http://chronicle.com

Kolowich, S. (2013, May 9). As MOOC debate simmers at San Jose State, American U. calls a halt. The Chronicle of Higher

Education. Retrieved from http://chronicle.comKolowich, S. (2013, May 21). MOOC professors claim no responsibility for how courses are used [Web log post]. Retrieved from http://chronicle.com/blogs/wiredcampus/mooc-professors-claim-no-responsibility-for-how-courses-are-used/43881?cid=megamenu

Kolowich, S. (2013, May 24). Harvard professors call for greater oversight of MOOCs [Web log post]. Retrieved from http://chronicle.com/blogs/wiredcampus/harvard-professors-call-for-greater-oversight-of-moocs/43953

Kolowich, S. (2013, May 28). Outsourced lectures raise concerns about academic freedom. The Chronicle of Higher Education.Retrieved from http://chronicle.com

Kuh, G. D., & Gonyea, R. M. (2003). The role of the academic library in promoting student engagement in learning. College & Research Libraries, 64(4), 256-282.

Lai, H.C., Chang, C. Y., Wen-Shiane, L., Fan, Y. L., & Wu, Y. T. (2013). The implementation of mobile learning in outdoor education: Application of QR codes. British Journal of Educational Technology, 44(2), E57-E62. doi:10.1111/j.1467-8535.2012.01343.x

Lee, Y., Choi., J., & Kim, T. (2012). Discriminating factors between completers of and dropouts from online learning courses. British Journal of Educational Technology, 44(2), 328-337. doi:10.1111/j.1467-8535.2012.01306.x

Lloyd, A. (2004). Working (in)formation: Conceptualizing information literacy in the workplace. Lifelong learning: Whose responsibilty and what is your contribution?: Refereed papers from the 3rd International Lifelong Learning Conference. Yeppoon, Central Queensland, Australia (pp.218-224).

Lloyd, A. (2010). Information literacy landscapes: Information literacy in education, workplace, and everyday contexts. Oxford: Chandos Publishing.

Mackey, T. P., & Jacobson, T. E. (2011). Reframing information literacy as a metaliteracy. College & Research Libraries, 72(1), 62-78. Retrieved from http://crl.acrl.org

Mangan, K. (2011, May 8). A seminar connects law students around the world. The Chronicle of Higher Education. Retrieved from http://chronicle.com

Montgomery, S. E. (2010). Online webinars! Interactive learning where our users are: The future of embedded librarianship. Public Services Quarterly, 6(2/3), 306-311. doi:10.1080/15228959.2010.497467

Montiel-Overall, P., & Grimes, K. (2012). Teachers and librarians collaborating on inquiry-based science instruction: A longitudinal study. Library & Information Science Research, 35(1), 41-53. doi:10.1016/j.lisr.2012.08.002

New, J. (2013, April 29). Fighting to reinvent teaching and keep costs down. The Chronicle of Higher Education. Retrieved from http://chronicle.com

OCLCResearch. (2013, April 5). MOOCs and libraries: New opportunities for librarians [Video file]. Retrieved from http://www.youtube.com/watch?v=3ebkaSjXtmk

OCLCResearch. (2013a, April 9). MOOCs and libraries: Copyright, licensing, and open access [Video file]. Retrieved from http://www.youtube.com/watch?v=7FvR4K3eddU

OCLCResearch. (2013b, April 9). MOOCs and libraries: Welcome from the University of Pennsylvania libraries [Video file]. Retrieved from http://www.youtube.com/watch?v=fU8Mle0Tar8

OCLCResearch. (2013c, April 9). MOOCs and Libraries: Who are the masses? A view of the audience [Video file]. Retrieved from http://www.youtube.com/watch?v=6u-MO1hMKSxc.

OCLCResearch. (2013d, April 9). MOOCs and libraries: Why MOOCs? Why Penn? Why now? [Video file]. Retrieved from http://www.youtube.com/watch?v=guQy-TudlFCI.

Open Education Database. (2013, May 16). Librarians: Your most valuable MOOC supporters [Web log post]. Retrived from http://oedb.org/library/features/librarians-your-most-valuable-mooc-supporters/ Oremus, W. (2013, September 18). Free online classes are an unsustainable gimmick: Here's a better idea. Slate. Retrieved from www.slate.com

Pickard, E., & Logan, F. (2013). The research process and the library: First-generation college seniors vs. freshmen." College & Research Libraries. Retrieved from http://crl.acrl.org

Piper, P., & Tag, S. (2011). Theme-based information literacy instruction. College & Undergraduate Libraries, 18(4), 319-332. doi:10.1080/10691316.2011.624956

Pritchard, P. A. (2010). The embedded science librarian: Partner in curriculum design and delivery. Journal of Library Administration, 50(4), 373-396. doi:10.1080/01930821003667054

Rinehimer, C. (2013, May 28). Commentary: The student and the spark [Web log post]. Retrieved from http://chronicle.com/article/The-Studentthe-Spark/139459/?cid=wb&utm_source=wb&utm_medium=en

Rivard, R. (2013, May 14). Georgia Tech and Udacity roll out massive new low-cost degree program. Inside Higher Ed. Retrieved from http://www.insidehighered.com/news/2013/05/14/georgia-tech-and-udacity-roll-out-massive-new-low-cost-degree-program

Roff, S. (2011). Visualizing history: Using museum skills to teach information literacy to undergraduates. College & Undergraduate Libraries,I 4), 350-358. doi:10.1080/10691316.2011.624958

Rudasill, L.M. (2010). Beyond subject specialization: The creation of embedded librarians. Public Services Quarterly, 6, 83-91. doi: 10.1080/15228959.2010.494577

Rudin, P. (2008). No fixed address: The evolution of outreach library services on university campuses. The Reference Librarian, 49(1), 55-75. doi:10.1080/02763870802103761

Rushby, N. (2013). Editorial: Open access. British Journal of Educational Technology, 44(2), 179-182. doi:10.1111/bjet.12027
Scaramozzino, J. M. (2010). Integrating STEM information competencies into an undergraduate curriculum. Journal of Library Administration, 50(4), 315-333. doi:10.1080/01930821003666981

Scarboro, A. (2012). Student perception of good teaching. International Journal of New Trends in Arts, Sports & Science Education, 1(1), 49-66. Retrieved from http://www.ijtase.net/

Schwartz, M. (2013, May 10). Massive open opportunity: Supporting MOOCs in public and academic libraries. Library Journal Academic Newswire. Retrieved from http://lj.libraryjournal.com

Shank, J. D. (2006). The blended librarian: A job announcement analysis of the newly emerging position of instructional design librarian. College & Research Libraries, 67(6), 514-524. Retrieved from http://crl.acrl.org

Shank, J. D. (2013). Goodbye cybrarians, hello moocbrarians: Envisioning the role of librarians in MOOCs [Powerpoint slides]. Retrieved from http://www.slideshare.net

Shank, J. D.,& Bell, S. (2011). Blended librarianship: [Re]envisioning the role of librarian as educator in the digital information age. Reference & User Services Quarterly. 51(2), 105-110.

Showers, B. (2012, January 6). The constant innovator: The academic library as a model of change management [Web log post]. Library Journal Academic Newswire. Retrieved from http://lj.libraryjournal.com

Sull, E. C. (2013, January 31). Student engagement in the online classroom. The Chronicle of Higher Education. Retrieved from http://chronicle.com

The Ed Techie. (2013, May 30). You can stop worrying about MOOCs now [Web log post]. The Ed Techie. Retrieved from http://nogoodreason.typepad.co.uk/no_good_reason/2013/05/you-can-stop-worrying-about-moocs-now.html

The Ed Techie. (2013, June 26). What quality measures apply to MOOCs? [Web log post]. The Ed Techie. Retrieved from http://nogoodreason.typepad.co.uk/no_good_reason/2013/06/what-quality-measures-apply-to-moocs.html

University of Pennsylvania Libraries. (2013).Coursera and MOOCS: Copyright resources to support publishing and teaching. Retrieve from http://guides.library.upenn.edu/content.php?pid=244413&sid=3375306

University of Tennessee Media Resources. (2013). UT, TBR partner with Coursera to pilot technology for courses [press release]. Retrieved from http://www.tennessee.edu/media/releases/053013_coursera.html

Valibrarian. (2013, February 19). ACRL VWIG Panel: MOOCs and Librarians [Video file]. Retrieved from http://www.youtube.com/watch?v=SinXCiMF_Cs&feature=youtu.be

Verpoorten, D., Westera, W., & Specht, M. (2012). Using reflection triggers while learning in an online course. British Journal of Educational Technology, 43(6), 1030-1040. doi:10.1111/j.1467-8535.2011.01257.x

Wang, M., Shen, R., Novak, D., & Pan X. (2009). The impact of mobile learning on students' learning behaviours and performance: Report from a large blended classroom. British Journal of Educational Technology, 40(4), 673-695. doi:10.1111/j.1467-8535.2008.00846.x

Weiner, S. (2008). The contribution of the library to the reputation of a university. Journal of Academic Librarianship, 35(1), 3-13.

York, A. C., & Vance, J. M. (2009). Taking library instruction into the online classroom: best practices for embedded librarians. Journal of Library Administration, 49, 197-209. doi:10.1080/01930820802312995

Young, J. R. (2013, May 20). What professors can learn from 'Hard Core' MOOC students. The Chronicle of Higher Education. Retrieved from http://chronicle.com

Appendices

Appendix A: Additional Resources

There are a number of blog entries and multimedia resources of interest regarding MOOCs and librarians. The following list constitutes a number of valuable articles and other resources:

• TED talks not only form valuable elements of MOOC content; the TEDtalks website (http://www.ted.com/talks) also contains a TEDtalk from Daphne Koller, the co-founder of Coursera. (Her TEDtalk can be accessed here: http://www.ted.com/talks/daphne_koller_what_we_re_learning_from_online_education.html.) Another TEDtalk of interest will be "Peter Norvig: The 100,000-Student Classroom" (Link: http://www.ted.com/talks/peter_norvig_the_100_000_student_classroom.html).

• Elizabeth Dill posted "MOOCs: Where Are the Librarians?" on the Humanities, Arts, Science, and Technology Alliance and Collaboratory Scholars blog (HASTAC.org) on August 14, 2013. In her post, she writes, "I find it hard to believe that in all of the MOOC furor no one is considering a crucial part of education: the research component, the research component." With perhaps an understandable bias, Dill—a librarian—equates librarians in the MOOC setting as a benchmark necessary to achieve and uphold educational standards.

• The associate vice presidents for outreach at Penn State University, and executive director of their World Campus, Wayne Smutz—like Elizabeth Dill—sees potential in MOOCs and knows they will not stand as the be-all, end-all solution for education that the hype can often make them out to be. He states, "MOOCs aren't likely to solve the fundamental student learning challenges that colleges and universities face, and they certainly won't take the place of a college education." However, he notes the critical components of online student success, which MOOC instructors may then wish to bring into their courses and course design. Of these six keys, three overlap quite nicely with librarianship: intensive support, the personal touch, and flexibility.

• The Ed Techie has two important posts, "You Can Stop Worrying About MOOCs Now" (May 30, 2013) and "What Quality Measures Apply to MOOCs?" (June 26, 2013), of interest. The former suggests critical issues looming regarding MOOCs, venture capitalists, return on investment (ROI), and commercial versus social enterprise goals within MOOCs. Ed Techie notes that for MOOC providers to consider "MOOC based learning on campus" we still just have blended learning (with which librarians and course instructors alike have experience) stating, "If you take the MOO out of the MOOC you're left with just a C, and no one's interested in just a C." The latter post states that those participating in MOOCs are "very different" and, perhaps strangely for some readers, pleas for MOOCs to be free of the "quality demands we have placed on higher education" so that experimentation through this unique, free relationship between student and educator may remain open. Librarians, too, may wish to have an open field for collaboration with MOOC faculty and experimentation with literacy content development and delivery. (The Ed Techie's assertion of the "differentness" of the MOOC student is also explored by Jeffrey R. Young in his article for Chronicle of Higher Education (May 20, 2013), entitled "What Professors Can Learn From 'Hard Core' MOOC Students," where he underscores the hugely important role that curiosity and passion play in student drive to participate in MOOCs.)

- In March 2013, the Online Computer Library Center, or OCLC, (OCLCResearch 2013a; OCLC Research 2013b; OCLCResearch 2013c; OCLCResearch 2013d) hosted a two-and-a-half-day conference, titled "MOOCs and Libraries: Massive Opportunity or Overwhelming Challenge," hosted at the University of Pennsylvania. Video content was posted on YouTube dated April 9, 2013. (See Table 1. Penn State is tied for the most number of MOOCs hosted by a single institution on Coursera.) Valuable resources available in the aftermath of that conference include a blog post from Brooklyn College librarians (Evans, 2013). See Panel 4, in particular. Recorded videos from the conference can be found on YouTube from the conference sessions:

    o The "MOOCs and Libraries" welcome speech from H. Carton Rogers III—the Vice Provost and Director of Libraries at the University of Pennsylvania: http://www.youtube.com/watch?v=fU8Mle0Tar8.
    o "Why MOOCs? Why Penn? Why now?" is a 23-minute talk led by Professor Ed Rock of Penn Law: http://www.youtube.com/watch?v=guQyTudlFCI
    o A panel of academics from several institutions, along with a representative from the Association of Research Libraries, led an hour-long session on copyright, licensing, and open access: http://www.youtube.com/watch?v=7FvR4K3eddU.
    o A second hour-long presentation from librarians and instructional designers, titled "MOOCs and Libraries: New Opportunities for Librarians," is also extremely relevant to the content in and context of this article: http://www.youtube.com/watch?v=3ebkaSjXtmk.

- The Association of College and Research Libraries' Virtual World Interest Group (VWIG) also posted a short video on YouTube on this topic called "MOOCs and Librarians": http://www.youtube.com/watch?v=SinXCiMF_Cs&feature=youtu.be.
- Two articles published by Library Journal are also worth reading: Ben Showers's "The Constant Innovator: The Academic Library as a Model of Change Management" (http://lj.libraryjournal.com/2012/01/opinion/backtalk/the-constant-innovator-the-academic-library-as-a-model-of-change-management-backtalk/) and Meredith Schwartz's "Massive Open Opportunity: Supporting MOOCs in Public and Academic Libraries" (http://lj.libraryjournal.com/2013/05/library-services/massive-open-opportunity-supporting-moocs/).
- The Open Education Database (http://www.oedb.org) published an article on May 16, 2013 entitled "Librarians: Your Most Valuable MOOC Supporters" and states, "Libraries are a major part of universities, but they're almost entirely missing from the MOOC conversation. That's a big mistake." Staff writers go on to describe the wealth of ways that librarians can participate in, contribute to, and help support MOOCs.

Chronicle of Higher Education (CHE) articles worth review:

- Josh Fischman discusses the "Rise of Teaching Machines" in his 2011 article for CHE's Digital Campus—exploring adaptive-learning technologies and their impact on student motivations, as well as noting resources engaged with these strategies, such as Knewton, Carnegie Mellon University's Open Learning Initiative, and Wake Forest University's "BioBook" project. More studies are needed on the outcomes of implementing this avenue of learning and content delivery, particularly for students in the community college environment. One may suspect that the concept of "teaching machines" outright replacing teachers is akin to the concept of

computers replacing librarians.
- Steve Kolowich has a number of thought-provoking and informative articles from 2013 regarding the complex debates over MOOC efficacy and host institution administration and return on investment available through the Chronicle of Higher Education, including:
    o "Why Some Colleges Are Saying No to MOOC Deals, At Least for Now";
    o "As MOOC Debate Simmers at San Jose State, American U. Calls a Halt";
    o "Wired Campus: MOOC Professors Claim No Responsibility for How Courses Are Used";
    o "Wired Campus: Harvard Professors Call for Greater Oversight of MOOCs"; and
    o "Outsourced Lectures Raise Concerns About Academic Freedom."

- Additional 2013 CHE articles of relevance here are:
    o Jennifer Howard's "Tomorrow's Academic Libraries: Maybe Even Some Books"; and
    o Laurie Essig's "It's MOOAs, Not MOOCs, That Will Transform Higher Education."

Relevant scholarly articles, while not always directly about MOOCs and librarianship, can provide for inspiration, reflection, and collaborative brainstorming. Readers may want to pursue:

- Sandra Roff's "Visualizing History: Using Museum Skills to Teach Information Literacy to Undergraduates" (2011), published in College & Undergraduate Libraries, may enlighten educators about creative efforts of librarians for traditional, credit-bearing courses and may provide a necessary spark to try new methods of engagement with their home institution's students as well as in the MOOC environment. As humanities and social science courses grow, the generation of visually appealing, and educational, customized materials for the MOOC setting—to help students "visualize history"—seems very appealing.
- Verpoorten, Westera, and Specht's "Using Reflection Triggers While Learning in an Online Class" (2012) discusses reflection triggers (RTs), which are used to provide opportunities for learners to contemplate and assess their learning. Rather than propagating the belief that reflection should occur at the end of a course or project, such as part of a portfolio, these authors advocate for reflection during the learning process, not as part of the aftermath (p. 1031). Within the context of online learning, technology has enabled opportunities for adaptive learning and MOOCs would likely benefit from adopting adaptive learning strategies into the scaffolding of their courses.
- Joyce Chao-chen Chen's "Opportunities and Challenges of MOOCs: Perspectives From Asia" (2013) explores issues of open access, archiving, and open educational resources, as well as multimedia instructional resources in use for "technology-based instruction" such as iTunesU, YouTubeEDU, and others. Librarians are often a great source for relevant resource suggestions, for faculty and students, and certainly working with a librarian to locate and mount such resources in a MOOC would be an appropriate collaboration. Also important in Chen's research is comparative data on locations of their MOOC students (p. 3), major MOOC developments in Asia (p. 5), highlighted opportunities that MOOCs provide (p. 6-8), cultural themes and differences (p. 9), and challenges and important competencies for MOOC teachers (p. 10-13).
- Jones, Regan, and Mitra (2011) consider "information literacy beyond the library" within the context of social enterprise and

workforce development. When discussing open education, we must note the critical opportunity for personal development and enrichment presented for MOOC students—"the marriage of concepts of information literacy and social enterprise produces opportunities that clearly represent a unique value-added proposition in the world of workforce development, education, and training for low-income workers" (p. 392).
• Youngju Lee, Jaeho Choi, and Taehyun Kim's "Discriminating Factors Between Completers of and Dropouts From Online Learning Courses" (2013) focuses on online course completion, and barriers to it. Suggestions and knowledge herein may be applicable to MOOCs and their estimated 10% completion rate.

Appendix B: MOOCs, MOOC Instruction, and Librarianship Survey

Q1 Informed Consent

This survey is about Massive Open Online Courses (MOOCs)—but also about librarianship. Your participation is completely voluntary, and you may leave blank any items that you do not feel comfortable answering. We sincerely appreciate your participation in this research effort. All data from this survey will be presented in aggregate and any quotes will not include any identifying information, unless your express permission is granted on the next screen ("Permission to Quote"). If you have any questions regarding this survey, please contact the Investigator: Laureen Cantwell, Instructional Services Librarian, University of Memphis (email: lcntwell@memphis.edu). By filling out this survey, you indicate that you have read, understand, and agree to these terms. Thank you for time and assistance! By selecting "Yes" below, you accept the Informed Consent details as outlined above.

Yes (1)
No (2)
• If No Is Selected, Then Skip To End of Survey

Q2 Permission to Quote

By selecting "Yes" below, you give the Investigator permission to quote from your responses. Please note that Permission to Quote is NOT a requirement to participate in this survey. If you select "No" your responses will ONLY be presented in aggregate and any quotes will NOT include any identifying information. If you have any questions or concerns, please contact the Investigator: Laureen Cantwell, Instructional Services Librarian, University of Memphis (email: lcntwell@memphis.edu). Thank you.

Yes, you have my permission to quote from my reply. (1)

No, you do not have my permission to quote from my responses. Please only use my entries for aggregate data and do not include any identifying information in any quotes used. (2)

Q3 Thank you for choosing to complete this survey. You should anticipate it will take about 10–20 minutes to complete, depending on the flow of your responses.

Q4 Your email address. (This information will be used to pair you with data gathered from your Coursera course page. Your contact information will not be published.)

Q5 Title(s) of courses taught through Coursera (past, present, upcoming). (This information will be used to pair you with data gathered from your Coursera course page. This information will be used within aggregate data. If you gave permission to quote on the previous screen, your course title(s) may be included in the quote information.)

Q6 Your institution. (This information will be used to pair you with data gathered from your Coursera course page. This information will be used within aggregate data. If you gave permission to quote on the previous screen, your institution's name may be included in the quote information.)

Q7 Your faculty status
Emeritus/Retired (1)
Tenured (2)
Tenure-track (3)
Instructor/Adjunct/Non-tenure track (4)
Other (5)

• Answer If Your faculty status. Other Is Selected:

Q8 If you selected "Other" please describe your position as an instructor within your institution.

Q9 Did/Will you receive any amount of course release for your role as Instructor of a MOOC on Coursera? If so, how much?

Q31 Did/Will you receive any pay from your institution for your role as Instructor in a MOOC on Coursera?
Yes (1)
No (2)

Q32 Other than pay and/or course release, have you been offered any other incentives from your institution to instruct/develop a MOOC?
Yes (1)
No (2)
• Q33 Please describe these incentives.

Q14 Are you currently teaching a MOOC (or MOOCs)?

Yes, one. (1)
Yes, several. (2)
No, my MOOC is finished. (3)
No, my MOOC is upcoming. (4)

• Answer If Are you currently teaching a MOOC (or MOOCs)? Yes, one. Is Selected Or Are you currently teaching a MOOC (or MOOCs)? Yes, several. Is Selected Or Are you currently teaching a MOOC (or MOOCs)? No, my MOOC is finished. Is Selected:

Q10 # of students enrolled in your MOOC(s). (If you teach/have taught more than 1 MOOC, please state final enrollment #s for each with the name(s) of the course(s).)

• Answer If Are you currently teaching a MOOC (or MOOCs)? No, my MOOC is finished. Is Selected:

Q11 # of students earning a Certificate in your MOOC(s). (If you teach/have taught more than 1 MOOC, please state #s for each course along with the name(s) of the course(s).)

• Answer If Are you currently teaching a MOOC (or MOOCs)? Yes, several. Is Selected:

Q15 How many MOOCs are you teaching currently?

Q13 How would you describe the level of your MOOC?
Introductory—no prior knowledge/study necessary (1)
Intermediate—some experience will be helpful (2)
Advanced—prior experience highly recommended (3)
Various levels—I teach several MOOCs (4)

• If Various levels—I teach se... Is Not Selected, Then Skip To How many hours of curriculum design a...(Continue at Q16)

• Answer If How would you describe the level of your MOOC? Various levels—I teach several MOOCs Is Selected:
Q34 What levels would you assign to the MOOCs you are teaching?

Q16 How many hours of curriculum design and course content preparation have gone into your MOOC(s)?

Q17 Have you also taught your MOOC(s) as in-person/online/non-MOOC course(s) at your institution?
Yes (1)
No (2)

• If No Is Selected, Then Skip To Have you gotten any special permission...(Continue at Q29)

• Answer If Have you taught your MOOC(s) as in-person/online/non-MOOC... Yes Is Selected:

Q18 How did you adapt your course(s) to for the Coursera/MOOC environment?

Q29 Have you gotten any special permissions from publishers (or others) to use copyright protected information in your MOOC(s)? (E.g., a book chapter, scholarly article, for use as a course material at no charge to enrolled Coursera students)
Yes (1)
No (2)

• If No Is Selected, Then Skip To End of Block

• Answer If Have you gotten any special permissions from publishers (... Yes Is Selected:
Q30 How did you obtain this permission? (E.g., what offices were involved?)

• Answer If Have you gotten any special permissions from publishers (... Yes Is Selected:
Q39 Did your institution incur a cost to accomplish access to the resource(s)? If there was a cost involved, what was it? (Estimates are fine)
Yes (1)
No (2)

Q12 Does your institution have a library (or libraries)?
Yes (1)
No (2)

• If No Is Selected, Then Skip To End of Block (Continue at Q24)

• Answer If Does your institution have a library (or libraries)? Yes Is Selected:

Q19 Do you use your institution's librarians and/or library/libraries for any of the following services? (Please check all that apply.)

	Purchasing materials	Locating resources at other institutions	Research instruction in my courses	Assistance developing course curricula	Assistance with emerging technology	Developing learning outcomes for courses	Copyright clearance for course materials	Information literacy instruction in my courses
I use my Library for:	☐	☐	☐	☐	☐	☐	☐	☐
I use my Librarian(s) for:	☐	☐	☐	☐	☐	☐	☐	☐

Q20 Have you ever had a librarian embedded into your courses at your institution? (NOT within your MOOC(s).) ("Embedded librarians" can serve for in-person, blended, and/or completely online courses; they may provide instruction, research consultations, writing/bibliographic reviewing assistance, or other kinds of assistance. Another definition and explanation can be found: http://library.uncg.edu/info/distance_education/embedded_librarian.aspx)
Yes. (1)
No. (2)

• If No. Is Selected, Then Skip To Q22 Have you involved your institution's ...

• Answer If Have you ever had a librarian embedded into your courses ... Yes. Is Selected:

Q21 Please describe any advantages and/or disadvantages of having an embedded librarian in your course(s).

Q22 Have you involved your institution's library and/or librarians in your MOOC(s)?
Yes. (1)
No. (2)

• Answer If Have you involved your institution's library and/or libra... Yes. Is Selected:

Q23 Please describe the involvement of the library and/or librarians in your MOOC(s). (This might involve: obtaining copyright clearance for course materials, working with publishers to create special access permissions for articles/book chapters, establishing information literacy components and/or learning outcomes, curricula development, course/instruction design, use of technology, and more.)

Q24 Do you feel students in your MOOC(s) can/do/will learn your course content?
Yes (1)
Maybe/Not sure yet (2)
No (3)

• Q25 Please elaborate on your answer.

Q40 Do you feel students in your MOOC(s) can/do/will become more information literate as a result of your course? (You can view the American Library Association's Association of College & Research Libraries (ACRL) Information Literacy Standards, Performance Indicators, and Outcomes here (www.ala.org/acrl/standards/information-literacycompetency#stan—link will open in a new window.)
Yes (1)
No (2)

Q27 Do you envision a future where librarians can/will be a part of the MOOC course environment?
Yes (1)
Maybe/Not sure yet (2)
No (3)

• Q37 Please elaborate on your answer.

Q36 If Coursera made a librarian available to your course, can you see yourself making use of the librarian?
Yes (1)
Maybe (2)
No (3)

• Q28 Please elaborate on your answer.

Q35 Please use this space to provide any additional thoughts about MOOCs, librarianship, instructing in MOOCs, etc., here.

Screenshots of videos accessible at the web addresses below

Figure 1. Cantwell, L. P. (November 2012). Global Education Conference: What Teachers Can Learn as Students in MOOCs. (See also the archived copy of this presentation via this link: http://www.screencast.com/users/LaureenHome/folders/Default/media/c31e218b-a4d2-401d-968e-88387cc2cfa8/embed).

Figure 2. MOOCs: What are they and how do they work? This figure is an embedded Prezi created by the author. It discusses MOOC basics, excitement and value, concerns, business and management of MOOCs (e.g., return on investment), and readiness assessment for MOOC hosting, with links to source material. (This Prezi and the survey used for this article are available on the author's website accessible through this link: http://prezi.com/embed/88b5f819f595f286fe64551a9d62fe9ba5ae88af/)

Table 1

Most prominent Coursera host institutions within the United States

Institution	# of courses hosted by institution based within the United States	% of Coursera courses hosted by institution based within the United States
Stanford University	22	6%
University of Pennsylvania	22	6%
University of Washington	14	3.8%
Georgia Institute of Technology	13	3.5%
Johns Hopkins University	13	3.5%
Duke University	11	3%
Princeton University	10	2.7%
University of Illinois, Urbana-Champaign	10	2.7%
Total courses hosted by these institutions	115	31%

Note. Data current as of May 15, 2013.

Table 2

Most prominent Coursera host countries based outside the United States

Country	# of courses hosted by country other than the United States	% of Coursera courses hosted by country other than the United States
United Kingdom	18	5%
Canada	13	3.5%
China & Hong Kong	11	3%
France	7	2%
Mexico	7	2%
Total courses hosted by these countries	56	15.5%
Total courses hosted outside U.S.	101	28%

Note. Data current as of May 15, 2013.

Table 3
Distribution of Coursera courses by sole or primary subject area/category

Course Subject Area/Category	# of courses with particular sole or primary subject area or category	% of Coursera courses with particular sole or primary subject area or category
Art	10	3%
Biology and Life Sciences	41	11%
Business and Management	28	8%
Computer Science categories (Artificial Intelligence, Software Engineering, Systems and Security, and Theory)	67	18%
Economics and Finance	17	5%
Education	35	10%
Health and Society	18	5%
Humanities	45	12%
Music, Film, and Audio	12	3%
Physics	11	3%
Total courses in these subject areas/categories	284	78%

Note. Data current as of May 15, 2013.

MOOCs for LIS Professional Development: Exploring New Transformative Learning Environments and Roles

Michael Stephens[1]

Thanks to SJSU SLIS student Margaret Jean Campbell for her invaluable assistance editing and formatting this piece. Thanks to Kyle Jones, PhD student at the University of Wisconsin-Madison's School of Library and Information Studies and SJSU SLIS lecturer, for his incredible work designing the site architecture and for co-istructing the Hyperlinked Library MOOC.

The rapid development of emerging disruptive technologies is a driving force behind the evolution of the library and information science (LIS) profession and is causing a redesign of the traditional approaches to LIS professional development. Historically fairly static, LIS environments have evolved into dynamic reflections of the enormous societal changes occurring as a result of open communications and access throughout the Web. In addition, 21st century LIS professionals must consider and prepare for the new roles they might play in network-enabled, large-scale learning environments. Several decades of research on self-directed learning (SDL) have shown the social, non-linear, and serendipitous process to be transformational. LIS professionals, who once relied upon yearly conferences, employer-provided seminars and workshops, and association newsletters in order to update their knowledge, have embraced SDL opportunities to expand their understandings and skill sets. The first wave of SDL and networked platforms for LIS professional development (Learning 2.0) may have been precursors to the connectivist learning environments designed into the free, not-for-credit, massive open online courses (MOOCs). Because these new environments of participatory and transformative learning offer the potential for LIS professionals to test emerging technologies, experiment and play with new roles, and self-select teams for collaborative artifact creation, the author has adapted his existing online graduate course, called the Hyperlinked Library, at San Jose State University's School of Library and Information Science (SJSU SLIS) in order to explore how LIS professionals can use emerging technologies and participatory practices to serve their communities. Launched in September 2013, the Hyperlinked Library MOOC pilot (#hyperlibMOOC) provides a sandbox in which LIS professionals and students can play the roles of learner, connector, and collaborator in a self-directed yet social learning experience. Results from the pilot course will contribute to a better understanding of how the not-for-credit MOOC can serve as a transformative environment for professional development.

---

[1] San Jose State University School of Library & Information Science

Key Words
LIS, professional development, information science, MOOC, connectivism, connectivist, collaboration, participatory learning, transformative learning, self-directed learning, collaborative learning, connected learning, SDL, andragogy, L2.0, learning 2.0

Introduction

Disruptive technologies continue to force the evolution of tried and true systems. Nowhere is this more evident than in the realm of education. The influx of technologies to connect learners to instructors and course material remotely has changed the very fabric of higher education, as well as continuing education and professional development. Dialing in, modem-based systems have given way to Internet-connected online learning environments, which in turn have evolved into experience-rich learning landscapes.

At the same time, those who support educational pursuits—librarians and information professionals—are faced with their own evolutionary transition. Disruptive technologies and trends impact library services as well. Recent library literature has featured coverage of e-book issues, the changing behaviors of information seekers, and the evolution of a profession once charged primarily with being the gatekeepers of collections into a profession that will include managing virtual communities for learning and research.

At the cutting edge of this horizon is the massive open online course (MOOC). MOOCs are touted by some as a means to transform teaching and learning for the 21st century, presenting an opportunity for global, open participation. Learners can access an educational opportunity from anywhere with peers from all over the world.

The emergence of network-enabled 24/7 learning presents challenges for those supporting learners, specifically librarians. What roles will and should they play in future large-scale virtual communities and learning programs? When learning resources are openly available on the Web and organized within a MOOC, are librarians needed to manage the resources and facilitate access?

With the opportunities for global online learning come some considerations. This article explores emerging thought concerning MOOCs within a framework of the roles the library and information science (LIS) professional can play as learner, connector, and collaborator in large scale courses. In addition, this article presents a new initiative to offer a large-scale, open course for librarians globally as a mechanism for professional development and continuous learning.

Methodology

The methodology used for this article is based on "futures research" (Glenn, 2003) and blends the methods of environmental scanning, trend research, and scenario planning. "The purpose of futures methodology is to systematically explore, create, and test both possible and desirable futures to improve decisions," notes Glenn (2003, p. 3), and it "provides a framework to better understand the present and expand mental horizons" (p. 3). Futures research "includes analysis of how those conditions might change as a result of the implementation of policies and actions, and the consequences of these policies and actions" (Glenn, p.3).

By combining a literature review with the qualitative methodologies of environmental scanning and trend research in this paper, we can outline various scenarios and the potential roles for LIS professionals in evolving and expanding learning environments.

Library service provider OCLC used such methodology in the 2003 OCLC Environmental Scan: Pattern Recognition report to its membership to identify and describe emerging trends that were impacting libraries (De Rosa, Dempsey, & Wilson, 2003). Reports and research from OCLC on the impact of social media, sharing and trust in a networked society, and the transformative power of libraries also use this methodology (De Rosa et al., 2003).

Scenario planning is a process of presenting and discussing multiple combinations of ideas as a way of quickly coming to a collection of plausible possibilities for the future (Johnson, Adams Becker, Cummins, Estrada, Freeman, & Ludgate, 2013). Scenario planning allows us to identify potential roles that LIS professionals might play based on current trends and scanning as well as on insights from the literature.

Literature Review

Self-Directed Learning (SDL), Professional Development, Learning 2.0, and MOOCs

A brief literature review of pertinent topics provides a foundation to explore the potential roles of LIS professionals in networked, participatory learning environments. These include roles in SDL, professional development, Learning 2.0, and the emerging MOOC environments.

Self-Directed Learning (SDL)

Candy's (1991) model of SDL included such defining characteristics as learner-created, learner-managed, and learning-motivated explorations. SDL is a key assumption of andragogy, a learning model that provides an alternative set of assumptions to the pedagogical models that focus on instructor dependency. Andragogy assumes that adult learners prefer a self-directed environment where they can draw upon their reservoirs of experience to explore task- and problem-oriented, real-world situations (Knowles, 1980). Some theories suggest that the ability to engage in SDL is situational (Grow, 1991), and the theory of transformative learning (TL) argues that an instructor functioning as a facilitator and provocateur can influence learners and groups toward greater SDL (Mezirow, 1997). SDL, as a component of both andragogy and TL, provides a theoretical framework for exploring the potential of MOOCs. Candy (1991) summarizes several decades of findings concerning SDL that include a social component or interaction with others:

- SDL features interaction with other people as a motivating factor.
- SDL is nonlinear in nature.
- SDL relies on serendipity.
- SDL is rarely a solitary activity; it is often social in nature. (p. 199)

Later acknowledging more findings, Candy (2004) argued that a better descriptor for SDL would be "learner control," in which learners "take control over a narrow range of choices" (p. 50). Candy (2004) also encouraged online education endeavors to allow the learner to explore beyond the range of choices in specified course material.

Professional Development for Library Staff

The literature focused on professional-development (PD) activities in libraries includes how-to style manuals for creating training programs as well as studies of the various ways library staff may participate in and benefit from PD. Emphasis is placed on concepts such as support of management, encouraging environments, employee circumstance, and quality of formal PD offerings (Chan & Auster, 2003; Havener & Stolt, 1994). Topics for learning in the library setting over the years included the reference interview, collection development, and the reader advisory. With the advent of technology in libraries, the emphasis for PD courses shifted, as did the delivery mechanisms. These include conferences, workshops, staff development days, and invited speakers.

Emerging technology also emphasized the need for LIS professionals to continue to learn and engage with new formats, mechanisms for delivery, and communication tools. Sayers (2007) concluded that academic libraries should maintain a positive emphasis on continuing support for PD to retain and recruit academic librarians.

Broadbent and Grosser (1987) surveyed special librarians and information center managers in Melbourne to gauge the effectiveness and challenges of PD activities. Results included suggestions to focus on teaching librarians to be learners in early coursework, to involve various institutions and associations in ongoing PD activities, and to increase institutional resources to support PD. Ultimately, however, it is administrative policy for PD that is needed for successful advancement of librarians' learning, argued Chan and Auster (2003). Their study also reported that a supportive manager and an environment that fosters learning are necessary for positive results (Chan & Auster, 2003).

Varlejs (1999) found that more than 75% of American Library Association members participated in SDL over more formal PD opportunities and noted for librarians an eagerness to learn is "an attribute central to one's professional life" (p. 194). Almost fifteen years later, the opportunities for library professionals to learn online have grown exponentially.

Learning 2.0

We could draw some interesting parallels between the development of Learning 2.0 (L2.0) programs and MOOCs as large-scale online learning programs. L2.0 programs, created in 2006 to include all library staff at the Public Library of Charlotte Mecklenburg County in a learning activity and available for replication via a Creative Commons license, have been reported by practitioners as a successful way to engage staff with emerging technology use in libraries (Stephens & Cheetham, 2012b). A globally offered L2.0 program, hosted by School Library Journal and facilitated by the author of this article, was intended to bring teacher librarians together in an atmosphere of exploration and chaos (Bromberg, 2008).

Delivered via a blog site or wiki, the self-directed and often replicated program of online learning modules has been lauded as transformational (Abram, 2008) and celebrated for its ability to bring staff together in a common goal: learning emerging technologies. "The Learning 2.0 program had a great impact on staff, who now know they are capable of learning new technologies," noted Lewis (2008) in a case study of an early program, and Gross and Leslie (2008) reported success in an academic library setting. A later, expanded case study by Gross and Leslie (2010) detailed the program's implementation and offered insights to make

Table 1. Professional Development (PD)

Traditional approaches	• How-to training program design manuals • Examples and studies of PD effectiveness • Emphasis on concepts: management support, work environments, employee circumstance • Topical focus: reference interview, collection management, reader advisory • Delivery: conferences, workshops, staff development days, invited speakers
Learning 2.0 (L2.0)	• Online learning modules • Self-directed learning (SDL) • Learner created and managed, self-motivated • Open educational resources (OER) • Creative Commons license
MOOCs and new culture of learning	• Online (blogs, wikis), participatory, connected SDL • Usually no cost and not-for-credit • Open educational resources (OER) • Interaction through forums, study groups, peer review • Automatic assessments

it more effective. Stephens and Cheetham (2011, 2012a, 2012b) mounted a large-scale study of L2.0 in Australia and detailed the benefits of the program for library staff and library service.

A Brief History of MOOCs

The term MOOC was first used in 2008 by George Siemens and Stephen Downes to describe a free, online course taught at the University of Manitoba for 2,300 students (Educause, 2011). Since then, a growing number of educational institutions have been experimenting with MOOCs, and an increasing number of individuals across the globe are enrolling in MOOCs. One reason for this growing interest is that MOOCS make content and learning more accessible and affordable. Many MOOCs are offered at no cost to students, who receive no course credit. Typically, they include open educational resources, easily accessible course sites (e.g., a blog or wiki), and interaction with other students via online forums, study groups, and peer review of assignments. In some MOOCs, student performance is automatically assessed via tools such as online quizzes.

Several new companies, including Coursera, EdX, and Udacity, recently started offering for-credit MOOCs that are not free. The New York Times reported that in fall 2012, Harvard University and the Massachusetts Institute of Technology (MIT) enrolled 370,000 students in MOOCs, while Coursera reached more than 1.7 million students (Pappano, 2012).

Although educators and scholars are debating the advantages and downsides of MOOCs, with many asserting that MOOCs have the potential to provide new insight regarding online learning, research regarding MOOCs is in its infancy. A recent study by The Chronicle of Higher Education found that 79% of MOOC instructors believe MOOCs are "worth the hype" (Kolowich, 2013). Daniel (2012), in "Making Sense of MOOCs: Musings in a Maze of Myth, Paradox and Possibility," explores emerging issues that educators should consider and scholars should research: technology platforms, for-profit versus not-for-profit models, effective pedagogy, and student success within large learning environments. A scan of recent research includes assessments of the experiences of students and professors in MOOC environments and evaluations of various MOOC platforms and their impact on student learning. Clearly, evaluating MOOC environments is an area ripe for exploration.

We can trace a thread of cohesion from SDL concepts woven into professional development opportunities for library staff to Web-based learning programs replicated and offered to thousands of library staff. The next frontier blends these concepts and can be exemplified in the development of a MOOC designed to enable social learning and offer a professional development opportunity.

New Environments for Learning: Hyperlinked, Connected, and Transformative

The Hyperlinked Library MOOC

Models persisting in LIS research indicate that the exploration and use of new information technologies has a beneficial impact on the profession and on library service. Clyde (2004) called for librarians to adopt emerging tools, such as blogs, because they could prove useful for their mission. And long before there were blogs or Facebook, Buckland (1992) noted that computing tools could be used for more than traditional tasks and urged librarians to learn to use the new tools to further their mission and improve library services. Delivering services to the end user—wherever they happen to be—was a goal Buckland (1992) offered, forecasting the onslaught of mobile and handheld devices that now offer always and anywhere access.

The author has worked for several years researching and refining a model of future library service called the Hyperlinked Library. This model is synthesized from data collected on emerging societal trends, scholarly and socio-technical publications, and burgeoning technologies used in library service. The methodology used to build the always-evolving, always-in-beta model and also used as a framework for this article is futures research (Glenn, 2003).

In an article for Serials Review, Stephens and Collins (2007) defined the Hyperlinked Library model as:

> ... an open, participatory institution that welcomes user input and creativity. It is built on human connections and conversations. The organizational chart is flatter and team-based. The collections grow and thrive via user involvement. Librarians are tapped in to user spaces and places online to interact, have presence, and point the way. (p. 255)

In September 2013, the San Jose State University's School of Library and Information Science (SJSU SLIS) launched its first open online course, the Hyperlinked Library MOOC (#hyperlibMOOC). It is adapted from the existing online graduate course offered to SJSU students enrolled in the Master of Library and Information Science (MLIS) program and is intended to serve as a professional development opportunity for librarians, library staff, and professionals who work in archives and other types of information centers. The SLIS MOOC is free and is not offered for academic credit. It explores how libraries are using emerging technologies to serve their communities.

This MOOC site was built using the open-source content management system WordPress along with a comprehensive suite of plug-ins, called BuddyPress, that provides the social experience. It was designed by Kyle Jones, one of the MOOC's co-instructors, and is powered by a number of additional plugins and themes to provide advanced functionality. Jones supervised a team of SJSU SLIS students during summer 2013 to build the site architecture and design the badge system. During the fall 2013 pilot, up to 400 MOOC students have the opportunity to explore the Hyperlinked Library model through recorded presentations and other content, as well as through practical assignments that encourage students to apply what they are learning. Badges are awarded as students move through the course, culminating with a certificate of completion.

Theoretical Framework for MOOCs

Connectivist learning theories offer a theoretical framework to approach learning experiences within open online networks. Kop (2011) reported on one of the first studies of a MOOC as a connectivist learning endeavor and defines connectivist learning as enhanced by four major types of activity:

1) aggregation – access to and collection of a wide variety of resources to read, watch, or play;
2) relation – after reading, watching, or listening to some content, the learner might reflect and relate it to what he or she already knows or to earlier experiences;
3) creation – after this reflection and sense-making process, learners might create something of their own (e.g., a blog

Figure 1

Welcome to the Hyperlinked Library
http://mooc.hyperlib.sjsu.edu/blog/welcome-to-module-1/

post, an account with a social bookmarking site, a new entry in a Moodle discussion) using any service on the Internet, such as Flickr, Second Life, Yahoo Groups, Facebook, YouTube, iGoogle, NetVibes, etc.; 4) sharing – learners might share their work with others on the network. This participation in activities is seen as vital to learning. (Connectivism section, para. 2)

Connected Learning

MOOCs have their foundations based on the pedagogical assumptions in connectivist learning theory, which recognizes that knowledge exists in dynamic relationships and external connections and expands with increased access to networks of people, materials, and tools (Clarà & Barberà, 2013). Jenkins (2012) uses the term "connected learning" to describe emerging methods of connected participation in online learning: "It's social. It's hands-on. It's active. It's networked. It's personal. It's effective. Through a new vision of learning, it holds out the possibility for productive and broad-based educational change" (para. 24). Connected learning includes three important components: a shared purpose, a production-centered approach, and an openly networked environment. Clarà & Barberà (2013) propose that MOOCs that encourage connected participation in joint activities, in environments facilitated by experts, offer the best opportunity for internalization and transformation. The Hyperlinked Library includes all three of the connected learning components as a foundation for the course:

Shared Purpose: MOOC students will explore the Hyperlinked Library model as a means of studying emerging technologies and emerging thought related to future libraries. Although each individual will bring his or her unique paradigm, the goal of looking forward is shared across all of those participating.

Production Centered: MOOC students will collaboratively create a series of artifacts indicative of their learning that can be used in their libraries and information centers. These include emerging technology planning guides and briefs relating to new service initiatives. Artifacts might be text-based or be shared via video, still image, infographic, etc.

Openly Networked: As noted above, the Hyperlinked Library functions as a WordPress- and BuddyPress-enabled community site accessible by anyone with a connection to the Web.

Transformative Learning

The MOOC will also incorporate concepts from TL. Mezirow (1997) describes a learning process that grows in quality as a result of critical reflection on experience: "Transformative learners move toward a frame of reference that is more inclusive, discriminating, self-reflective, and integrative of experience" (p. 5). In other words, as learners encounter new ideas, new approaches—and in the MOOC, new technologies—they constantly update and broaden their knowledge and understanding of the world around them. Applying this theory to new models of learning about information technologies provides a useful framework for understanding how information professionals and library staff integrate new tools into library service.

The act of blogging reflections by MOOC students supports this concept. Thomas and Brown (2011) noted this in A New Culture of Learning:

Blogging is also a personally transformative experience. Because a person's blog is subject to change and revision by others, the influence of the collective can powerfully and meaningfully shape the blogger's view of the world, just as the blogger, at the same time, can shape the collective. (p. 66)

Transformation, then, potentially occurs as individuals encounter new paradigms and as groups encounter each other's shifting paradigms.

MOOC Meets Learning 2.0

The parallels between the MOOC movement, connectivism, and L2.0 programs merit consideration. Might we argue that L2.0 programs, offered in hundreds of organizations since 2006, are connectivist precursors to the evolving, open, and large-scale learning landscapes we're experiencing now?

The Hyperlinked Library will incorporate certain emphases culled from the author's L2.0 research. The L2.0 model has an emphasis on play, experimentation, and social interaction with other learners as part of the programs. The group becomes the learning collective. Thomas and Brown (2011) note that a collective is "a community of similarly minded people who [help an individual] learn and meet the very particular set of needs that [s/he has]" (p. 21).

A focus on play, innovation, and experimentation is needed for 21st century learning success, argue Thomas and Brown (2011). Jenkins, Purushotma, Clinton, Weigel, and Robison (2006) defined play as "the capacity to experiment with one's surroundings as a form of problem-solving" (p.4) and argued that play is one of the most important emerging social literacies and valued skills for the changing landscape of education. The L2.0 model combines play and opportunities to explore new technologies into a unique, self-directed yet social, and connected learning experience.

This will be replicated within the MOOC. Weekly modules covering concepts such as community engagement, transparency, privacy, and user experience will provide MOOC participants the opportunity to explore, experiment, and reflect on the ideas and challenges associated with these topics. The potential is present for learners to "play" with the ideas and potential solutions to problems encountered in their own information environments via reflection and the creation of course artifacts. Concurrently, the instructors expect participants to critically reflect on their own practice within this new learning environment.

Scenarios for Future Roles

SDL encompasses the idea that learning can be situational and that people may behave differently in a range of learning environments and in relation to different subject matter (Grow, 1991). Leadership in online learning environments may involve fluidly transitioning through many roles in relation to users and participants. According to Grow (1991), one can expect to fluctuate from dependency through self-direction as a learner to coaching through consultancy as a leader. In addition, connectivist and connected learning approaches that purposefully challenge participants to play learner, connector, and collaborator in sustained, shared activities are being explored as optimum MOOC environments (Clarà & Barberà, 2013; Jenkins, 2012). This section explores the roles the LIS professional can play in large-scale courses as learner, connector, and collaborator—roles that may prove valuable beyond MOOCs to other places, virtual and physical, where LIS professionals practice. There must also be consideration for students in LIS programs to gain experience with these roles and environments.

Learner

The first role an LIS professional should play in these new learning environments is that of learner. This role is grounded in the "now" of these scenarios. As Jenkins (2012) notes, taking an active role in learning is part of the connected learning approach. Reading current news and articles about MOOCs might give librarians background knowledge, but actively participating has the potential to provide more depth of experience. Burkhardt (2012) writing for his library-focused blog argued, "There are a lot of good reasons though for librarians to sign up for a MOOC themselves" (para. 1). His reasons include exploring innovations in higher education and planning for future scenarios by updating skills, learning from great teachers, and allowing librarians to do something for themselves (para. 2).

This interest in continuous learning should be instilled in future LIS professionals from the moment they enter graduate school. Thomas and Brown (2011) note, "In the new culture we describe, learning thus becomes a lifelong interest that is renewed and redefined on a continual basis" (p. 32). Moving forward, an LIS professional might continue to utilize MOOCs as a means to keep current with emerging ideas and issues in librarianship as well as specific subject areas of interest.

The Hyperlinked Library MOOC may be the beginnings of a model that evolves into a rich set of learning communities offering lifelong learning for LIS professionals. Future research will gauge the effectiveness of the model.

Connector

The LIS professional may also find the role of connector to be a prominent part of future duties. A connector is someone who can facilitate a group to make connections between learning, ideas, and practice. Also, this person is a leader of sorts who connects people within organizations and lets those connections grow.

Because MOOC content is typically free and open on the Web, the role of librarians seems nullified in this environment. Instead of locating and sharing resources, LIS professionals working actively within large learning environments may help learners locate and connect with others in the community who may share similar or discordant ideas. This person may also connect groups to ideas and resources to further their conversations.

In the Hyperlinked Library, groups of MOOC participants will self-select into "tribes" of people interested in the same topic, avenue of librarianship, or service population. The moniker was chosen to relate to Godin's concepts of groups and leaders. Godin (2008) posits that a tribe is simply "a group of people connected to one another, connected to a leader, and connected to an idea…a group needs only two things to be a tribe: a shared interest and a way to communicate" (p. 1). In the MOOC, SJSU SLIS students, who are not participating in the MOOC, serve as participatory learning guides (PLGs), who keep an eye on the sharing, connected learning, and joint activities within assigned groups of participants. PLGs also submit periodic critical reflections on MOOC effectiveness and participant progress. We might also call PLGs "connectors."

The role of connector, then, is one that encourages participation, sharing, and the furthering of connectivity and joint action in a group. Godin (2008) shares an illu-

Table 2. Professional Development (PD) in a MOOC Environment

Roles that LIS professionals may play	
Learner	· Active participation as a learner brings more depth of experience than passive reading · Technological skills automatically exercised and updated through participation · Access to wide variety of mentors and teachers · Self-directed exploration available 24/7
Connector	· Locating, curating, and sharing information is social and participatory—anyone can be the leader or connector on any topic or number of topics · Discordant ideas and perspectives have new possibilities for interaction through active and open connectors · Unrestricted opportunity to follow a passion, share, create, participate in, and lead groups or "tribes"
Collaborator	· Working together to solve problems, sharing expertise with technologies, building artifacts, organizing connected experiences · Working with outside-MOOC entities · MOOC participatory learning guides and interactive tools function as collaborators with learners · Creating participatory learning tools is acting as a collaborator

minating example that inspired this concept in the MOOC:

> In the spring of 2008, I announced a paid summer internship for students. More than 130 well-educated students from all over the world applied. As an experiment, I set up a private Facebook group for the applicants and invited each on to participate. Sixty of them joined immediately. No tribe existed yet—just sixty strangers in an online forum. Within hours, a few had taken the lead, posting topics, starting discussions, leaning in and leading. They called on their peers to contribute and participate. And the rest? They lurked. They sat and they watched. They were hiding, afraid of something that wasn't likely to happen. Whom would you hire? (p. 57)

The same could be said for LIS professionals. How they encourage and facilitate a community's interaction might be a primary factor in future hiring decisions. The work of Skokie Public Library in Illinois to facilitate and connect the community is indicative of this set of skills (Buhmann, Greenwalt, Jacobsen, & Roehm, 2009). SkokieNet evolved from a static HTML site in 1995 to a Drupal platform that supports several websites and a community portal and information network. The development of an environment for vibrant online community interactions, supported by the library, happened through the efforts of far-sighted library directors and the collaboration of a consortium of area libraries.

Collaborator

The role of collaborator within learning environments is the third scenario for librarians. The collaborator might work with learners to create an artifact or instruct learners on various technologies that might assist them in fulfilling course requirements. They might also collaborate with other entities on campus, in the community, or in other information settings to further the goals of the course. In the Hyperlinked Library MOOC, the PLGs will also perform the role of collaborator. A summer class of SJSU SLIS students worked to build resources for MOOC participants to utilize together as they navigate the course site.

This is a notable trend. From a recent policy brief on the future of American libraries from the American Library Association, Hendrix (2010) sees the confluence of two major trends, a focus on user and library adoption of popular emerging technologies and an emphasis on human relationships:

> Combining these two schools of thought yields a fundamental and increasingly popular prediction about the future of libraries: collaboration will become a common and important focus. The concept of collaboration arises in almost all conversations concerning the future direction of American libraries. Libraries and librarians are expected to partner with many types of institutions, organizations, and individual users to provide both traditional and cutting-edge services and flexible, usable physical and online environments. (p. 15)

Bitter-Rijpkema, Verjans, and Bruijnzeels (2012) survey the impact of emerging, disruptive technologies on library learning and note the job description of the public librarian is moving "from information to knowledge worker with a focus on innovative co-creation of meaning" (p. 39). Libraries of all kinds are adding digital creation labs and makerspaces. The skills of the collaborator and co-creator will be necessary for these environments.

Conclusion

Utilizing literature, scanning the current environment of higher education in flux, and developing scenario-based roles of future information professional work within large-scale learning environments are some ways to understand the sweeping changes disruptive technologies have brought to our landscape.

As we go forward, research centered on the Hyperlinked Library MOOC in fall 2013 will contribute to a better understanding regarding how free, not-for-credit MOOCs can serve as professional development tools as well as test some of the underlying theory and models the MOOC is based on. There is an eagerness to evaluate the SLIS MOOC, identify areas where the model is effective, and provide recommendations regarding how to improve the design of MOOCs in the future.

References

Abram, S. (2008). The 23 things - Learning 2.0. Stephen's Lighthouse. Retrieved from http://stephenslighthouse.com/2008/02/05/the-23-things-learning-2-0/

Bitter-Rijpkema, M. E., Verjans, S., & Bruijnzeels, R. (2012). The Library School: Empowering the sustainable innovation capacity of new librarians. Library Management, 33(1/2), 36-49.

Broadbent, M., & Grosser, K. (1987). Continuing professional development of special library and information center managers. Journal of Education for Library and Information Science, 28(2), 99-115. Retrieved from http://www.jstor.org/stable/40323621

Bromberg, P. (2008, July 21). All together now. SLJ's 2.0 program begins today, July 21 [Web log post]. Retrieved from http://librarygarden.net/2008/07/21/all-together-now-sljs-2-0-program-begins-today-july-21/

Buckland, M. (1992). Redesigning library services: A manifesto. American Library Association. Retrieved from http://sunsite.berkeley.edu/Literature/Library/Redesigning/html.html

Buhmann, M., Greenwalt, T., Jacobsen, M., & Roehm, F. (2009). On the ground, in the cloud. Library Journal, 134(12), 35-37.

Burkhardt, A. (2012, August 13). 4 reasons librarians should join a MOOC [Web log post. Retrieved from http://andyburkhardt.com/2012/08/13/4-reasons-librarians-should-join-a-mooc/

Candy, P. C. (1991). Self-direction for lifelong learning: a comprehensive guide to theory and practice. San Francisco: Jossey-Bass.

Candy, P. C. (2004). Linking thinking: Self-directed learning in the digital age. Canberra, ACT: Department of Education, Science and Training.

Chan, D. C., & Auster, E. (2003). Factors contributing to the professional development of reference librarians. Library & Information Science Research (07408188), 25(3), 265. doi:10.1016/S0740-8188(03)00030-6

Clarà, M., & Barberà, E. (2013). Learning online: massive open online courses (MOOCs), connectivism, and cultural psychology. Distance Education, 34(1), 129-136. doi:10.1080/01587919.2013.770428

Clyde, L. A. (2004). Weblogs and libraries. Oxford: Chandos Publishing.

Daniel, J. (2012). Making sense of MOOCs: Musings in a maze of myth, paradox and possibility. Journal of Interactive Media in Education (JIME). Retrieved from http://www-jime.open.ac.uk/jime/article/view/2012-18

De Rosa, C., Dempsey, L., & Wilson, A. (2003). The 2003 OCLC environmental scan: Pattern recognition (Executive Summary). A. Wilson (Ed.). Dublin, OH: OCLC Online Computer Library Center, Inc. Retrieved from http://www.oclc.org/content/dam/oclc/reports/escan/downloads/escansummary_en.pdf

Educause. (2011). 7 things you should know about MOOCs. Educause Learning Initiative. Retrieved from http://net.educause.edu/ir/library/pdf/ELI7078.pdf

Glenn, J. C. (2003). Introduction to the futures research methods series. In J. C. Glenn & T. J. Gordon (Eds.), Futures research methodology, V2.0 (pp. 1-61). AC/UNU Millennium Project, American Council for the United Nations University. Available from The Millennium Project website: http://www.millennium-project.org/millennium/FRM-v2.html

Godin, S. (2008). Tribes: We need you to lead us. New York: Penguin Group (USA) Inc.

Gross, J., & Leslie, L. (2008). Twenty-three steps to learning Web 2.0 technologies in an academic library. The Electronic Library, 26(6), 790-802. doi: 10.1108/02640470810921583

Gross, J., & Leslie, L. (2010). Learning 2.0: A catalyst for library organisational change. The Electronic Library, 28(5), 657-668. Retrieved from ECU Publications Pre. 2011 http://works.bepress.com/julia_gross/9

Grow, G. (1991). Teaching learners to be self-directed: A stage approach. Adult Education Quarterly 44(2): 109 - 114. Retrieved from http://www.longleaf.net/ggrow/SSDL/Model.html#SituationalLeadership

Havener, W., & Stolt, W. A. (1994). The professional development activities of academic librarians: Does institutional support make.... College & Research Libraries, 55(1), 25. Retrieved from https://www.ideals.illinois.edu/bitstream/handle/2142/41730/crl_55_01_25_opt.pdf?sequence=2

Hendrix, J. C. (2010, February). Checking out the future. Perspectives from the library community on information technology and 21st-century libraries (Policy Brief No. 2). ALA Office for Information Technology Policy. Retrieved from http://www.ala.org/offices/sites/ala.org.offices/files/content/oitp/publications/policybriefs/ala_checking_out_the.pdf

Jenkins, H. (2012, March 1). Connected learning: A new paradigm [Web log post]. Retrieved from http://henryjenkins.org/2012/03/connected_learning_a_new_parad.html

Jenkins, H., Purushotma, R., Clinton, K., Weigel, M., & Robison, A. (2006). Confronting the challenges of participatory culture: Media education for the 21st century. Chicago, IL: The MacArthur Foundation

Johnson, L., Adams Becker, S., Cummins, M., Estrada, V., Freeman, A., & Ludgate, H. (2013). NMC Horizon Report: 2013 Higher Education Edition. Austin, TX: The New Media Consortium. Retrieved from http://www.nmc.org/pdf/2013-horizon-report-HE.pdf

Knowles, M. S. (1980). My farewell address...andragogy – no panacea, no ideology. Training & Development Journal, 34(8), 48.

Kolowich, S. (2013, March 18). The professors who make the MOOCs. The Minds Behind the MOOCs. The Chronicle of Higher Education. Retrieved from http://chronicle.com/article/The-Professors-Behind-the-MOOC/137905/?cid=wb&utm_source=wb&utm_medium=en#id=overview

Kop, R. (2011). The challenges to connectivist learning on open online networks: Learning experiences during a massive open online course. The International Review of Research in Open and Distance Learning, 12(3), 19-38. Retrieved from http://www.irrodl.org/index.php/irrodl/article/view/882/1689

Lewis, L. (2008, February 5). Library 2.0: Taking it to the street. Paper presentation from VALA 2008 Conference & Exhibition. Melbourne, Australia. Retrieved from http://www.valaconf.org.au/vala2008/papers2008/35_Lewis_Final.pdf

Mezirow, J. (1997). Transformative learning: Theory to practice. New Directions for Adult and Continuing Education, 1997(74), 5-12. Retrieved from http://www.ecolas.eu/content/images/Mezirow%20Transformative%20Learning.pdf

Pappano, L. (2012, November 2). The year of the MOOC. Education Life. New York Times. Retrieved from http://www.nytimes.com/2012/11/04/education/edlife/massive-open-online-courses-are-multiplying-at-a-rapid-pace.html?_r=0

Sayers, R. (2007). The right staff from x to y: Generational change and professional development in future academic libraries. CAVAL Research and Advocacy. Library Management, 28(8/9), 474-487. Retrieved from http://www.lib.cuhk.edu.hk/conference/aldp2007/programme/aldp2007_full_paper/RichardSayers.pdf

Stephens, M., & Cheetham, W. (2011). The impact and effect of learning 2.0 programs in Australian academic libraries. New Review of Academic Librarianship, 17(1), 31-63.

Stephens, M., & Cheetham, W. (2012a). Benefits and results of learning 2.0: A case study of CityLibrariesLearning – discover*play*connect. Australian Library Journal, 61(1), 6-15.

Stephens, M., & Cheetham, W. (2012b). The impact and effect of learning 2.0 programs in Australian public libraries. Evidence Based Library and Information Practice, 7(1), 53-64.

Stephens, M., & Collins, M. (2007). Web 2.0, library 2.0, and the hyperlinked library. Serials Review, 33(4), 253.

Thomas, D., & Brown, J. S. (2011). A new culture of learning: Cultivating the imagination for a world of constant change. Lexington, KY: CreateSpace.

Varlejs, J. (1999). On their own: Librarians' self-directed, work-related learning. The Library Quarterly, 69(2), 173-201. Retrieved from http://www.jstor.org/stable/4309298

Efficiency, Economy, and Social Equity in Online Education at America's Community Colleges

Marco Castillo

> *In this paper, I utilize social equity as a guiding administrative value to assess the implications of the expansion of online education in America's community colleges. Online education holds promise for our nation's community colleges and can serve as a useful tool for state and local governments seeking to reduce costs while expanding educational offerings to traditional and non-traditional students. Nevertheless, while the traditional administrative values of efficiency and economy are served by the use of this pedagogical approach, there remain a variety of open questions regarding the social equity implications of an expansion of this instructional modality.*

In response to the rapid pace of change in the economy, more people are entering or returning to college to develop the skills necessary to remain competitive in today's workforce (Merrick & Thurow, 2009). While an increasing demand for education may be seen as a positive development for society, this demand is testing the capacity of our nation's publicly funded community colleges. This growing demand has prompted community colleges to find new ways to expand their capacity and educational offerings in the face of stagnant or shrinking budgets. One way they have done this is through the expansion of online education.

In this paper, I utilize social equity as a guiding administrative value to assess the implications of the expansion of online education in America's community colleges. I highlight that online education holds promise for our nation's community colleges and can serve as a useful tool for state and local governments seeking to reduce costs while expanding educational offerings to traditional and non-traditional students (Stumpf, McCrimon, & Davis, 2005). While the traditional administrative values of efficiency and economy are served by the expansion of this pedagogical approach, there remain questions regarding the social equity implications of expanding online education at America's community colleges. In this paper, I highlight two major problems with the expansion of online education at community colleges that seem to counter the value of social equity. First, I address questions regarding the quality of online education, noting both theoretical and empirical evidence that community college students may in some instances be receiving a product that is not of sufficiently high quality when compared to traditional instruction. Second, I focus upon issues of proper "fit" between community college students and the online education product, noting that vast segments of the community college population may not be well suited for online education, regardless of product quality. Taken together, these problems raise serious questions regarding the wisdom and social equity implications of implementing online education in a wholesale fashion at the community college level. I follow with a discussion on ways that online education may be implemented in a fashion that minimizes these problems, thus reflecting the values of social equity to a greater extent.

While it seems clear that online education holds promise for bringing new efficiencies and added value to community colleges, such benefits are dependent on proper program implementation that takes the aforementioned factors into consideration. Suboptimal implementation that overlooks questions of instructional quality and student fit may result in the opposite of the intended effects, increasing costs for state and local governments as well as community college students, hampering student progress through increased course failures and higher attrition rates, and other unintended negative effects (Feenberg, 1999).

The History and Mission of Community Colleges

America's community colleges are in large part products of early twentieth century progressivism. Along with other social and educational institutions that arose during the Progressive Era, community colleges developed as organizations intended to promote social equality and social mobility through the expansion of access to higher education (Vaughan, 2006). Community colleges (then termed "junior colleges") benefited from an overall increase in public spending in education during this era, as greater investments in K-12 education later resulted in a growing demand for accessible forms of post-secondary education for the growing number of graduates from America's high schools (Cohen, 2003, p. 6). This growing demand was reinforced by a move on the part of research universities to shed the task of teaching college freshmen and sophomores to a new type of educational institution that would occupy a space between the K-12 schools and traditional four-year colleges (Cohen, 2003, p. 6). The result of these converging forces and factors was the formation and expansion of America's community colleges.

Community colleges continued to grow in size and scope throughout the twentieth century and were bolstered by other key developments. Community colleges experienced a boost in enrollment during the Great Depression as they expanded their educational mission to include more applied job training programs to ease the effects of unemployment. After World War II, the passage of the Servicemen's Readjustment Act (i.e., the GI Bill) further aided in the expansion of community colleges as many veterans opted for the shorter, applied, and community-based program of study they offered. The Truman administration boosted the legitimacy of America's community colleges through its formation of Truman's Commission on Higher Education for American Democracy; the commission released the Truman Commission Report which extolled the value of what would come to be known as a community college education. The community colleges would receive yet another boost in the 1960s, as the baby boomer generation increased the demand for all forms of postsecondary education. The resulting passage of the Higher Education Act in 1965 provided additional financial support for all higher education institutions, including community colleges (Community Colleges: The History of Community Colleges). Toward the end of the twentieth century, it was clear that community colleges had grown to become an essential part of higher education. While they remained committed to their mission of providing the first two years of a liberal arts postsecondary education, they would go on to expand their offerings to include professional education, workforce retraining, and community development (Vaughan, 2006, p. 26).

The beginning of the twenty-first century brought with it a host of economic challenges that placed increasing stresses on federal, state, and local governments that affected their ability to fund necessary public services. Threats of terrorism, the exportation of America's manufacturing base, and the bursting of the housing bubble among other factors have placed severe budgetary stresses on both federal and state governments. Public services across the board have suffered and higher education is no exception to this rule. Yet, the demand for community college services is still expanding, prompting elected officials and administrators to find ways to do more with less. One way states and localities have sought to expand the availability of community college education in the face of budgetary crisis is through the expansion of online education.

The Promise of Online Education

It is increasingly evident that a broad array of students is interested in online education. One reason for this is that online education holds the potential to increase the convenience of pursuing education, especially for non-traditional students. Non-traditional students, broadly defined as financially independent working students outside of the 18–23-year-old age bracket, may particularly benefit from online education due to the scheduling flexibilities made possible by this option. Online education may also help non-traditional students with jobs minimize their potentially greater opportunity costs, as their pursuit of an education may require them to forgo a substantial income. Online education can also bring financial benefits to colleges by allowing them to utilize their current capital and labor resources more effectively. In her report titled Cost Efficiencies in Online Higher Education, Katrina A. Meyer of the University of Memphis notes that online education can allow for three cost-saving economic substitutions—capital for labor, lower-cost labor for higher-cost labor, and capital for capital. With the substitution of capital for labor, technology can be utilized to leverage the work of higher-cost, full-time faculty over a broader population of students, creating economies of scale. Through collaborations between full-time faculty and lower-cost part-time faculty and teaching assistants, these efforts can be even further leveraged in the online setting. Capital for capital substitution allows colleges to shift resources from traditional capital expenditures such as buildings and new classrooms to technological expenditures, such as the computer servers, software, and class management systems, which many argue are more cost-effective (Meyer, 2006).

The potential cost savings for community colleges and students are substantial. A Pew Charitable Trust study found that by redesigning courses to take advantage of online technologies, institutions could reduce course-related costs by an average of 37% (Meyer, 2008, p. 60). The potential benefits from online education are many. However, as with all innovations, there are some potential shortcomings to this educational approach that should be noted.

Online Education and Social Equity

Clearly, there is a host of benefits that can be brought to colleges as a result of the expansion of online education. However, we should note that these benefits are primarily related to efficiency and economy in the delivery of education. While efficiency and economy are important factors to consider, they are not the only important or relevant ones. Indeed, it is easy to make this oversight, particularly in an age of fiscal austerity in the public sector. Public administration scholar George Frederickson (2010) observed this tendency and proposed adding a third equally important value—social equity—into the study and practice of administering public organizations. He notes:

> Social equity values have to do with the fairness of the organization, its management, and its delivery of public services. Social equity asks these questions: For whom is the organization well-managed? For whom is the organization efficient? For whom is the organization economical? For whom are our public services more or less fairly delivered . . . In the pursuit of efficiency, public officials will try to make the entire organization and its delivery of public services efficient or economical, assuming that all of the public served by the organization will benefit, more or less in equal measure, from greater efficiency or economy. [However], [i]t is clearly evident that the public is highly varied—rich and poor, old and young, fortunate and unfortunate, urban and suburban—and that while public services may, in a general sense, be more efficient or economical, in the specific sense, these public services will almost certainly be efficient and economical for some more than others (p. xv).

In the case of the expansion of online education at America's community colleges, it is critical that policymakers consider how this pedagogical approach will specifically affect the diverse community college student population. While online education may be a product that is demanded by an increasing number of students and can produce cost savings for schools and states, we must ask ourselves—is expanding online education in the best interest of community college students? Is online education a beneficial product for the community college student population? Does online education primarily benefit the budgets of community colleges and their funding states and localities more so than community college students themselves? In fact, do these economic benefits to schools and states come at the expense of some segments of the community college student population?

Theoretical Dilemmas

I will first highlight the theoretical conflicts that may exist between online education as an instructional modality and the major theories of learning. Learning theory is a diverse field, and it is impossible to review the totality of this field in a single research article. Nevertheless, for the purposes of this article, I will summarize the main learning theories with the aim of noting their implications for online learning at community colleges. Learning theories seek to provide us with a variety of views regarding how learning takes place in the individual (Harasim, 2012). While a variety of learning theories abound, they can be basically categorized into three major schools of thought: behaviorism, cognitivism, and most recently constructivism. Each of these schools takes a different perspective on how learning occurs and thus each may have important implications for the quality of instruction delivered via online models.

Behaviorism. The earliest school of thought in learning theory was behaviorism. Behaviorism as a learning theory was derived from the broader psychological school of behaviorism developed by psychologist B.F. Skinner. It emphasized that all human actions and activity, both external actions as well as internal processes, should be regarded as behaviors; as such, they can be best modified by finding a way to alter individual behavior patterns or changing the environment in order to change behavior patterns (Anderson, 2008, p. 6). Learning would be considered a change in observable behavior under this model, caused by external stimuli in the environment (Skinner, 2011). While this school of thought was influential, critics noted that there were many forms of learning that were not observable through human behavior. As such behaviorist learning theory gradually gave way to cognitivist theories of learning.

Cognitivist Theories. Cognitivist theories of learning arose in response to the shortcomings of behaviorist schools of thought. In response to the criticism that behaviorism had become too dependent on external incidences of behavior to explain learning, cognitivists developed a new theory emphasizing the internal components of learning. Cognitive theories posit that learning involves the use of memory, motivation, and thinking and reflection (Anderson, 2008, p. 7). Cognitivists emphasized that learning was an internal process rather than an external behavior and that one's ability to learn is dependent on factors such as the capacity of the learner, the intensity of effort exerted during the learning process, and the prior knowledge of the learner. For cognitive theorists, learning is an internal mental process and pedagogy needs to be developed around this process.

Constructivism. More recently, educators have moved toward constructivism as a theory of learning and guiding pedagogy. Constructivist learning theory emphasizes that learning is a process by which the individual builds new ideas based on prior knowledge and experience. Under constructivist models, learners interpret data according to their personal reality and this interpretation is the foundation of learning. The external world is observed, data is processed and interpreted, and then the individual forms his or her understanding of this data which becomes personal knowledge. Learners learn best when new information can be placed in the context of what learners already know and can be applied in a real-world setting so that this data acquires a personal context and meaning for the individual (Anderson, 2008, p. 7).

It is important for us to note that as in other academic areas, there are competing schools of thought about educational theory and no single one should be understood as having the final word on how individuals learn. The important point to note for our purposes is that proponents of online education posit that none of these theories are inherently incompatible with online learning. Behaviorist, cognitivist, and constructivist schools of thought can all be reflected in properly structured online learning models. In fact, some have highlighted how online learning strategies can be tailored to address specific aspects of each of these frameworks. For instance, online learning can utilize behaviorist strategies by emphasizing the teaching of facts in the online environment. Cognitive learning theory can be reflected in online models by devising assignments and strategies that emphasize critical thinking and learning processes. Finally, constructivist learning theory can be reflected in the online learning environment through the use of assignments that teach higher-order thinking that emphasize "why" questions and help students devise new knowledge that is relevant to them (Janicki & Liegle, 2001).

Yet, critics argue that that online learning is not nearly as compatible with traditional learning theories. For instance, behaviorists hold that responding to and altering the behaviors of learners is essential to the learning process and that online learning makes this process cumbersome. The lack of a physical presence and a personal relationship between students and instructors makes it difficult to provide feedback to students, hampering the instructor's ability to modify student behaviors in the way necessary for learning to occur (Stephenson, 2001). Other well established learning theories, such as Lev Vygotsky's social development theory, emphasize the need for expert guidance and social interaction in the learning process, both of which may be hindered in the online learning environment. Finally, new learning theories that have been developed to support online learning, such as connectivism, have been derided by some as having weak theoretical foundations and being insufficient substitutes for the traditional learning theories used to justify pedagogical innovations (Kop & Hill, 2008).

Online Education Quality

We should also consider the social equity implications of delivering an educational product that may be of lower quality than traditional instruction to community college students. Proponents of online learning point toward the generally positive findings among broad based studies addressing the quality of online education. One of the earliest of such studies presented in Thomas L. Russell's book The No Significant Difference Phenomenon shows that there were no significant differences in student outcomes between online education and education delivered in person (Russell & IDECC Organization, 2001). While Russell's research generally does not find advantages to online learning, it supports the thesis that online learning is no worse than traditional instruction. Other studies go further, noting that online education may actually be superior in quality to face-to-face instruction. In 2010, the United States Department of Education conducted a meta-analysis of research studies comparing the effectiveness of online learning to face-to-face instruction. While most of the studies found no significant difference between these modes of instruction, the study did note that when there was a difference, it tended to be positive and in favor of online education. These findings stand alongside other broad based studies presenting a positive outlook for online education. For instance, online education advocacy organizations such as the Sloan Foundation have released a variety of studies illustrating the growth of online education, the diffusion of this instructional method, the relatively high levels of student satisfaction, with this learning modality, and the general sense of enthusiasm expressed for online education on the part of college administrators (Allen & Seaman, 2011).

Despite these generally positive reports, there are some findings within these same studies that give us reason for pause. While the findings of the 2010 meta-analysis of online education conducted by the United States Department of Education were generally positive, the authors accept that multiple explanations may be given for these effects (Means et al., 2009, p. xiv). The authors noted that higher levels of student achievement in online classes may be a product of several factors, including greater attention given to course design, greater time-on-task for students enrolled in hybrid classes (which combine face-to-face and online components), and other pedagogically innovative techniques utilized in, but not exclusive to, online settings. There are also basic methodological shortcomings in this study that qualify its findings. The authors of the study note that, "[A]lthough the types of research designs used by the studies in the meta-analysis were strong (i.e. experimental or controlled quasi-experimental), many of the studies suffered from weaknesses such as small sample sizes, failure to report retention rates for students in the conditions being contrasted, and, in many cases, potential bias stemming from the authors' dual roles as experimenters and instructors" (Means et al., 2009, p.xviii). Likewise, the Sloan Consortium's 2011 study titled Going the Distance: Online Education in the United States, while championing the virtues of online education, does include some problematic findings. For instance, while the number of online programs and courses has grown at colleges nationwide, the acceptance of online learning by faculty has been flat since it was first measured in 2003. The report notes that less than one-third of chief academic officers believe that their faculty accept the value and legitimacy of online education. This is virtually the same percentage as when this statistic was first collected in 2003. Moreover, the report also finds that academic leaders at private for-profit institutions perceive a higher faculty acceptance rate while traditional nonprofit colleges have the lowest, supporting the possibility that some of the support for online education is driven by the financial pressures at smaller private colleges (Allen & Seaman, 2011, p. 13). While these statistics may simply be a product of reactionary opposition to online learning, it is possible that these gaps in support may be indicative of real problems in the substance and/or the implementation of online instruction.

Student Fit

In addition to these theory- and research-based criticisms, there are questions about the aptness of community college students for the highly independent form of learning that is required in online education. Even if online education can be shown to be of similar quality to traditional face-to-face education, the question remains as to whether this form of learning is suitable for the community college student population. Recent demographic data shows us that community colleges have an increasingly diverse student population. Among this population are a growing number of adult learners—students who have already operated successfully in their various career paths and are seeking educational opportunities to advance in these paths or to shift into others (Chen, 2009). Adult learners, defined as those age 25 or older, have a set of characteristics that distinguish them from traditional age students. They are more likely to work full time, support a family, and take longer to complete their degree requirements than their younger counterparts (American Association of Community Colleges). Moreover, adult learners in community colleges are more likely to perform well on their coursework than their younger counterparts (Knowles, Holton, & Swanson, 2012). It may be reasonable to posit that these adult learners may be better prepared for the independent form of learning required in online instruction. These learners may be more responsible, more academically prepared, and more resilient, allowing them to benefit from the flexibilities of the online educational modality.

Yet, this very same diversity poses a risk for another growing subset of the community college student demographic. Community colleges have long had diverse student populations in terms of race and socioeconomic status. But recent trends show us that that the socioeconomic and racial composition of America's community colleges is becoming more heavily skewed toward minority students, with the majority of black and Hispanic undergraduate students attending these colleges (American Association of Community Colleges). Moreover, the community college population is changing in terms of socioeconomic status, with community colleges having a shrinking population of students from the highest socioeconomic quarter and a growing population of those from the poorest quarter (Kahlenberg, 2010). Finally, community colleges still serve a significant number of traditional age students with academic deficiencies and in need of developmental education (Mullin, 2012). Taken together, it is clear that community colleges educate a significant number of students with various educational risk factors and needs that may not be met in the online setting.

We need to take into consideration the bifurcated nature of the community college student population as we consider expanding this educational modality. There is reason to believe that online education can be highly valuable and helpful for adult learners and better prepared community college students. But community colleges are also responsible for educating a large subset of students who have graduated from lower performing public schools. These students may enter community colleges with a set of educational deficits that may make them vulnerable in the online environment. The effect of this harm may be compounded when we consider the generally limited financial resources community college students have to spend on education. Taking these factors into consideration could help us form an online education policy that will benefit students who are good candidates for this modality while protecting community college students with greater educational risk factors and needs.

Thus, there are a variety of factors that need to be taken into consideration as we seek to implement online education at America's community colleges. Issues of product quality stand at the forefront. Online education is still at an early (and some might even say experimental) stage of development and research suggests that there are still serious questions about the quality of online education as a whole. Moreover, even if proper quality can be established, there are still serious questions about the fit of community college students for online education, particularly given the diversity of the community college student population. The degree to which online education contributes to the advancement of social equity in the provision of community college education will depend on the care with which these policies are implemented at the ground level. In the forthcoming section, I propose a set of propositions that can be utilized to help us develop information enabling us to form policies that expand online education in a more socially equitable fashion.

Propositions and Policy Implementation

The key social-equity-based argument against the expansion of online education in community colleges is the proposition that community college students will do worse in online classes than they would in traditional face-to-face classes. If this is true, online education becomes a socially inequitable endeavor that inherently harms the most vulnerable of the higher education student population. Therefore, I offer the following proposition for future investigation:

Proposition 1: Academically at-risk community college students of low socioeconomic status will have a higher course failure rate in wholly online classes than in traditional face-to-face classes.

Establishing this proposition as true would require us to seriously reconsider any wholesale move toward this instructional approach at the community college level. Nevertheless, as I stated previously, there are subpopulations within the community college student body that may benefit from this instructional approach. Therefore, I offer the following proposition to help us learn more about the nuances of the effect of this instructional approach:

Proposition 2: Non-traditional community college students will perform as well in online classes as in traditional face-to-face classes.

If this proposition can be established as true, it would change the practical implications of the prior proposition. While wholesale moves toward online education may result in socially inequitable outcomes, targeted moves that focus on the needs of a smaller subset of community college learners may achieve some of the cost efficiencies desired by administrators while bringing new conveniences and flexibilities to non-traditional community college students. Nontraditional community college students may be able to benefit from online education without suffering the academic harm that traditional community college students may experience, resulting in a net positive benefit for all parties.

Finally, while the evidence suggests that wholly online instruction may not be efficient and/or effective for all community college students, there is evidence that technology can be utilized to achieve some of the aforementioned efficiency and economy benefits while maintaining or even improving the quality of instruction. Therefore, I offer the following proposition:

Proposition 3: Academically at-risk community college students of low socioeconomic status will perform better in hybrid classes than in traditional face-to-face classes and wholly online classes.

A positive finding for this proposition would have important and positive implications for public officials, community college administrators, and students interested in expanding online education. Hybrid education could reduce overhead costs and improve economies of scale for community colleges, allowing them to actualize at least some of the potential cost efficiencies. This could be accomplished while improving the student learning experience due to the utilization of online technologies and the increased focus on course redesign efforts.

Conclusion

Community colleges have a rich history of serving the public. Since their inception in the early part of the twentieth century, community colleges have pursued their mission of bringing education and its benefits to the poor and working class, thus advancing the value of social equity in America. While originally focused on providing a more general form of education, community colleges have since expanded as organizations, now providing a traditional education along with training for a host of specific jobs and technical careers. Community colleges have grown as organizations and as institutions and they are now a critical avenue by which the poor and working class can gain access to higher education and advance socially and economically in society.

Community colleges play an important role in American society, but like many other public institutions, their ability to fulfill their role is threatened by modern fiscal restraints. Clearly, technological advancements can help bring new efficiencies to community colleges, and it appears that online education can help community colleges meet the growing demand for higher education. But there is equal evidence that this technological and pedagogical innovation needs to be handled carefully in order for it to deliver on its promise. Those charged with implementing online education need to be cognizant of the proper use and the limits of this new instructional approach, lest they find themselves harming the very population they intend to help and protect.

References

Allen, I. E., & Seaman, J. (2011). Going the distance: Online education in the United States, 2011. Sloan Consortium. Retrieved from http://www.eric.ed.gov/ERICWebPortal/contentdelivery/servlet/ERICServlet?accno=ED529948

American Association of Community Colleges. (n.d.). Students at community colleges. American Association of Community Colleges. Retrieved from http://www.aacc.nche.edu/AboutCC/Trends/Pages/studentsatcommunitycolleges.aspx

Anderson, T. (2008). The theory and practice of online learning. Edmonton: AU Press.

Chen, G. (2009). Changing student demographics: Rising number of professional students. Community College Review. Retrieved from http://www.communitycollegereview.com/articles/75

Cohen, A. (2003). The American community college (4th ed.). San Francisco: Jossey-Bass.

Community colleges: The history of community colleges, the junior college, and the research university. (n.d.). Stateuniversity.com. Retrieved from http://education.stateuniversity.com/pages/1873/Community-Colleges.html

Feenberg, A. (1999). Distance learning: Promise or threat? Education at a Distance, 12(1). Retrieved from http://www.usdla.org/html/journal/DEC99_Issue/dl.htm

Frederickson, H. G. (2010). Social equity and public administration: Origins, developments, and applications. Armonk, NY: M.E. Sharpe.

Harasim, L. M. (2012). Learning theory and online technologies. New York: Routledge.

Janicki, T., & Liegle, J. O. (2001). Development and evaluation of a framework for creating Web-based learning modules: A pedagogical and systems perspective. Journal of Asynchronous Learning Networks, 5(1), 58-84.

Kahlenberg, R. (2010). The community college summit: Innovations. The Chronicle of Higher Education. Retrieved from http://chronicle.com/blogs/innovations/the-community-college-summit/27361

Knowles, M. S., Holton, E. F., & Swanson, R. A. (2012). The adult learner: The definitive classic in adult education and human resource development. London: Routledge.

Kop, R., & Hill, A. (2008). Connectivism: Learning theory of the future or vestige of the past? The International Review of Research in Open and Distance Learning, 9(3), 1-13.

Means, B., SRI International Center for Technology in Learning, & United States Department of Education. Policy and

Program Studies Service. (2009). Evaluation of evidence-based practices in online learning: A meta-analysis and review of online learning studies. Retrieved from http://www2.ed.gov/rschstat/eval/tech/evidence-based-practices/finalreport.pdf

Merrick, A., & Thurow, R. (2009). The jobless go back to school and, they hope, work. The Wall Street Journal, p. A14.

Meyer, K. (2008). If higher education is a right, and distance education is the answer, then who will pay? Journal of Asynchronous Learning Networks, 12(1), 45-68.

Meyer, K. A. (2006). Cost-efficiencies in online learning. New York: Wiley/Jossey-Bass.

Mullin, C. (2012). Why access matters: The community college student body (No. 2012-01PBL). Washington, D.C.: American Association of Community Colleges.

Russell, T. L., & IDECC Organization. (2001). The no significant difference phenomenon: A comparative research annotated bibliography on technology for distance education: As reported in 355 research reports, summaries and papers. [S.l.]: IDECC.

Skinner, B. F. (2011). About Behaviorism. New York: Random House Digital.
Stephenson, J. (Ed.). (2001). Teaching & learning online: New pedagogies for new technologies. London: Routledge.

Stumpf, A. D., McCrimon, E., & Davis, J. E. (2005). Carpe diem: Overcome misconceptions in community-college distance learning. Community College Journal of Research and Practice, 29(5), 357. doi:10.1080/10668920590921552

Vaughan, G. B. (2006). The community college story. American Association of Community Colleges.

Mindful Meditation for Online Learning: Lighting the fire by dimming the lights: Helping college students relax and focus to prepare for online learning

Brenda Freshman, Carol A. Molinari

As more college courses are delivered online to adapt to students' busy schedules, instructors are challenged to find creative ways to promote online learning. This paper explores the use of meditation to prepare college students for online learning by examining whether and how meditation increases students' focus and concentration. A structured meditation exercise was administered to an undergraduate and graduate online course at a public university. Student reflections and comments suggest personal and cognitive benefits of meditation for online instruction. Ways to integrate meditation into online courses are discussed to encourage instructors to include meditation in their instruction methodology. This pilot intends to inspire future study and debate regarding the value of meditation for promoting online learning.

Key words: student focus, stress reduction, pedagogy, self-directed learning, self-awareness.

Introduction

As more college students work while they take courses, college educators are increasingly challenged to design courses that meet the demands of school and work. Not surprisingly, more and more courses are being offered online and in hybrid formats (Allen & Seaman, 2010). These delivery changes require instructors to re-think ways to design and manage their courses to promote learning, especially in the online environment. Today's thoughtful educator asks, "How can I help students mentally prepare themselves so that they are ready for online learning?"

This paper examines the use of meditation as a way to prepare busy college students for online learning. Meditation was selected for two main reasons. First, meditation promotes cognitive activities that include concentration, focus, understanding, and recall (Jenson, Vangkilde, Frokjaer, & Hasselbalch, 2012; Koraza et al., 2012; Hussain & Bhushan, 2010; Van den Hurk, Giommi, Gielen, Speckens, & Barendregt, 2010). Second, meditation is also a personal relaxation activity that helps clear away other external stimuli while it increases attention and improves clarity and quality of thought (Sears, Kraus, Carlogh, & Treat, 2011). This paper will discuss the rationale, methods, preliminary results, and recommendations of this meditation pilot study to help prepare the student cognitively and emotionally for online learning.

Literature Survey

Online Learning and Meditation

Helping students focus, interact, and engage with each other are effective ways to promote learning. These are activities which require intellectual and personal growth (Bain, 2004). Most higher education faculty understand ways to develop students' thinking through reasoning, analysis of evidence, use of abstract ideas, and applied problem solving. However, the promotion of self-awareness and personal responsibility is less understood and evident in higher education. Yet such personal development appears to be critical in online learning. In an overview of student abilities necessary for effective distance learning, Cunningham (2010) states that "self-directed learning is key to successful on-line distance education" (p.1). He also highlights the value of self-awareness and self-discipline. The literature base in this area further supports the importance of self-regulation (Allen et al., 2004; Fahme, 2011; Radovan, 2011; Sutton & Nora, 2008), active participation (Conaway, Easton, & Schmidt, 2005; Hacker & Niederhouse, 2000), and cognitive development (Sutton & Nora, 2008; Yang, Huna-Yuan, & Lin,2009) in online education. Conversely, impediments such as anxiety and stress have been shown to constrict task performance (Eysenck, Payne, & Derakshan, 2005) and to reduce satisfaction and learning in online courses (Sun, Tsai, Finger, Chen & Yeh, 2008).

Meditation was selected as an activity to promote online learning based on evidence that the practice reduces stress and increases self-efficacy. Previous studies have consistently found meditation to be effective in anxiety and stress reduction (Chu, 2010; Davis & Hayes, 2011; Jenson et al., 2012), improving focus and attention (Koraza et al., 2012; Ray, Baker, & Plowman, 2011; Tang et al., 2007), and developing emotional regulation (Holzel et al., 2011; Zautra et al., 2008). While these benefits of meditation relate to family, work, and personal settings, there was little evidence in the literature of its benefits in academic settings. Therefore, this qualitative analysis of online students' meditation experience is proffered as a preliminary thread of new inquiry.

Meditation: Variations and Descriptions

A consistent meditation practice as part of one's daily routine has documented benefits both for the mind and body. Although there are many varieties of meditation practice, three specific types appear to be most prevalent in the academic literature: 1) visualization; 2) transcendental; and 3) mindfulness. While there might be some overlap to the practice and impact of each of these meditation styles, there are clear distinctions of method and focus which will be very briefly outlined. With visualization or guided imagery, an individual will be guided either by suggested visual cues (recorded, in person or written) or mental ones (i.e. take a journey in the mind's eye).

Transcendental meditation (TM) has roots in the ancient Vedic traditions of India. About 50 years ago, the Maharishi promoted and taught the TM technique to US audiences and other peoples throughout the globe (www.tm.org). This practice involves sitting comfortably in a chair and practicing a technique of mantra-based mental relaxation. Teachers of TM adhere to sacred and proven traditions; in turn, individuals learn this technique by becoming a student of a trained TM instructor.

According to Dwividi (2000), the construct of "mindfulness" dates back to the 6th century Buddhist term in the Pali language "Sati." In this context Sati (as described in the Satipathan Sutta) is comprised of 4 aspects: 1) awareness of functions and parts of the body, 2) awareness of feelings and sensations, 3) awareness of cognitions, and 4) awareness of mental impediments. Recently, Holzel et al.

(2011) reviewed the literature that related to the effects of mindfulness meditation. The categories of: a) attention regulation, b) body awareness, c) emotional regulation, and d) change in perceptions of self are strikingly similar to early Buddhist principles. The goal of mindfulness meditation "is to maintain attention to current internal and external experiences with a nonjudgmental stance, manifesting acceptance, curiosity and openness." (p.549).

Jon Kabat-Zinn (1990) developed the meditation technique termed mindfulness-based stress reduction (MBSR). This MBSR intervention is comprised of three elements, 1) video presentation of didactic information on mindfulness, stress and pain management and everyday implementation of the MBSR technique to alleviate these challenges, 2) mindfulness exercises, and 3) reflective discussion and sharing. Kabat-Zinn's video and exercises served as the online meditation activity used in this study and will be discussed in the methods section.

Meditation: Evidence of Benefits

Although much of the current research on mindfulness meditation has occurred in clinical settings for patients with anxiety or pain, some research has taken place in work and school environments. Ho's (2011) investigation of meditation experience and relationships with self-directed learning (SDL), organizational innovation (OI), and organizational performance (OP) has particular relevance to this study. Survey results of Taiwanese technology managers found that meditation experience promoted the openness to challenge, inquisitive nature, and self-understanding factors of SDL. Other studies that involved non-clinical populations such as college students, administrators, employees, and mediators have indicated improved attention (Ray et al., 2011; Shapiro, Schwartz, & Bonner, 1998; Tang et al., 2007; Van den Hurk et al., 2010), stress reduction, and emotional regulation (Aftanas & Golosheykin, 2005; Chu, 2010; Jenson et al., 2012).

Many studies have been conducted in clinical settings with patients suffering from mental and physical maladies. These investigations demonstrated stress reduction effects (Carlson, Speca, Faris, & Patel, 2007) and emotion and pain regulation (Zautra et al., 2008) as positive correlates to meditation practice. Other studies reported the following benefits of meditation: increases in well-being (Carmody & Baer, 2008; Chiesa & Serretti, 2009) and improved cognitive functioning (Sears et al., 2011). While not all studies support the advantages of the practice—for example, King and Coney (2006) found no significant differences in cognitive function between experienced meditators and non-meditators—nonetheless, the growing research supports the positive value of meditation in a variety of settings.

Methods

A structured meditation exercise was piloted in two online courses at the undergraduate and graduate levels offered in a Healthcare Management program during Fall 2011. The purpose of the exercise was to assess whether and how meditation influenced students' learning and personal growth. Students responses and reflections about the activity provided the data used in this qualitative analysis.

The meditation exercise included viewing the You Tube video of a talk by Jon Kabat-Zinn (1990) from the University of Massachusetts Medical School that was sponsored by Google. It discusses the scientific evidence of mindfulness practices and behaviors as they relate to stress reduction and healing. Students were given instructions to guide them in a brief meditation followed by several open-ended questions that related to their personal experience of meditation and any perceived benefits. The following describes the instructions given to students:

> You will review two web sites that will provide background and research the effects of meditation on health, stress reduction, and healing.
>
> http://www.4mindfulnessmeditation.com/ will provide a brief overview of mindfulness meditation.
>
> http://www.youtube.com/watch?v=r-SU8ftmmhmw
>
> This is a 1 hour and 14 minute You Tube video of a talk by Jon Kabat-Zinn from the University of Massachusetts Medical School that was sponsored by Google.
>
> Practice and Reflection:
> In a quiet place where you will not be interrupted, sit comfortably, up right in a chair with legs uncrossed, or in a yoga lotus position on the floor. Make sure your back can remain straight. Have a watch or clock nearby and practice just breathing and watching your thoughts for 3-5 minutes. Before you begin, notice how your body and mind feel. Try to go as long as possible. Then respond to the following questions - keep responses to each 200-250 words:
>
> 1. Did you notice a change in how your body and mind felt after the meditation was complete? If so, describe this change.
> 2. Discuss two benefits you experienced after meditating.
> 3. Discuss two potential problems of meditation.

Student Sample

This meditation exercise was conducted in two online professional courses in Healthcare Management: one undergraduate and one graduate. There were 31 students in each course with 19 women and 12 men in the graduate course; and 29 women and 2 men in the undergraduate course. Both classes were racially and ethnically diverse and reflective of the racial and ethnic characteristics of the selected public university and academic program. Two thirds of the graduate and undergraduate students were non-white; with an estimated 25% international students from Africa, Asia, and Middle East.

Plan of Analysis

The open-ended questions were systematically analyzed to identify common student responses related to their meditation experience. Responses were listed and categorized to reflect common themes. A count of responses for each category was tallied and sorted by class (undergraduate vs. graduate) and for graduate students by gender. Initially, gender was examined among graduate students only as undergraduates were overwhelmingly female; however, no significant differences were found between male and female graduate responses and thus findings are reported only by class. Due to the small number of students in this pilot, significant tests were not performed. However, the following tables describe their responses.

Results

The following tables summarize responses for graduate and undergraduate students regarding their meditation experience and perceived benefits and problems.

Table 1. Did you notice a change in how your body and mind felt after the meditation was complete? If so describe.

	Clear-minded	Relaxed/Calm	Better Memory	Aware of physical environment
Graduates (n=31)	52%	36%	26%	20%
Undergraduates ((n=31)	33%	34%	48%	25%

Table 2. Discuss two benefits of meditation.

	Lower stress	Clear focus	More emotional stability	Improved concentration	Helped to process information
Graduates (n=31)	43%	35%	40%	33%	24%
Undergraduates (n=31)	40%	37%	10%	23%	15%

Table 3. Discuss two potential problems of meditation.

	Time	Managing self-awareness	Acceptance by others	Less productivity	Clash with cultural/religious beliefs
Graduates (n=31)	47%	35%	25%	28%	15%
Undergraduates (n=31)	45%	24%	14%	21%	7%

Discussion

Patterns or re-occurring themes observed after meditation.

Graduate students were most likely to report being clear-minded and undergraduates were most likely to report better memory following meditation. Both groups reported feeling relaxed and peaceful and aware of their physical environment.

Perceived benefits derived from meditation.

Lower stress and gaining a clear focus were consistently reported in both classes as a benefit of meditation. Graduates were more likely than undergraduates to report gaining emotional stability, improved concentration, and information processing as benefits. Perceived potential problems from meditation.

Time required to meditate was consistently reported as a potential problem by all students. This relates to the lower productivity reported by graduate students and undergraduate women. Graduate students were more likely to report problems related to managing difficult feelings that emerge from heightened self-awareness than undergraduates. Several graduate and undergraduate students noted that meditation could clash with an individual's cultural and religious beliefs and thus lead to some level of intrapersonal conflict. Given the racial and ethnic diversity of both classes this is an important point to consider.

General Comments

The following are examples of general comments from students related to the meditation

Graduate students

- This is my first semester in grad school and my first online class ever. As you can imagine, I was nervous and somewhat intimidated, especially since I did not know what to expect. That is the main reason why I started meditating.
- Have to practice it, do it more than once to get the benefit there is a learning curve to mindfulness meditation.
- During the exercise, I felt my muscles relax and my head felt lighter, as if everything was warm and melting away. In my mind, I felt in tune with my body. I was able to focus and think more clearly in daily situations. I even noticed I was more able to pick up on smaller details. Also, my thoughts were, how can I express this, like an early 1920's silent movie where everything is moving fast, and the words are showing the next slide. What I am trying to say is that even though, my thoughts were racing, I was able to clearly process and interpret the content of each thought.

Undergraduate students

- There is a feeling of inspiration, health of the body, and circles of empowerment. In general, the aftermath of meditation presents the body with some form of awareness concerning your soul and energy.
- There is more responsibility to direct ourselves in online courses. Meditation can greatly benefit us in these online courses by clearing our minds to gain a mental focus.
- Online learning is time consuming and very demanding but can be very interesting and become a learning opportunity if one is able to take things one at a time and become very discipline to time management. That is the strength of meditation.

Recommendations to Apply Lessons Learned

Students' feedback and reflections indicate that meditation promotes relaxation, reduces stress, and thus fosters readiness to learn. With these benefits in mind, the following are suggested ways to integrate meditation into an online course:

1. Start an online course with a meditation exercise. This can provide the opportunity for students to relax and mentally focus on the course content and instruction. The meditation exercise can also serve as an ice-breaker to help learners focus and share personal experiences. Some ways to set up this exercise include posting student responses to a discussion board or conference to help students to get acquainted with each other in a non-threatening and personal way.
2. Place the meditation exercise at the middle or end of the course as a stress reducer to help students relax and focus, especially before tests or other busy times in the course.
3. Be clear with students regarding the purpose of meditation to online learning. It is important to explain how meditation promotes relaxation and attention, otherwise the students may feel distracted or confused by the meditation exercise, which may impede learning.
4. Offer credit for completion of the assignment to increase student participation in the meditation exercise. Linking a reward for this activity will encourage students to seriously consider and complete the meditation exercise.

Review student comments and reflections about the meditation; check for feedback especially related to perceived benefits, problems, and ways to improve the exercise. These can provide insightful feedback in terms of whether and how the meditation exercise helped students relax, focus, manage their time, and engage with others in the online learning environment.

Limitations and Future Studies

There were several limitations to this pilot investigation and these will be discussed together with suggestions for further study. First, the study was limited to one program in a single university. It is important to examine a broad sample of online students from undergraduate and graduate programs in a variety of universities to assess whether perceived benefits of meditation are similar, different, or not present among other students. Another point to consider is to select programs with culturally diverse students since perceptions about meditation are likely to be influenced by cultural beliefs and values. Thus, examining meditation across a broad array of online programs with diverse students would provide a student sample that can be examined across key demographic factors to assess their effects on perceptions and benefits of meditation.

Second, this pilot used subjective responses to open-ended questions following the meditation without any pre-assessment. A pre- and post-design to evaluate the effects of meditation such as mindfulness, self-awareness, self-regulation, and stress can strengthen the validity of these preliminary results. Additionally, using established quantitative tools vs. the qualitative ones used in this pilot can also minimize some internal validity threats. For example, using the Kentucky Inventory of Mindfulness Skills (Baer, Smith, & Allen, 2004) or the Langer Mindfulness/Mindlessness Scale (Haigh, Moore, Kashdan, & Fresco, 2011), as well as validated emotional intelligence inventories or stress assessments can provide appropriate tools for this type of inquiry.

Third, this study did not look at the impact of meditation on learning of course content. Future investigations may examine the relationships between meditation and student grades for online courses to assess if meditation can improve student online learning and grades. It is important to apply some or all of these for future studies to enhance their rigor and validity.

Conclusion

This study sought to promote dialogue and initiate inquiry focused on the function and benefits of meditation to prepare students for online instruction and learning. As more college courses are being delivered online, it is increasingly important for the academic community to assess student learning processes related to online instruction. This pilot used meditation as an innovative process to prepare online learners by helping them to relax, focus, and engage with fellow learners and the instructor in course activities. The current investigators want to encourage others to build on these preliminary steps by using pre- and post-evaluation designs, established quantitative measures, and larger sample sizes with the intent to build a student data base that can inform future dialogue and study regarding the value of meditation for online learning.

References

Aftanas, L., & Golosheykin, S. (2005). Impact of regular mediation practice on EEG Activity and During Evoked Negative Emotions. International Journal Of Neuroscience, 115(6), 893-909. doi:10.1080/00207450590897969

Allen, M., Mabry, E., Mattrey, M., Bourhis, J., Titsworth, S., & Burrell, N. (2004). Evaluating the effectiveness of distance learning: A comparison using meta-analysis. Journal of Communication, 54(3), 402-420.

Allen, I. E., & Seaman, J. S. (2007). Changing the landscape: more institutions pursue online offerings. On The Horizon, 15(3), 130-138.

Baer, R. A., Smith, G. T., & Allen, K. B. (2004). Assessment of mindfulness by self-report: The Kentucky Inventory of Mindfulness Skills. Assessment, 11(3), 191-206.

Bain, K. (2004). What the best college teachers do. Cambridge, MA: Harvard University Press.

Carlson, L. E., Speca, M., Faris, P., & Patel, K.D. (2007). One year pre–post intervention follow-up of psychological, immune, endocrine and blood pressure outcomes of mindfulness-based stress reduction (MBSR) in breast and prostate cancer outpatients. Brain, Behavior, and Immunity, 21(8), 1038-1049.

Carmody, J., & Baer, R. A. (2009). How long does a mindfulness-based stress reduction program need to be? A review of class contact hours and effect sizes for psychological distress. Journal of Clinical Psychology, 65, 627–638. doi: 10.1002/jclp.20555

Chiesa, A., & Serretti, A. (2009). Mindfulness-Based Stress Reduction for stress management in healthy people: A review and meta-analysis. Journal Of Alternative & Complementary Medicine, 15(5), 593-600. doi:10.1089/acm.2008.0495

Chu, L. (2010). The benefits of meditation vis-à-vis emotional intelligence, perceived stress and negative mental health. Journal of the International Society for the Investigation of Stress, 26(2), 169-180.

Conaway, R. N., Easton, S. S., & Schmidt, W. V. (2005). Strategies for enhancing student interaction and immediacy in online courses. Business Communication Quarterly, 68(1), 25-35.

Cunningham, J. (2010). Self-direction: A critical tool in distance learning. Common Ground Journal, 7(2), 89-100.

Davis, D., & Hayes, J. (2011) What are the benefits of mindfulness? A practice review of psychotherapy-related research. Psychotherapy, 48(2), 198-208.

Dwivedi, K. N. (2000). Mindfulness in mental health. Psychiatry Online. Retrieved from www.priory.com/psych/mindfulness.htm

Eysenck, M., Payne, S., & Derakshan, N. (2005). Trait anxiety, visuospatial processing and working memory. Cognition & Emotion, 19(8). 1214-1228.

Fahme, D. (2011). Analysis of communication barriers to distance education. Online Journal of Communication and Media Technologies, 1(1), 1-15.

Hacker, D. J., & Niederhauser, D. S. (2000). Promoting deep and durable learning in the online classroom. New Directions for Teaching and Learning, 2000(84), 53-63.

Haigh, E. A. P., Moore, M. T., Kashdan, T. B., & Fresco, D. M. (2011). Examination of the factor structure and concurrent validity of the Langer Mindfulness/Mindlessness Scale. Assessment, 18(1), 11-26.

Ho, L. (2011). Meditation, learning, organizational innovation and performance. Industrial Management & Data Systems, 111(1), 113-131.

Hölzel, B. K., Lazar, S. W., Gard, T., Schuman-Olivier, Z., Vago, D. R., & Ott, U. (2011). How does mindfulness meditation work? Proposing mechanisms of action from a conceptual and neural perspective. Perspectives On Psychological Science, 6(6), 537-559. doi:10.1177/1745691611419671

Hussain, D., & Bhushan, B. (2010). Psychology of meditation and health: Present status and future directions. International Journal of Psychology & Psychological Therapy, 10(3), 439-451.

Jensen, C. G., Vangkilde, S., Frokjaer, V., & Hasselbalch, S. G. (2012). Mindfulness training affects attention—Or is it attentional effort? Journal of Experimental Psychology, 141(1), 106-123.

Kabat-Zinn, J. (1990). Full catastrophe living: Using the wisdom of your body and mind to face stress, pain, and illness. New York: Bantam.

King, G., & Coney, J. (2006). Short term effects of meditation versus relaxation on cognitive functioning. Journal Of Transpersonal Psychology, 38(2), 200-215.

Koraza, E. H., Sato, J. R., Lacerda, S. S., Barreiros, M. A., Radvany, J., Russell, T. A., Sanches, L. G., Mello, L. E., & Amaro, E. (2012). Meditation training increases brain efficiency in an attention task. NeuroImage, 59(1), 745-749.

Radovan (2011). The relation between distance students' motivation, their use of learning strategies, and academic success, Turkish Online Journal of Educational Technology, 10(1), 21-222.

Ray, J. L., Baker, L. T., & Plowman, D. A. (2011). Organizational mindfulness in business schools. Academy of Management Learning and Education, 10(2), 188-203.

Sears, S. R., Kraus, S., Carlough, K., & Treat, E. (2011). Perceived benefits and doubts of participants in a weekly meditation study. Mindfulness, 2(3), 167-174.

Shapiro, S. L., Schwartz, G. E., & Bonner, G. (1998). Effects of Mindfulness-Based Stress Reduction on medical and premedical students. Journal of Behavioral Medicine, 21(6), 581-599.

Sun, P., Tsai, R. J., Finger, G. Chen, Y., & Yeh, D. (2008). What drives a successful e-learning? An empirical investigation of the critical factors influencing learner satisfaction. Computers & Education, 50, 1183-1202.

Sutton, S. C., & Nora, A. (2008). An exploration of college persistence for students enrolled in web-enhanced courses: A multivariate analytic approach. Journal of College Student Retention, 10(1), 21-37.

Tang, Y., Ma, Y., Wang, J., Fan, Y., Feng, S., Lu, Q., Yu, Q., Sui, D., Rothbart, M. K., Fan, M., & Posner, M. (2007). Short-term meditation training improves attention and self-regulation. Proceedings of the National Academy of Sciences of the United States of America, 104(43), 17152-17156.

Van den Hurk, P. A., Giommi, F., Gielen, S. C., Speckens, A. E., & Barendregt, H. P. (2010). Greater efficiency in attention processing related to mindfulness meditation. The Quarterly Journal of Experimental Psychology, 63(6), 1168-1180.

Yang, J. F., Huna-Yuan, L., & Lin, N. C. (2009). Modes of delivery and learning objectives in distance education. International Journal of Instructional Media, 36(1), 55-71.

Zautra, A. J., Davis, M. C., Reich, J. W., Nicassario, P., Tennen, H., Finan, P., & Irwin, M. R. (2008). Comparison of cognitive behavioral and mindfulness meditation interventions on adaptation to rheumatoid arthritis for patients with and without history of recurrent depression. Journal Of Consulting And Clinical Psychology, 76(3), 408-421.

Curriculum design for flexible delivery: an assessment of e-learning approaches

Jayanath Ananda[1]

Technological advancements have pushed the boundaries of tertiary education design and delivery across the globe. Flexible teaching and learning delivery approaches have proliferated in recent times without much attention to pedagogically-driven learning designs. This paper reviews various pedagogical designs used as part of e-learning and blended learning models in business education. It also maps the tenets of learning theories to selected e-learning designs. Tertiary educators face several challenges when implementing e-learning designs in business education. They include a traditional structured approach to learning, difficulties in catering to diverse student cohorts equitably, and choosing effective technologies that underpin a particular e-learning pedagogy.

Keywords: learning theories, business education, online pedagogies, e-learning, conversational framework, web 2.0, flexible learning

1. Introduction

Curriculum design for flexible delivery is at the forefront of a teaching and learning renewal of tertiary education, particularly in business education. Flexible delivery of teaching and learning covers a wide array of approaches including online teaching and e-learning, block-mode teaching delivery and distance education. Hunter et al. (2010) stress that if continuous improvements have not been made to business education, the society will lose significant economic contributions made by business graduates. On the one hand, there is a growing awareness in business education that the traditional approach to teaching and learning fails to meet industry demands (van Over & Stover, 1994; Westerbeck, 2004) and lags behind in equipping business students with skills to leverage the use of networks, optimal links and information (Hughes, 2006). The most common pitfalls include the strong emphasis on technical content, inadequate application of knowledge and generic skills such as group work, communication, problem-solving, critical thinking and leadership (Albrecht & Sach, 2001; Carr & Mathews, 2002). On the other hand, today, tertiary education institutions offering business programmes face increased competition and chronic funding challenges (Hunter et al., 2010) forcing them to introduce flexible and innovative courses as a marketing strategy to bolster student enrolment.

Technological advancements have pushed the boundaries of tertiary education institutions towards new forms of knowledge construction and social interaction. The emergence of Web 2.0 based learning tools, which can augment superior computational and communication capabilities and foster collaboration and social interaction, have provided an impetus for a growing body of work on curriculum design for e-learning (Bower et al., 2009). Web 2.0 can be broadly defined as a second generation

---

[1] School of Economics, La Trobe University

or more personalised communicative form of the World Wide Web that emphasises active participation, connectivity, collaboration and sharing of knowledge and ideas among users (Lee & McLoughlin, 2011). Web 2.0 is often associated with the use and practice of social software where multiple users can collaborate with one another, micro-contents such as blog posts, text-chats, video-clips, open web tools and other sophisticated web interfaces (Bower et al., 2009; Dabbagh & Reo, 2011). Tapscott and Williams (2010) state that "universities are losing their grip on higher learning as the internet is, inexorably, becoming the dominant infrastructure for knowledge—both as a container and as a global platform for knowledge exchange between people" (p.18).

The rapid spread of globalization and enormous developments in information technology (IT) have also led to dramatic changes in the business environment and business courses need to be responsive to these changes (Mohamed, 2009). Burdett (2003) highlights the importance of incorporating strategies such as group work into business teaching pedagogy[2] to ensure deep learning outcomes. It is also envisaged that a blend of technical and interpersonal skills are required to navigate and succeed in the modern working place (Hunter et al., 2010). New models and novel approaches to business education have been called for, which include the interests of industry, students and academia (Anderson and Rask, 2008). One of the approaches that has received attention in business education reforms is the use of e-learning and blended learning approaches.

The Joint Information Systems Committee (JISC) defines e-learning[3] as 'learning facilitated and supported through the use of information and communication technologies' (Beetham, 2004, p.1). E-learning has also been presented as a continuum of face-to-face learning, which contains no e-learning, to distance education which can be fully e-learning (Bates & Poole, 2003). Blended learning which combines both face-to-face learning and forms of e-learning is placed in the middle of this continuum. Commonly cited reasons for incorporating e-learning into curricula include increased flexibility of learning environments, improvement of quality by increased access to information, reduced cognition load and authentic learning, ability to tap into the global market, widening access, competition and strategic reasons (Normand & Littlejohn, 2006).

Despite the initial enthusiasm, e-learning has not lived up to its expectations in both the university and corporate sectors (Driscoll, 2008; Granić et al., 2009). Past evidence of technology introduction to teaching and learning indicates that often such technology has been embraced with naïve enthusiasm only to be later discarded (Lowerison et al., 2008). It is also clear that the predicted decline in face-to-face teaching, due to the introduction of online teaching technologies, has not occurred (Beetham, 2004). However, the potential of online technologies has not yet been fully harnessed for learning.

Pedagogical problems, organizational barriers, technical issues and financial problems have been cited as the main impediments of e-learning development (Driscoll, 2008). A diverse array of

---

[2] Although the term pedagogy is often regarded as the art and science of teaching, it is not without critics (Beetham & Sharpe, 2007).

[3] Although the meaning is relatively uncontested, there is no universally accepted definition for e-learning. Online learning is regarded as more narrow in scope than e-learning (Beetham, 2004).

theoretical perspectives which is alien and overwhelming to academics outside the field of education is another factor contributing to the lack of applications in pedagogically-driven e-learning designs (McNaught, 2003). The mere presentation of subject matter using multimedia does not, of itself, lead to better learning (Mayes & Freitas, 2004). Central to the issue is the mapping of sound pedagogical principles as outlined by Biggs (2000) into the e-learning curriculum design. Biggs (1996) emphasised that learners use their own activities to construct knowledge and the teaching design should specify the desired levels of understanding and activities that they need perform. There is little evidence of various learning theories being applied to effective pedagogically driven e-learning (Beetham et al., 2001; Clegg et al., 2003; Conole et al., 2004). There is also a need for studies that examine the extent to which the emergent technologies such as Web 2.0 support the educational process and to identify ways in which they can enhance student learning (Oskoz & Elola, 2011).

This paper focuses on e-learning in business education and how it can be adapted to diverse contexts including multi-campus teaching delivery. The paper reviews the specific pedagogical principles that can be used in designing business subjects for flexible delivery predominantly based on online technologies. The remainder of this paper is organised as follows. An overview of learning theory is presented in the next section. Then the tenets of learning theory are mapped to e-learning pedagogy. In the next section, some challenges and potential applications of e-learning to business education are discussed with special reference to multi-campus and flexible delivery. Some concluding comments are provided in the final section.

2. Overview of learning theories

Theories of learning outline three broad traditions to learning: behaviourism, cognitivism and constructivism (Mayer, 2003). These traditions are derived from broader fields, not just education, and are regarded as historical stages of enquiry into knowledge. The behavioural approach to learning posits that knowing is the result of objective experience whereas the cognitive approach purports knowing as the mental processing of information. The behavioural approach places a high emphasis on prescriptive instructions on well-defined learning objectives and rewarding learners as they progress incrementally toward larger learning goals (Lowerison et al., 2008). The constructivist approach subscribes to the view that learning is a subjective construction of knowledge. The basic premise is that meaning is not imposed or transmitted by direct instruction, but is created by students' learning activities (Biggs & Tang, 2007).

Anderson and Krathwohl (2001) provide a taxonomy of learning which incorporates a knowledge dimension and a cognitive process dimension. The knowledge dimension relates to the subject matter contents and incorporates factual knowledge (discrete pieces of elementary information), conceptual knowledge (interrelated representations of more complex knowledge forms), procedural knowledge (the skills to perform processes) and metacognitive knowledge which is the knowledge and awareness of one's cognition as well as that of others. The cognitive process dimension includes remembering, understanding, applying, analysing, evaluating and creating. These levels represent a continuum from lower order thinking skills to higher order thinking skills (Anderson & Krathwol, 2001).

Various interpretations of the three learning theory traditions described above have been discussed in the literature. For example, Greeno et al. (1996) highlight three broad perspectives which make vastly different assumptions about what is crucial for understanding learning – the associationist perspective (learning as an activity); the cognitive perspective (learning as achieving understanding); and the situative perspective (learning as social practice). These three perspective (associationsist, cognitive, and situative) correspond to behaviourism, cognitivism, and constructivism in learning theory traditions, respectively. The associationist perspective, which encompasses the research traditions behavioural theory and neural networks[4] (Mayes & de Freitas, 2004), contends that knowledge is organised accumulation of associations and skill components. Moreover, not only are the formation, strengthening and adjustment of association pivotal to learning but so is the reinforcement of connections through feedback. Albeit controversial, the associationist view also assumes that knowledge and skills need to be taught from the bottom up where smaller units are mastered as a prerequisite for more complex units. The cognitive perspective emphasises underlying processes of interpreting and constructing meaning and focuses on schema theory, information processing theories, the level of processing in memory, mental models and metacognitive processes. In sharp contrast to the associationist perspective, the cognitive perspective places a strong emphasis on the structures of understanding when acquiring new knowledge. The situative perspective advocates that learning must be personally meaningful and always subject to influences from the social and cultural setting in which the learning occurs. One branch of situative learning emphasises the importance of context-dependent learning[5] where every effort is made to make the learning activity authentic to the social context (Mayes & de Freitas, 2004).

Biggs (1999) emphasised the importance of consistency between the curriculum, teaching methods, the learning environment and the assessment procedures when designing curricula. Accordingly, a good pedagogical design is one with complete consistency of the above elements. The logical process should align the intended learning outcomes with learning and teaching activities and then design assessment tasks which will genuinely test whether the outcomes have been reached (Mayes & de Freitas, 2004). Albeit simple in theory, the application of Biggs' approach to curriculum design is not straightforward. Biggs (2009) advocates a constructivist approach prompting the designer to always focus on what the learner is actually doing. Hence, the guiding assumption about learning upon which various teaching methods and learning activities are built is constructivist theory.

Given the numerous interpretations of learning traditions and online pedagogies, applying learning theories to curriculum design becomes a non-trivial task. The core question for the curriculum designer is which learning theory and which perspective is useful for a specific teaching and learning context. Essentially, the task involves unpacking various online pedagogies so that their learning tradition roots can be uncovered. The next section applies these learning theories to selected online pedagogies.

---

[4] Neural networks posit knowledge states as patterns of activation in a network of elementary units (Mayes and de Freitas, 2004).

[5] For example, Problem-based Learning (PBL).

3. Applying learning theories to online pedagogies

The core research question addressed in this paper concerns the pedagogical approaches to e-learning design in business courses with diverse student cohorts. The focus is on what questions practitioners should ask when making e-learning design decisions. This invariably involves reflecting on the intended learning outcomes, the assumptions about the role of technology, the learning context and teaching modes. Contextual elements (Kember, 1997), in particular, appear to have different levels of influence on teaching and learning (Gonzalez, 2009). Salmon (2002) contends that "there are no e-learning models per se but only e-enhancements where technology is used to achieve better learning outcomes," or a more cost-efficient way of bringing the learning environment to learners (Mayes & de Freitas, 2004). When applying theory to online pedagogies, it is also important to take into consideration the contextual factors including diverse student cohorts and teaching delivery modes and how they enable non-specialists to engage in effective e-learning curriculum design. Therefore, mapping learning theory onto various pedagogical approaches is the logical precursor to any attempt to identify pedagogies that are best suited for a particular teaching and learning context.

Table 1 summarises selected online pedagogies, their learning theory foundations and the relevance to flexible curriculum design. My intention here is to apply learning theory to a few chosen pedagogies that are relevant to diverse student needs or cohorts. The diverse needs include consideration of academic year (whether undergraduate or postgraduate), learning context (type of group, relationship) and the nature of the task. Online pedagogies that subscribe to a behavioural tradition include most current e-learning tools, e-training modules and some intelligent tutoring models. Certain business courses by nature are interdisciplinary and thus pedagogical approaches that enhance learning through association and reinforcement, whilst building advanced complex tasks in a step-by-step manner, are useful. When catering to student groups with differing backgrounds and circumstances (e.g. full-time student versus part-time student who is employed), pedagogies that subscribe to cognitive traditions can be highly relevant. Under this learning theory tradition, several online pedagogies including Laurillard's conversational model and Salomon's distributed cognition model are described. Among the plethora of pedagogies that draw from constructivism, several relevant to business courses are discussed.

Pedagogies based on a behavioural perspective include instruction-based e-training models through which simulation of a process is carried out and problems or routines that have been carefully sorted according to the difficulty level are presented. These pedagogies are based on the premise that behavioural modifications are possible via stimulus-response pairs and trial and error learning. Instructional approaches are considered to be more appropriate when students have not yet formed an understanding about a particular topic (Magliaro et al., 2005). Most current e-learning development models which use digital media such as podcasting, Lectopia, lecture presentation, quizzes and web-based self-assessment subscribe to behaviourism. Intelligent Tutoring Systems (ITS) (Anderson & Reiser, 1985) and learning objects models (Wiley, 2000) also align with the behavioural theory as they essentially follow an instructivist approach (Mayes & de Freitas, 2004). Howev-

Table 1: Selected e-learning pedagogies and their learning theory traditions

Learning theory (primary)	Learning theory (secondary)	Main features	e-learning pedagogy/ tools	Possible application to research question	References
Behaviourism	Behaviourism	Behaviour can be modified through stimulus-response pairs and trial and error learning. Learning through association and reinforcement with a pedagogical focus on adaptive response	Most current e-learning development; Lecture presentations, Podcasting, Lectopia, library resources, quizzes, self-assessment	Useful when introducing new concepts, theories and facts. Relevant when designing inter-disciplinary courses for multi-student cohorts where competence in complex tasks can be built in a stepwise process.	
	Associanist/Instructional Systems Design (ISD)	The competence in advanced and complex tasks is built step by step from simpler units of knowledge and skill, finally adding coordination to the whole structure.	E-training, learning objects, some intelligent tutoring models		Mayes & de Freitas (2004)
Cognitivism	Cognitive/Constructivist	Learning is understood as achieving understanding through dialogue and collaboration. New knowledge must be built on the foundations of already existing frameworks, through problem-solving activity and feedback	Laurillard's Conversational Model Dialogic pedagogies	Highly relevant in catering to different student groups and group-specific tasks (abstract or concrete) as learner groups may differ in their understanding and application of concepts.	Laurillard (2002) Mayes & de Freitas (2004) Bower et al. (2009)
	Cognitive	Learning as transformation in internal cognitive structures with a pedagogical focus on processing and transmission of information through communication, inference and problem solving	Salomon's distributed cognition Intelligent Learning Systems		Salomon (1993)
Constructivism	Constructivist	Learning as subjective construction of knowledge with a task-oriented pedagogical focus. Favours hands-on, self-directed activities oriented towards design and discovery. Focuses on a	Toolkits and other support systems that enable constructivist principles	The use of toolkit is largely driven by the subject content	Papert (1986; 1991); Conole et al. (2004)

Table 1 (Cont'd)

Community of Practice/Situative perspective/ Socially situated learning Co-constructivist	Learning as developing social practice Learning as social participation emphasising interpersonal relationships involving imitation and modelling	CSALT networked learning model Peer-assisted dialogic pedagogies	The emphasis on organisational context and educational setting has a greater relevance to curriculum design	Goodyear (2001); Greeno et al. (2000); Mayes & de Freitas (2004)
Activity-based	Influenced by activity theory and focuses on an activity system and structures of activities. The Zone of Proximal Development (ZPD) – Allows students to extend beyond what they could have achieved in isolation	Dialogic pedagogy Students on a networked learning course collaborating on a project (e.g. A Wiki project)	Collaborative group activities and projects can embed generic skills such as team work	Vygotsky (1978) Jonassen (2000)
Experiential	Learning as the transformation of experience into knowledge, skills and attitudes. Reflection as a means of transforming experience	Asynchronous communication which is not time-bound and communication archives offer increased opportunities for reflection	Asynchronous communication tools such as Discussion forums	Kolb (1984)
Socially-mediated/Constructivist	A stimulus is given in the form of an online activity where individuals post contributions. Interactions among participants take place through cross posting and responding to other's contributions. A summary, feedback or critique is offered by a moderator.	Salmon's e-tivities or Salmon e-moderation model	Useful in framing the course designing process as it provides five logical steps of student engagement process.	Salmon (2002) Salmon (2004)

er, pedagogies of behavioural origins often do not take advantage of the benefits derived from more socio-constructivist learning designs where the active engagement of students and socially constructed meanings are sought (Bower et al., 2009).

An approach which draws on both constructivist and cognitive theories is Laurillard's (2002) conversational framework. The conversational framework emphasises the importance of discursive or conversational flows to enable higher learning. It has been very influential in the development of e-learning in the UK. In this model, learning is understood as achieving understanding through dialogue and collaboration. The framework contends that learners form thorough understanding by apprehending the structure of discourse, interpreting forms of representation, acting on descriptions of the world, applying feedback, and reflecting upon the goal-action-feedback cycle (Bower et al., 2009). The conversational framework highlights five different media types to guide course designs: narrative; productive; interactive; communicative; productive, and adaptive (Laurillard, 2002). Table 2 describes these media types and related e-learning tools.

One of the main criticisms of the Laurillard framework is whether it is able to sustain the individual/group dialogue to enhance generic skills (Goodyear, 2002; Mayes & de Freitas, 2004). From a learning context point of view, narrative media types have the advantage of allowing the learner to access information at a time and in a place suitable for the learner. Since information is presented in more than one medium, the framework can overcome physical/sensory access problems. However, information overload and the need for a wider repertoire of information skills can be potential downsides. In communicative media types, learners have to communicate and take turns more explicitly drawing on different skills from spoken communication. The ability to record these dialogues for later reflection is an added advantage. However, demand for prompt responses in synchronous communicative tasks can be a burden for the learner.

A third approach that draws on both constructivist and Communities of Practice principles (Mayes & de Freitas, 2004) is the CSALT (Centre for Studies in Advanced Learning Technology) networked learning model (Goodyear, 2001). It emphasises the distinction between the tasks designed by the tutor and the activities carried out by the learner. The model disaggregates the implied pedagogy into a hierarchy comprising four levels: pedagogical tactics (the lowest level), pedagogical strategy, high level pedagogy, and philosophy (the highest level). The upper levels of pedagogy are considered conceptual while the lower levels are regarded as procedural or operational. Interestingly, the CSALT model, whilst integrating an element of the systems approach, places an emphasis on the organisational context and asserts its importance, particularly in the education setting. The pedagogical framework and the educational setting are contained within the organisational context. An educational setting is comprised of educator-designed tasks, student activities, and the 'learning environment'[6] including educational technology. With a strong footing in collaborative learning, the CSALT model demonstrates that learning outcomes can be linked with specific learner groups and their activities (Mayes & de Freitas, 2004). Goodyear (2001) also emphasises the transformational and personal development aspects of networked learning (Mayes & de Freitas, 2004). Considering the merits

---

[6] This can include the Personal Learning Environment (PLE) which can be a knowledge network, a cognitive space or technology associated with individual learning.

Table 2: Laurillard media type and e-learning tools

Media type	Description	e-learning tools
Narrative	Since formal learning depends more on interaction with representations than with the 'real world,' learners should produce representations of their own (notes, mind maps, class presentations and answers to comprehension questions)	On-screen text, image, video files, PowerPoint slides, DVDs, web pages, animations Multimedia authoring tools, word and image processing tools Electronic whiteboards, wikis, blogs, shared write/draw systems
Productive	Supports skills of analysis and application allowing learners to manipulate data consciously and explicitly, using their own parameters and protocols	Spreadsheets and other statistical tools, databases, qualitative analysis tools, online calculators
Interactive	Supports developing information skills and supporting research tasks. A special category of interactive tools are quizzes with feedback.	Quizzes, search engines, gateways and portals, interactive maps
Communicative	Asynchronous communication between individuals and groups can be used to promote reflective learning and allow ideas to be built collaboratively whereas synchronous communication has the benefits of immediacy and high motivation.	<u>Asynchronous</u>: Email, text, discussion forums, mailing lists, wikis, video and audio messages <u>Synchronous</u>: Online chat, video conferencing, instant messaging, mobile phones
Adaptive	Supports tasks that depend on continuous adaptation to user input where learners receive intrinsic feedback to their actions. Valuable in embedding experimental learning and higher order learning skills (e.g. problem solving, evaluation, research, etc.)	Simulations, virtual worlds, models, computer games, interactive tutorials

Source: Modified from Sharpe and Oliver (2007).

of each learning stage and activity, Bower et al. (2009) developed an online pedagogy framework that focuses on four general learning design principles: transmissive; dialogic; co-constructive; and collaborative. This framework allows the learning design to be driven by the cognitive and collaborative requirements rather than the ever-changing technology (Bower et al., 2009).

Salmon's (2004) e-moderating model of course design splits student engagement into five stages: access and motivation, online socialisation, information exchange, knowledge construction, and development. This model describes the stages of progressing towards successful online learning both for students and e-moderators (Mayes & de Freitas, 2004). The model has been widely used as a way of sequencing activities in courses that rely on collaborative computer-mediated discussions (Sharpe & Oliver, 2007). Although the model does not align with a learning theory directly, it implies a commitment to constructivist tasks and the greatest possible degree of dialogue.

Whilst descriptions of forms of learning settings that support quality learning outcomes are common in the literature, detailed descriptions about learning processes in forms that can be easily applied by teachers are less available (Oliver et al., 2007). In this section, an attempt was made to examine the learning theory traditions of selected e-learning pedagogies. The intention here was not to provide an exhaustive discussion of various online pedagogies but to hand pick a few online pedagogies that may be relevant to business curriculum design targeted at diverse student cohorts. The next section discusses some of the main challenges of applying e-learning pedagogies to curriculum design from a business education perspective.

4. Challenges, contextual influences and potential applications to business education

Traditional approaches to business education often fail to harness the full power of information technology and they support the notion that the individual is 'a lone seeker of knowledge' (Kilpatrick et al., 2003). Often, technology is a simple 'add on' to the course. This idea stems from the notion that teaching is a highly structured and prescriptive form of instruction whereby learning objectives and activities are defined in a more concrete format. Such traditional didactic approaches tend to result in surface learning (Ramsden, 2002) where the emphasis is on coverage of content and the assessment system which tests and rewards low-level outcomes in the classroom (Hunter et al., 2010). Such surface learning approaches fail to meet the general market expectations for business graduates (Jackson, 2009).

To address some of these pressing issues, universities are exploring ways in which information and communication technologies can: (a) enhance students' learning, (b) address issues of multi-campus and flexible delivery, and (c) implement pedagogically-sound methods (Design for Learning, La Trobe University, 2009). Today, most business subjects offered in Australian universities have an online component delivered through various Learning Management Systems (LMS) such as Moodle and Blackboard. These subjects can be regarded as web-supplemented rather than e-learning which is fully online. Currently, many universities are moving towards blended learning approaches where a combination of face-to-face learning and forms of e-learning is used. The majority of subject offerings with a web presence follow an instructional design pedagogy and behavioural theory. Providing lecture presentations, tutorial material, podcasting, audio lectures using Lectopia and library resources are common elements of web-supplemented business subjects. What is less clear in current offerings is how web-supplemented elements enshrine and support such stated graduate capabilities as writing skills, creative problem-solving skills, and critical thinking skills.

There is evidence that much of the technology incorporation into curricula is prompted by practical challenges such as catering to large classes (Davies et al., 2005). However, different types of problems are inherent to the concurrent delivery of a subject in several campuses[7]. The concurrent delivery or multi-campus delivery of subjects is not uncommon in most business courses in Australia. In such circumstances, all students must have satisfactory access to subject resources whether they are metropolitan or regional, full-time or part-time. Blended learning approaches such as block-mode delivery have become popular in recent times as they cater to different learning styles and time challenges faced by part-time students. The main advantage of such an approach is the accessibility of material for part-time students who are unable to make a time commitment during normal teaching hours. Block-mode delivery tends to contain intensive sessions with a heavy content focus. The obvious downside of such an approach is there is little time for classroom discussion and reflection due to intense time pressures. Block-mode delivery combined with e-learning or online learning can bring about new possibilities of extended interaction (Bretag & Hannon, 2007).

To incorporate technology successfully into the curriculum requires the purpose of the course to be negotiated and made explicit (Sharpe & Oliver, 2007). According to this premise, 'one off' rational course design processes have been problematic. Integrating technology into curriculum requires careful consideration on what it attempts to support. For example, it is the type of activity or collaborative task and thinking processes in which students engage that determines the quality of learning and technology is simply the mediator for the task or collaboration (Bower et al., 2009). Laurillard (2009) asks the question: how do we ensure that pedagogy exploits the technology and not vice versa? Without a strong theoretical understanding about the nature of formal learning, technology is at risk of being merely used to enhance conventional learning designs.

From the discussion presented in section 3, it is apparent that one single pedagogical approach may not satisfy both the theoretical and practical considerations in flexible delivery curriculum design in business courses. Each e-learning pedagogy contains both positive and negative features when embedding technology into curricula. Out of the e-learning pedagogies reviewed, Laurillard's (2002) conversational framework offers much promise for business curriculum design. Drawing from both constructivist and cognitive learning theory traditions, the framework offers a logical process highlighting appropriate e-learning media types to guide course designs. However, in multi-campus delivery contexts, it is important to be cognisant of the limitations imposed by the use of multiple media forms because the IT infrastructure and accessibility may not be uniform across various campuses of the same university. Salmon's (2002) e-moderation model is particularly useful in framing the course designing process as it offers logical steps of student engagement.

---

[7] Ocak (2010) highlights the practical problems and impediments of blended learning from a faculty point of view.

E-learning activities need to be integrated into assessment in order to be regularly used by students (Sharpe & Oliver, 2007). This is consistent with Biggs' (1999) constructive alignment notion. Lowerison et al. (2008) argue that learning theories have to be adjusted to the realities of online teaching. Previous reviews of e-learning models have emphasised the need to refine the methodological frameworks that position various e-learning models in the pedagogical space (Mayes & de Freitas, 2004). Conole and Oliver's (2002) approach requires practitioners to describe their own uses of technology and then formalise this to help them decide whether they are using the appropriate technology.

Emerging web technologies present new opportunities and challenges for both students and educators. They include Web 2.0 tools such as social bookmarking, Wikis, shared document creation, blogs, microblogging, presentation tools, image creation and editing, podcasting, video editing and sharing, screen recording, mindmapping and digital storytelling. Although most new technologies are not designed specifically for educational purposes, educators and students can leverage these tools to enhance the learning experience. New technologies are prompting many educators to rethink pedagogy and current teaching and learning models. Conole (2007) argues that the gap between the potential of technologies to support learning and the reality of how they are actually being used may be due to a lack of understanding about how technologies can be used to harness specific learning advantages. She presents a taxonomy that characterises components of a learning activity—context, pedagogy, and task (p. 85)—and these could be used to support practitioners to make informed choices in their designing for learning.

Implementing flexible learning approaches involves a different set of challenges. Technology issues are the most common challenge in many e-learning contexts. They include the learning infrastructure (hardware, software, delivery mechanisms, and processes that deliver and manage learning programmes), which is pivotal to e-learning success. As mentioned earlier, the learning infrastructure of all campuses of the university may not have the same quality or capacity. This is highly relevant in multi-campus delivery of subjects. Learning infrastructure contributes to the complexity of e-learning in several ways. Key factors contributing to the complexity of the technology infrastructure include technology dependencies[8], customisation issues, integration challenges, and learner volumes (Shank et al., 2008). Multi-campus settings with differing IT capabilities exacerbate these infrastructure challenges. In fully-online delivery, certain student cohorts may not be able to access 'bandwidth-hungry' applications. Web 2.0 tools and the changing needs of the learners, especially those who have grown up with the internet and a plethora of social media networks, also provide unique challenges to educators. The abundance of choice and content creates anxiety for both students and teachers. Change from the top-down instructional approaches that have dominated business education to more flexible ones that focus on the learner is needed.

---

[8] The implementation requires the full support and expertise of the IT department to ensure the chosen applications run efficiently within the organisation's existing platforms, client workstations and computer networks, disk space, and bandwidth support (Shank et al., 2008).

5. Conclusion

Technological advancements and changing student needs have transformed teaching and learning worldwide. Business courses, in particular are forced to respond to some unique challenges in the face of educational reform and curriculum renewal in the tertiary sector. This paper reviewed the literature on e-learning pedagogies that have been used as part of blended learning and flexible delivery. An attempt has been made to link the e-learning pedagogies with their underpinning learning theories. The literature on online pedagogies is voluminous. Each pedagogy emphasises a different aspect of learning and most pedagogies often draw from more than one learning theory tradition. This paper draws together and presents the key pedagogies for e-learning in business education in a coherent form.

Adapting e-learning to business education contexts requires careful consideration to what the subject wants to achieve, namely deep learning outcomes. On the one hand, new web technologies expand the opportunities to design subjects informed by sound pedagogies that will instil graduate attributes and deliver deep learning outcomes. They also prompt educators to rethink current teaching and learning pedagogies. Particularly, pedagogical principles strongly support collaborative learning that emanates from a constructivist paradigm. On the other hand, institutional context, organisational structures and infrastructure issues can hamper e-learning success. E-learning in business education is still evolving and more research is needed to better understand how technology can be used to harness specific learning advantages.

References

Albrecht, W. S., & Sach, R. J. (2001). The perilous future of accounting education. The CPA Journal, 71(3), 16-23.

Anderson, L., & Krathwohl, D. (2001). A taxonomy for learning, teaching and assessing: A revision of Bloom's taxonomy of educational objectives. New York: Longman.

Andersen, P. H., & Rask, M. (2008). Taking action: new forms of student and manager involvement in business education. Marketing Intelligence & Planning, 26(2),145-165.

Anderson, J. R., & Reiser, B. J. (1985). The LISP tutor. Byte, 10, 159-175.

Atkinson, R. (2006). Web 2.0: Next-g, s sequel, or more of the same? HERDSA News, 29(2), 20-22.

Bates, A. W., & Poole, G. (2003). Effective teaching with technology in higher education: Foundations for success. San Francisco: Jossey-Bass.

Beetham, H., Jones, S., & Gornall, L. (2001). Career development of learning technology staff: Scoping study final report, JISC Committee for Awareness, Liaison and Training Programme. Retrieved fromhttp://www.jisc.ac.uk/publications/reports/2001/cdssfinalreport.aspx

Beetham, H. (2004). Review: Developing e-Learning models for the JISC practitioner communities. JISC Pedagogies for e-learning programme: Initial review. Retrieved from http://www.jisc.ac.uk/whatwedo/programmes/elearningpedagogy/outcomes

Beetham, H., & Sharpe, R. (2007). An introduction to rethinking pedagogy for a digital age. In H. & R. Sharpe (Eds.) Rethinking pedagogy for a digital age: Designing and delivering e-learning (pp.1-25). London: Routledge..

Biggs, J. B. (1996). Western misconceptions of the Confucian-heritage learning culture. In D. A. Watkins & J. B. Biggs (Eds.), The Chinese learner: Cultural, psychological, and contextual influences (pp. 45-68). Hong Kong; Melbourne, Australia: Comparative Education Research Centre; Australia Council for Educational Research.

Biggs, J. (1999). Teaching for quality learning at university: What the student does. Buckingham: The Society for Research into Higher Education and Open University Press.

Biggs, J. B. (2000). Teaching for quality learning at university, SRHE & Open University, Buckingham.

Biggs, J. B., & Tang, C. (2007). Teaching for quality learning at university: What the student does (3rd ed.). Berkshire: Society for Research into Higher Education and Open University Press.

Bower, M., Hedberg, J., & Kuswara, A. (2009). Conceptualising Web 2.0 enabled learning designs. In Same places, different spaces. Proceedings ascilite 2009 Auckland (pp.1153-1162). Retrieved from http://www.ascilite.org.au/conferences/auckland09/procs/bower.pdf

Bretag, T., & Hannon, J. (2007). Online close and personal: Developing a community of inquiry using computer mediated communication. In M. Hellsten & A. Reid (Eds.), Researching international pedagogies for teaching and learning, Netherlands: Springer.

Burdett, J. (2003). Making groups work: University students' perceptions, International Education Journal, 4(3),177-191.

Carr, S., & Mathews, M. R. (2002). Accounting curriculum change: Is it a rational academic exercise? Working Paper, Charles Sturt University, Bathurst, NSW.

Clegg, S., Hudson, A., & Steele, J. (2003). The emperor's new clothes: Globalisation and e-learning in higher education. British Journal of Sociology of Education, 24(1), 39-53.

Conole, G. (2007). Describing learning activities: tools and resources to guide practice. In H. Beetham & R. Sharpe (Eds.), Rethinking pedagogy for a digital age: Designing and delivering e-learning (pp.81-91). Oxford: RoutledgeFalmer.

Conole, G., Dyke, M., Oliver, M., & Seale, J. (2004). Mapping pedagogy and tools for effective learning design. Computers & Education 43, 17-33.

Conole, G., & Oliver, M. (2002). Embedding theory into learning technology practice with toolkits. Journal of Interactive Educational Media, 8. Retrieved from http://www.jime-open.ac.uk/

Dabbagh, N., & Reo, R. (2011). Back to the future: Tracing the roots and learning affordances of social software. In M.J.W. Lee & C. McLoughlin (Eds.), Web 2.0-based e-learning: Applying social informatics for tertiary learning (pp. 1-20). Hershey, PA: Information Science Reference.

Davies, A., Ramsay, J., Lindfield, H., & Couperthwaite, J. (2005). A blended approach to learning: Added value and lesson learnt from students' use of computer-based materials for neurological analysis. British Journal of Educational Technology, 36(5), 839-49.

Design for Learning (2009). Design for learning: Curriculum review and renewal. Melbourne: La Trobe University.

Gonzalez, C. (2009). Conceptions of, and approaches to, teaching online: A study of lecturers teaching postgraduate distance courses. Higher Education, 57, 299-314,

Goodyear, P. (2001). Effective networked learning in higher education: Notes and guidelines (Deliverable 9). Bristol: Joint Information Systems Committee (JISC). Retrieved from http://csalt.lancs.ac.uk/jisc/docs/Guidelines_final.doc

Goodyear, P. (2002). Psychological foundations for networked learning, Chapter 4. In C. Steeples & C. Jones (Eds.), Networked learning: perspectives and issues (pp. 49-75). Berlin: Springer Verlag.

Granić, A., Mifsud, C., & Ćukušić, M. (2009). Design, implementation and validation of a Europe-wide pedagogical framework for e-learning. Computers & Education, 53, 1052-1081.

Greeno, J. G., Collins, A. M., & Resnick, L. (1996). Cognition and learning. In D.C. Berliner& R.C. Calfee (Eds.), Handbook of educational psychology (pp.15-46). New York: Simon & Schuster Macmillan.

Hughes, G. D. (2006). How business education must change. MIT Sloan Management Review, 47(3), 88.

Hunter, J. D., Vickery, J., & Smyth, R. (2010). Enhancing learning outcomes through group work in an internationalised undergraduate business education context. Journal of Management & Organization, 16, 700-714.

Jackson, D. (2009). Undergraduate management education: It's place, purpose and efforts to bridge the skills gap. Journal of Management and Organization, I(2), 206-223.

Kembler, D. (1997). A reconceptualisation of the research into university academics' conceptions of teaching. Instructional Science, 7(3), 255-275.

Kilpatriack, S. I., Barrett, M. S., & Jones, T. (2003). Defining learning communities. International Education Research Conference, Auckland, New Zealand.

Kolb, D. (1984). Experiential learning: Experience as the source of learning and development. Englewood Cliffs, NJ: Prentice-Hall.

Laurillard, D. (2002). Rethinking university teaching: A framework for the effective use of learning technologies (2nd ed.). Oxford: RoutledgeFalmer.

Laurillard, D. (2009). The pedagogical challenges to collaborative technologies. International Journal of Computer-Supported Collaborative Learning, 4(1), 5-20.

Lee, M. J. W., & McLoughlin, C. (2011). Web 2.0-based e-learning: Applying social informatics to tertiary teaching. Hershey, PA: Information Science Reference (IGI Global).

Lowerison, G., Cote, R., Abrami, P. C., & Lavoie, M. (2008). Revisiting learning theory for e-learning. In S. Carliner & P. Shank (eds.), The e-leaning handbook: Past promises and present challenges. San Francisco: John Wiley.

Magliaro, S. G., Lockee, B. B., & Burton, J. K. (2005). Direct instruction revisited: A key model for instructional technology. Educational Technology Research & Development, 53(4), 41-55.

Mayer, R. E. (2003). Learning and instruction. Upper Saddle River, NJ: Merrill Prentice-Hall.

Mayes, T., & de Freitas, S. (2004). Stage 2: Review of e-learning theories, frameworks and models. JISC e-Learning Models Desk Study. Retrieved from http://www.jisc.ac.uk/whatwedo/programmes/elearningpedagogy/outcomes

McNaught, C. (2003). Identifying the complexity of factors in the sharing and reuse of resources. In A. Littlejohn (Ed.), Reusing online resources: A sustainable approach to e-learning (pp. 199-211). London: Kogan Page.

Mohamed, E. K. A. (2009). Optimizing business education: a strategic response to global challenges. Education, Business and Society: Contemporary Middle Eastern Issues, 2(4), 299-311.

Normand, C., & Littlejohn, A. (2006). Flexible delivery: A model of analysis and implementation of flexible programme delivery. Enhancing Practice, The Quality Assurance Agency for Higher Education. Retrieved from www.enhancementthemes.ac.uk

Ocak, M. A. (2010). Why are faculty members not teaching blended courses? Insights from faculty members. Computers & Education, 56(3), 689-699.

Oliver, B., Jones, S., Ferns, S., & Tucker, B. (2007). Mapping curricula: Ensuring work-ready graduates by mapping course learning outcomes and higher order thinking skills. Evaluations and Assessment Conference, Brisbane.

Oskoz, A., & Elola, I. (2011). Meeting at the wiki: The new arena for collaborative writing in foreign language courses. In M.J.W. Lee & C. McLoughlin (Eds.), Web 2.0-based e-learning: Applying social informatics to tertiary teaching (pp. 209-227). Hershey, PA: Information Science Reference (IGI Global).

Papert, S. (1986). Constructionism: A new opportunity for elementary science education. Unpublished proposal to the National Science Foundation.

Papert, S., & Harel, I. (1991). Situating constructionism. In S. Papert & I. Harel (Eds.), Constructionism (pp. 1-11). Norwood, NJ: Ablex Publisihng Corporation.

Ramsden, P. (2002). Learning to lead in higher education. London: Routledge.

Salmon, G. (2002). E-tivities: The key to active online learning. London: Kogan Page.

Salmon, G. (2004). E-moderating: The key to teaching and learning online. (2nd ed.). London: RoutledgeFarmer.

Salomon, G. (1993). No distribution without individuals' cognition. In G. Salomon (Ed.), Distributed cognitions: Psychological and educational considerations (pp. 111-138). New York: Cambridge University Press.

Shank, P., Precht, L. W., Singh, H., Everidge, J., & Bozarth, J. (2008). Infrastructure for learning: Options for today or screw-ups for tomorrow. In S. Carliner & P. Shank (Eds.), The e-learning handbook: Past problems, present challenges (pp. 109-166). San Francisco, CA: John Wiley & Sons.

Sharpe, R., & Oliver, M. (2007). Designing courses for e-learning. In H. Beetham & R. Sharpe (eds.), Rethinking pedagogy for a digital age: Designing and delivering e-learning (pp.41-51). London: Routledge.

Tapscott, D., & Williams, A. (2007). Wikinomics: How mass collaboration changes everything, Atlantic Books.

Van Over, D., & Stover, D.L. (1994). Object-oriented design: A new approach to curriculum development. Journal of Information Systems Education, 6, 22-26.

Vygotsky, L.S. (1978). Mind in society. Cambridge, MA: Harvard University Press.
Westerbeck, T. (2004). Brave new world, bold new b-school. BizEd, July/August, 36-40.

Wiley, D. A. (2000). Connecting learning objects to instructional design theory: A definition, a metaphor and a taxonomy. Retrieved from http://www.elearning-reviews.org/topics/technology/learning-objects/2001-wiley-learning-objects-instructional-design-theory.pdf

Rethinking Distance in an Era of Online Learning

Jennifer Glennie[1], Tony Mays[2]

This paper explores the ways in which technology in general, and online provision in particular, has contributed to a blurring of boundaries between different modes of educational provision, but makes a case for the retention of the notion of "distance" and how the challenges of distance may be overcome through conscious decisions made and budgeted for at the programme design stage. The argument made here results from an ongoing discussion within the South African Institute for Distance Education (SAIDE) in reflection on work at institutional, national and cross-border levels. It proposes a model for mapping different forms of provision within a funding framework in South Africa that looks set to continue a distinction between distance and non-distance forms of provision. The paper suggests a hierarchy of issues that should be addressed in the quality assurance and accreditation of distance programmes with varying degrees of ICT integration.

Key words: technology; online; distance education; SAIDE; quality assurance; accreditation

The Context

There is need to expand the capacity and effectiveness of the post-schooling system in many countries in Africa generally, and in South Africa in particular. However, most traditional contact-based institutions have already reached their capacity to support full-time students. In addition, there is increasing demand for more flexible provision of learning opportunities which allow lifelong learning to take place alongside other life commitments such as work, family and community engagements. There is evidence that designed and implemented well, distance provision can reach larger numbers and cater for more diverse student needs; and do so in ways that maintain or improve quality while achieving some cost-per-student savings through economies of scale (and for students, savings on costs of residence and travel). For these reasons, national policy in South Africa foresees and encourages expansion in provision of high quality distance education.

Although distance education can offer a way of breaking out of 'the iron triangle defined by the vectors of access, quality and cost' (Daniel & Kanwar, 2006, p.7) by increasing access, improving quality and cutting costs, it is also true that often distance education is not properly planned, does not deliver what it promises, and is not cost-effective. This is because it is complicated to plan and manage, and because the mistakes are less easy to conceal and/or overcome with a large, dispersed student body. Systemic evaluations of distance provision have provided evidence that much provision is far from ideal (CHE 2004). In addition, there seems to be a widespread assumption that education

---

[1] Director: South African Institute for Distance Education (SAIDE)
[2] Senior Programme Specialist – HE: SAIDE

delivered by means of ICT integration can improve the quality of educational provision in developing countries, not least in institutions of higher learning. Governments and higher education institutions in such countries are spending enormous sums of money in this regard. The "roll-out" of ICTs into schools, higher education institutions and community learning centres, together with more provision of on-line distance education courses, are increasingly advocated as the means to increase access to education and improve the quality of its delivery. The suggestion is that, particularly in countries which face serious educational shortcomings and whose educational institutions remain underdeveloped, Information and Communication Technologies (ICTs) can make the difference.

However, even accepting the assumption that ICT integration can make an important contribution, the question of the quality of educational delivery and support using ICTs requires much deeper analysis. Simply "throwing computers at higher education institutions" is not enough. While issues of the provision of ICT hardware, the improvement of connectivity, and the upgrading of communications and general technology infrastructure are clearly important, it is only when actual issues of the improvement of teaching and learning are addressed that claims made for the educational potential of ICTs can be confirmed or refuted. In South Africa, we are increasingly at this juncture.

Institutions now have a much wider range of possibilities to consider about what content to use, how to mediate it and how to assess learning. Depending on the learning context, the nature of their target learners and their vision and mission, institutions might opt for a minimal engagement with ICT in which the ICT supports other forms of teaching or, at the other extreme, a form in which ICT is integral to the design of the programme. All institutions will likely need to use a variety of ICT to maintain and improve communications, for example, but whether or not to use the affordances of ICT for a highly interactive form of engagement during the teaching process will have profound implications both for cost of provision and for the access and competences required of both students and staff. Institutions need to select appropriate technologies to use in appropriate ways, taking into account their differing contexts of provision: a one-size-fits-all approach will not be possible.

The rapid pace of technological change and increasing globalization have resulted in an exponential increase in access to sources of information, which means that teachers, whether contact or distance-based, can no longer be expected to be the sole content authority for the teaching-learning interaction. The roles and responsibilities of the lecturer, learner, and support services may be significantly changed in the online environment in particular as described by many research studies (Yang & Cornelious, 2005; Oliver, 1999). Digital technologies open up many possibilities for a more interactive engagement, but whether the affordances of ICT are used in this way must be a conscious design decision: ICT can be used simply to transmit content more efficiently. However, in institutions which consciously seek to use ICT to teach differently, the role of the lecturer is changing to that of facilitator, learning environment designer, co-learner, and may also include content curation (Plomp, 1999). The role of the learner in such institutions and programmes is then also changing, moving towards more self-directed, independent study and greater collaboration and engagement both with peers inside the institution and others outside the walls of the classroom or lecture hall (Berge, 2000; Kahn, 2012; Richardson). Burbules and Callister (1996) observe in particular that "hypertexts actively invite and facilitate multiple, alternative readings of the same material"; they suggest that "more than just a new way of organizing information, hypertext influences the information it organizes ... Form and content become interdependent." However, they also recognize that these potential new learning possibilities need form and content within which they can be realized—if engagement with hypertext is not, as we put it earlier, subordinated to disciplinary inquiry, then the activity it produces will dissolve in intellectual chaos, arbitrariness and "a limitless bricolage of fragments" (as cited in SAIDE, 2006).

Migration to an ICT-supported approach, whether for contact or distance or blended provision, should therefore be considered carefully and be undertaken within the context of the institutional environment as a whole.

The key point to be made here is that the way in which we use technology models particular values and uses for our students and places particular kinds of demands both on them and on their teachers. Therefore, we need to make conscious choices to use appropriate technologies in appropriate ways, taking cognizance of both our learning purposes and the technology profile of our target learners and staff (Mays, 2011). In our view, technology needs to support the teaching and learning process and not drive it.

Distance education provision and technology use

Distance Education (DE) providers have traditionally been early adopters of new technology, and different generations of DE provision have emphasised different systems and technologies issues, for example:

- 1st generation: correspondence—emphasis on mailing systems
- 2nd generation: specially prepared self-study material—emphases on materials development, storage, dispatch
- 3rd generation: print + multi-media and two-way communication—introduced importance of teams/ learner support
- 4th generation: ICTs and two-way interaction—added concerns for social learning/multi-skilling
- 5th generation: communities of learning—highlights multi-skilling/decentralised decision-making: Learning Management Systems/Personal Learning Environments (extrapolated from Heydenrich and Prinsloo, 2010).

While in North America, distance education seems to have become almost synonymous with video-based and/or online learning, in sub-Saharan Africa the traditional model for distance provision has been print-based correspondence or print-based and contact supported. However, with growing access to ICT facilities by staff and students and increasingly available and affordable connectivity, this is changing.

It should be noted that small scale virtual learning environments with high levels of interactivity are usually not affordable for scaled provision. At the other end of the scale, (largely) unmediated MOOCs generally have too low retention and throughput to be an effective model for DE provision for which institutions receive subsidy and students pay fees. Effective technology supported DE delivery for formal studies must rather take into account the needs, capacities and costs to students and staff and provide the necessary support for success. Thus the effective integration of ICTs must involve a careful analysis of learning and teaching needs and contexts so that the most appropriate use can be made of the most appropriate technologies (including print) to support the learning process.

Recently within South Africa's dedicated distance provider, the University of South Africa - Unisa, there has been recognition of the need to think and plan more holistically in terms of the 'student walk' through the institution (Louw, 2007) and the fit or lack thereof between student and institution expectations, preparedness and responsiveness at each key step of the walk (Prinsloo, 2009). Key steps in the student walk have been identified as follows: marketing and orientation; the process of application (and the need for guidance and counselling so that prospective students make informed choices); registration (including RPL); teaching and learning (including orientation to the process); formative assessment; consolidation and summative assessment; second assessment opportunity and finally graduation and alumni management. Different combinations of ICT might be used in different ways in different steps of this process (Mays, 2011).

How do assumptions about learning shape how ICT is used?

It is suggested that both the selection and the manner in which resources and technology are used to support learning are influenced by explicit or implicit assumptions about the nature and purpose of teaching and learning. This is illustrated in Table 1.

The table suggests that assumptions about the nature and purpose of teaching and learning, whether or not made explicit, will influence the choices teachers make about the selection and use of both resources and technology. Although different approaches might be needed by different students at different stages in their learning journey, the overall trend is towards favouring practices towards the right of the table. This has profound implications for the ways in which learning programmes are designed, supported and assessed and consequently also for the expectations of students and staff.

For the purpose of highlighting quality issues that are involved in ICT-supported distance education, it is necessary to provide conceptual clarity on what constitutes distance education.

Concept of distance education

Currently distance education students in South and Southern Africa rarely, if ever, have the opportunity to engage directly with their teachers or peers as contact sessions are often few and far between. ICT can be used to address this but, as noted previously, this calls for a conscious design decision with consequences for how such programmes are resourced. Distance education focuses on the teaching, learning, support, assessment, technology, and learning management systems design that aim to provide educational opportunities to students who are not physically "on site". In distance education, learners are separated from the instructional base or teacher, either in space or time, for a significant portion of their learning (ADEA Working Group on Distance Education and Open Learning). As an approach, distance education does not preclude some face-to-face contact, but such learning opportunities do not necessarily take place at school or in the presence of a teacher; neither do they have to be based on a "group structured" programme. There is greater freedom of space and time, and there is also much learner flexibility in the learning process.

Whereas online learning opportunities may be offered both to campus-based and remote students, distance education is premised on a very diverse and geographically distributed student body, a high level of independent learning and decentralised support for students who may never attend the central campus. So in our opinion, online provision and distance provision cannot be conflated: though the former can be designed specifically to meet the needs of the latter. Designing a programme for a target audience who can be assumed to have access to computer labs or a wifi network on a central campus raises different requirements from the design of a programme for distributed students who may not have that access. Even if registration requirements stipulate that students must have specific ICT devices and specific levels of connectivity, there is need to think about how distributed students can gain access to technical support (for example an online support centre; a call centre).

Where registration requirements are clear and a technical support structure is in place, the design of the learning programme itself usually makes certain assumptions about what students already know or can do: designing a programme for local students studying on a flexible study basis, or students distributed across a province, or students distributed across a whole country or region, or students anywhere in the world, raises important design questions about what examples to use; what resources to refer to; the type of language that might be appropriate; how a large and distributed student population might be divided into smaller groups for collaborative assignments (perhaps deliberately pairing students from different environments); and what learning styles and strategies might be appropriate (perhaps a greater range of options for a more diverse range of participants). So when Evans and Pauling (2010) rightfully question whether the notion of "distance education" is still relevant, we would argue that it remains useful at the programme design stage to think about where prospective students will likely be located. We believe that "geographic distance" can still exacerbate "transactional distance" (Moore, 1993, 1996) in an online environment, and activities and support strategies need to be designed accordingly.

Distance education can thus be construed as a collection of methods (including but not limited to online) for the provision of structured learning as well as a mode of delivery that avoids the need for learners to discover the curriculum by attending classes frequently and for long periods. Distance provision aims to create a quality learning environment using an appropriate combination of different learning resources, tutorial support, peer group discussion, and practical sessions (real or virtual or a combination of both). Literature shows that some of the key aspects that constitute an effective learning environment, whether it is in face-to-face or in distance education settings are that learners should be encouraged to engage with the content, to collaborate and interact during learning, to reflect on what they learn and to relate it to practice (CHE 2007; Strydom and Mentz 2010). In distance education, creating an effective learning environment entails designing activities that promote mastery of knowledge/concepts by learners; mastery of skills through doing; interacting with peers and the environment to gain deeper insights; and reflecting on what is learnt to gain wisdom without necessarily requiring teachers and learners to be in the same place at the same time. Students do not necessarily need to be "online" to do some of these things.

Distance versus technology-mediated conventional education: the narrowing gap

As noted by SAIDE in an earlier report:

> Technologies can be applied in a range of ways, to support an almost limitless combination of teaching and learning strategies, and it is essential to keep options as open as possible. This flexibility should form the cornerstone of all planning processes. (SAIDE, 2000: iv)

The wealth of possibilities offered by mixed-mode learning is increasingly being realised by educational institutions. Thus, due to increased use of technology the distinction between distance education and face-to-face delivery is increasingly becoming blurred as is the distinction between distance learning and elearning. At the same time, the advent of information and communication technology and its increasing ubiquity is making it more and more feasible to interact with a course facilitator and with peer learners at a distance, both synchronously and asynchronously. Distance education providers are increasingly harnessing the affordances of this technology to enhance their teaching and learning processes. So on the one hand we have a blurring of boundaries, but on the other we have a funding and policy framework in South Africa that looks set to continue to maintain a distinction for some time to come. The challenge then is where, on the continuum of endless possibilities, to draw a line between what constitutes technology-mediated contact provision and distance education. SAIDE acknowledges the complexity at the interface of distance education and technology-supported learning, and has developed a grid that serves to illustrate a number of delivery modes lying on the two continua of spatial distance on one hand and technology use on the other. Figure 1 illustrates various delivery permutations based on the two variables.

In addition to the spatial and technological dimensions illustrated in Figure 1, a third (human) dimension needs to be considered across all forms of provision. This is the underpinning educational approach and the extent to which this is fit for its purpose in terms of the target audience, the purpose and level of the course being offered, as well as the extent to which an equivalent learning experience is offered across different contexts of learning and practice. A diverse range of ICTs are now available to enable this, including more informal social networking, but they need to be selected and utilised purposefully for this potential to be realised. In an insightful paper on emergent learning and the affordances of learning ecologies in Web 2.0, Wiliams, Karousou and Mackness (2011) caution:

> although social networking media increase the potential range and scope for emergent learning exponentially, considerable effort is required to ensure an effective balance between openness and constraint. It is possible to manage the relationship between prescriptive and emergent learning, both of which need to be part of an integrated learning ecology. (p.39)

Notwithstanding the growing mix of modes and methods, the realities of funding in South Africa in the short to medium term as well as a concern to differentiate provision in order to address relevant quality issues mean that the regulatory framework in South Africa will continue to distinguish between 'contact' and 'distance' provision for the foreseeable future. This in turn calls for the adoption of a single simple definition of 'distance education' that will apply

Figure 1: Mapping different examples of provision

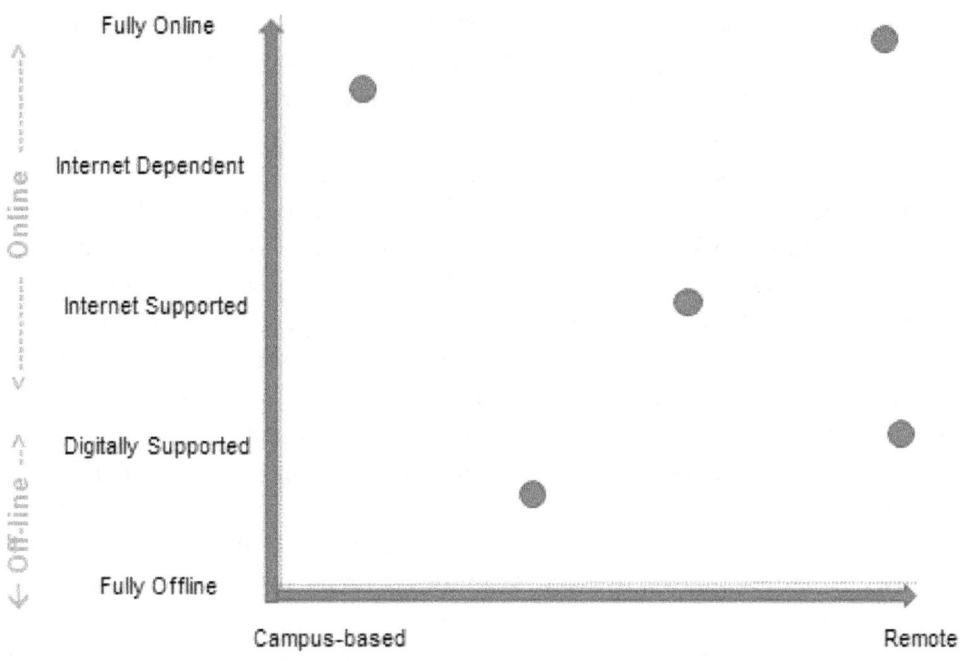

across all statutory and regulatory bodies. Taking cognizance of the finding from the South African Survey of Student Engagement (Strydom & Mentz, 2010) that, on average, undergraduate students in contact programmes in South Africa spend 40% of their time involved in scheduled campus-based activities, for the purposes of this discussion, the term 'distance education' therefore refers to all modes of provision, including blended and technology-supported learning provision, in which students spend 30% or less of the stated Notional Learning Hours in undergraduate courses at NQF Levels 5 and 6, and 25% or less in courses at NQF Level 7 and initial post-graduate courses at NQF Level 8, in staff-led and conventional face-to-face, campus-based structured learning activities.

Within this framework, "distance education" therefore refers to practices towards the right-hand side of the grid in Figure 1 in which it is assumed that students will rarely, if ever, be in the same time and place as their teacher. This has profoundly different implications for student and staff roles and also for what facilities need to be put in place and maintained at the extremes of practice, notwithstanding that there may be some programmes converging towards a blended mode of provision. Critical for the current discussion is a consideration of how ICTs are utilised to facilitate active student engagement with the curriculum, to provide a wide range of learning support strategies and to enable reliable assessment that is consistent with the overall purpose of the programme, without necessarily requiring teachers and students to be in the same place at the same time. We are thus looking to uses of technology that involve far more than simply providing "print behind glass." Probably the most important and perhaps the most difficult transition to the online/blended mode for both the instructor and learner is that of adjusting to the online communication medium, be it used synchronously or asynchronously. This includes concepts and practice surrounding teaching and learning interaction, engagement, and facilitation.

Programme design needs to be guided by an upfront decision concerning the level of mediation that is to be employed in the online component of the course by the responsible academic. In addition, large student numbers would indicate the employment of tutors to manage small virtual group online interaction. In the first instance, interactions would typically be tutor to learner, and learner to learner. However, the online environment offers greater potential for an expanded environment, including with expertise residing outside of the institution. Figure 2 illustrates one model of the many possible interactions.

Not all aspects of Anderson's model above will necessarily feature in all programme designs. For example, the development of simulations and games or virtual labs is time-consuming and may not be appropriate to all contexts. However, it does seem to make sense for all programmes to create opportunities for greater student-content interaction (through the design of meaningful activities with automated feedback for example); opportunities for student-teacher interaction outside of normal office hours by email and through online fora; as well as student-student interaction as students can often support one another in the learning process and an online community of learning can help overcome the sense of isolation that often characterizes distance provision.

Although perhaps more extreme in Sub-Saharan Africa for a host of historical and current reasons, similar challenges regarding how to teach effectively are evident elsewhere as society adapts to the increasing availability of and demand for information enabled by the ubiquitous availability of technology. Laurillard (2002, 2006) suggests that there is consequently a need to rethink the way we teach in the new knowledge society including adopting a more professional research-based teaching approach that parallels the professional approach the sector has always adopted towards research; placing a greater emphasis on the development of the long-term high-level cognitive skills of scholarship and utilising technology to promote meaningful interaction and engagement.

Expansion of distance education provision in higher education is increasingly being associated with more use of educational technology for these kinds of reasons. In South Africa, although there is currently only one dedicated distance education institution, there has been considerable increase in the number of students studying on distance education programmes at predominantly contact institutions, a process that is supported by evolving policy guidelines for post-schooling provision generally. The increasing use of ICTs for teaching and learning has made it possible for more providers to engage students that are not in the same place at the same time, i.e. reach students 'at a distance'. This has meant that many institutions/programme that would characterise themselves as contact/face-to-face are often moving into distance provision without necessarily making a conscious decision to do so. Stakeholder submissions to the research process for the Council on Higher Education report submitted in 2009 emphasised that face-to-face institutions could not ignore the wealth of possibilities offered by mixed-mode or blended e-learning (Council on Higher Education, (2009: 9-14)). This was seen to be essential in terms of opening access and increasing graduate output.

A growing body of literature provides insight into the possible advantages and the minimum requirements for integrating ICTs into learning provision more generally (Simonson, Smaldino, Albright, & Zvacek, 2003) and on the unique opportunities provided by the online environment in particular (Anderson & Elloumi, 2004). The literature suggests the need to recognize the increased diversity of the potential learners and to design with different learning needs in mind from the outset (Ehlers, 2004; Davis, 2007; as cited in Moore, 2007), including the need to address issues of cultural diversity (Gunawardena & LaPointe, 2007; as cited in Moore, 2007) and make the necessary investment in appropriate curriculum design ahead of marketing and registration (Butcher, 2001). It is then necessary to create awareness of the nature and demands of distance and technology mediated learning prior to registration (Simpson, 2004; Davis, 2007; as cited in Moore, 2007) and give attention to the ways in which both tutors and learners are prepared, monitored and supported in an online or technology mediated learning environment (McPherson & Nunes, 2004) throughout the learning process. The design of the learning process may usefully be informed by an understanding of adult and possibly self-learning theory (Davis, 2007; as cited in Moore, 2007; Hase and Kenyon 2001) and the changing expectations and preferred learning styles of students (Dede, Dieterle, Clarke, Ketelhut, & Nelson, 2007; as cited in Moore, 2007) and in particular the need for interaction, customization and reciprocity in learning partnerships (Beldarrain, 2006). Caplan, Thiessen, and Ambrock (as cited in Anderson & Elloumi, 2004) point to the need for multi-disciplined teams to develop these kinds of programmes which will obviously have implications for project management, time and cost and in turn models a particular form of professional practice.

Figure 2: A model for online learning (Anderson, 2008,61)

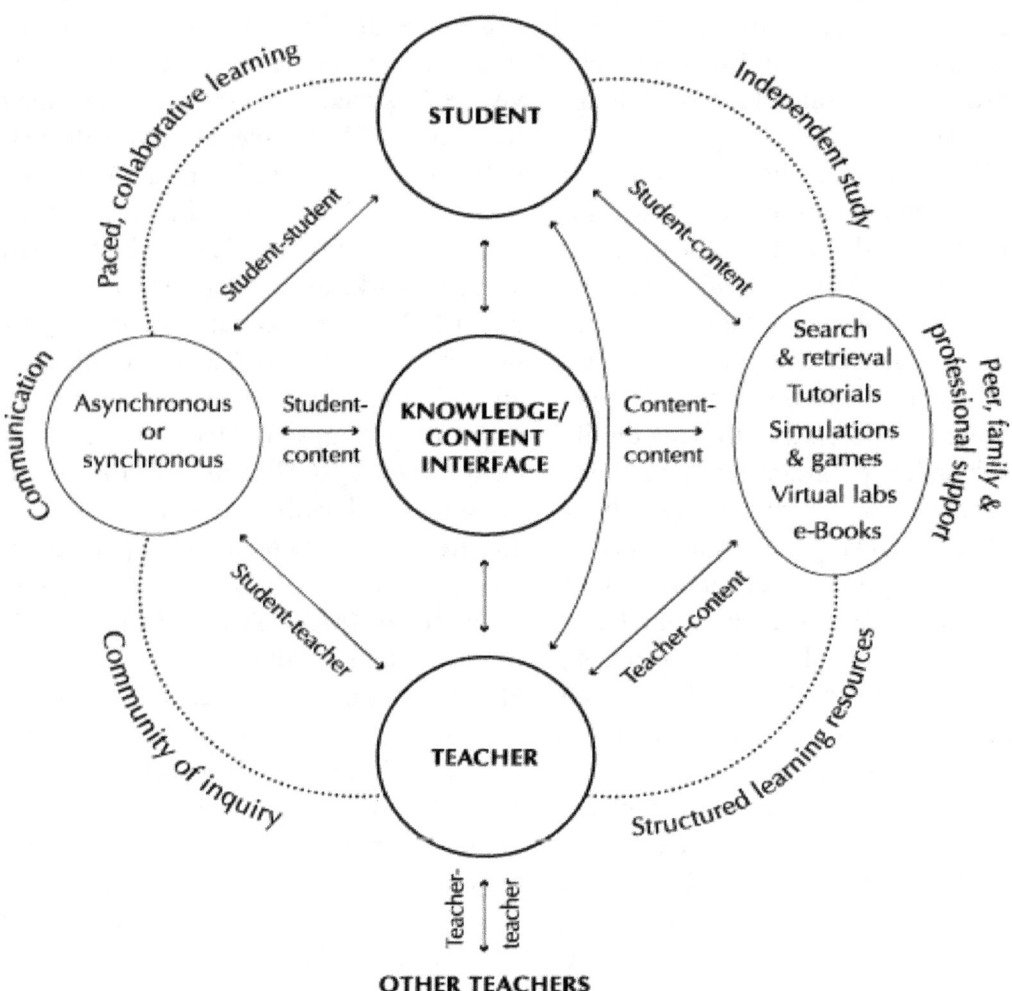

Welch, Drew, and Randall (2010) report on a SAIDE engagement with an on-line learning process to explore how to train tutors to support distance learning on-line. They noted the usefulness of Salmon's (2004) model for structuring a learning programme on-line overall and Gunawardena et al.'s (2006) Wiscom model for designing particular learning activities. They conclude that, designed appropriately, an on-line course can result in greater engagement and interaction but indicate that the approach needs to be thought about very carefully if large-scale provision is required. The recruitment, selection, training, monitoring and ongoing support of tutors working with sub-groups of the student population becomes a management task in its own right and has implications for the ways in which learning management systems are constructed. Thus a meaningful migration towards ICT integration involves much more than simply making resources available on line.

Accreditation of technology-enhanced distance education: an international perspective

Whilst distance education is gaining prominence in higher education, many challenges are faced in terms of enhancing the quality of delivery. Key challenges of distance learners to be addressed by a provider include overcoming the difficulty of students sharing their experiences with other students; providing opportunities to interact with teachers outside of normal hours; providing appropriate and timely interactive learning materials; making available expert guidance and support in order to derive maximum benefit out of the learning materials. Many of these traditional challenges can be addressed through appropriate use of technology, but only if the integration of technology is designed for the purpose and the impact on students, staff and systems taken into account and provided for.

The prominent quality assurer in higher education, David Woodhouse (2009) identifies key characteristics of distance education that often pose quality challenges to providers:

- more stakeholders or sites involved in the creation and delivery of a course or programme;
- longer chains of communication;
- often larger scale;
- more separate activities and roles to be co-ordinated;
- greater administrative needs (such as record keeping);
- more delegation of assessment in competency testing;
- achieving consistency of practice over a distributed organisation or a collaboratively delivered programme or course;
- a different interpretation of what constitutes teaching (for example, in the separation of roles in providing learning content and support);
- a more careful and deliberate process of planning and development of courses and systems than is common for conventional delivery;
- greater issues of credibility;
- complications raised by a transition from a largely correspondence-based ODL programme to an increasingly on-line system;
- QA processes that are accepted as integral to the ODL programme provide models for the assessment of quality in campus-based programmes.

Implications for the review of distance provision

In understanding mode of delivery, consideration needs to be given not only to the extent of temporal or spatial separation of teacher and learner, but also the extent to which digital technology is used to support the teaching and learning in a programme. The flexibility of the temporal dimension in technology-supported teaching and learning provides a great pedagogical strength. Interaction can either be synchronous (at the same time) or asynchronous (with delays). The asynchronous nature of many of the communication and collaboration technologies currently available allows learners to reflect and contribute more meaningfully in an online dialogue, thus developing and improving their critical thinking skills.

In fully online programmes all interactions with staff and students, educational content, learning activities, assessment and support services are integrated and delivered online. Blended programmes with some elements of online participation could also be digitally supported offline e.g. by use of CD/DVDs. In the context of a developing economy, this could alleviate excessive and expensive downloading of multimedia materials.

When designing or transforming a course for online delivery, the presence of the learning pathway becomes more important than ever and needs to be carefully designed and implemented, so that the navigation framework for the course is entirely clear.

The potential of the digital medium should be exploited to the full within the constraints of the target teaching and learning environment, ICT infrastructure and available budget. Multimedia (MM) elements could be incorporated where appropriate. However, careful consideration should be paid to the pedagogical purpose (the primary driver) of any MM learning object – this should always be supported by the appropriate use of ICTs.

When redeveloping materials for online delivery, it should not be assumed that the activities, assignments and assessment would necessarily be scheduled to take place online. The potential of the new environment should be exploited only if and when it is deemed to be relevant and appropriate. The instructions and guidance for each activity should be entirely explicit, as this environment will form the learner's primary source of reference for their engagement with the course.

With regard to online assessment, there are a variety of assignment and question types that are typically supported by virtual learning environments (VLE/LMS). However, it is important to note that the usual considerations around the validity and security of assessment apply. The deployment of automated online assessment can be used more easily for formative rather than summative assessment, unless a proctored examination venue is utilized, and a variety of appropriately structured and valid assessment forms are designed.

When engaging in a mediated online course, the teacher's presence is of paramount importance. Learners should also be given the opportunity at the beginning of a course to establish their own online presence and acknowledge other learners as part of their group embarking on this learning experience together. Again, this should be explicitly built in at the design stage.

Taking into account the flexible nature of materials presentation in an online environment, the layout and layering of the various pedagogical elements requires particular attention. The layering refers to the information that the student first sees on the online course landing page; what course elements are then available via a hyperlink, and how they are presented; what activities and assessment are designed to support learning; how these are supported by ICTs; and how the learners are to be engaged with the materials, their instructor and each other, all to be accomplished through making the most of opportunities afforded by the online environment. The elements of each section of a landing page would typically include: the title of the sub-topic; some textual narrative explaining what the section is about; a clear indication of what the learner is expected to undertake in this section; and how they should go about it. In order to keep the landing page uncluttered, the detail of any resources and activities is available via a link.

People considerations

When embarking on a new mode of delivery for a particular course, there are a number of additional elements to be considered in order to promote the success of an online/blended programme.

Learners: computer literacy skills should be ascertained and any remediation deemed necessary should be undertaken prior to their engagement with the online course. Of primary importance is the verification that each learner has reasonable access to the online environment. This would include provision for their device that is to be used to access their course, as well as regular internet access at a reasonable cost. They should also be provided with a brief orientation to their online environment that would include a training session in order for them to explore the features and functions of the software with which they are expected to engage, and importantly, an orientation to the pedagogical purpose within their course.

Lecturers/Tutors: should be equipped with the skills to facilitate the course online in a manner that supports and engages the learner in the changed environment.

Extended support team: it should be made explicitly clear to lecturers/tutors and learners who is available to support them, when those people are available, and what kind of support can be expected from them, and how they should be contacted. This information should be embedded in the start-up information for each programme. In order to achieve this, good inclusive relationships should be developed within the institution between academic and support staff in their quest to provide an effective online teaching and learning environment.

Towards a hierarchy of review

There is a hierarchy in evaluation implied by the discussion in this section:

• First, we need to look for a curriculum design that models good teaching and helps students develop the necessary competences for success, regardless of the mode of provision.
• Second, we need to look for learning pathways and learning activities that model the desired approaches to knowledge, learners and technology usage within a distance context of diverse and geographically distributed students.
• Third, we then need to establish whether the most appropriate technologies are used in the ways most appropriate to the learning intention, taking cognizance of the technol-

ogy profile of the leaners, their teachers, and their contexts of practice.

Acknowledgements

The ideas explored here have been the subject of ongoing debate within SAIDE. The authors acknowledge with thanks the contributions of our colleagues to these discussions and this paper: Alice Barlow-Zambodla, Maryla Bialobrzceska, Sheila Drew, Grieg Krull, Jenny Louw, Brenda Mallinson, Ephraim Mhlanga, Catherine Ngugi, Rebecca Pursell, and Tessa Welch.

References

Anderson, T. (2008). The theory and practice of online learning (2nd ed.). Athabasca: Athabasca University Press.

Anderson, T., & Elloumi, F. (Eds.). (2004). Theory and practice of online learning. Athabasca: Athabasca University.

Beldarrain, Y. (2006). Distance education trends: Integrating new technologies to foster student interaction and collaboration. Distance Education, 22(2), 139-153.

Berge, Z. (2000). New roles for learners and teachers in online higher education. Baltimore: University of Maryland System, UMBC. Retrieved from its.fvtc.edu/langan/BB6/BergeZane2000.pdf.

Burbules, N.C., & Callister, T.A. (1996). Knowledge at the crossroads: some alternative futures of hypertext learning environments. Educational Theory. 1, 23-50.

Butcher, N. (2001). Online learning: Possibilities and pitfalls in unit 10: Developing online materials. UNICCO online course development guide. Retrieved from http://www.saide.org.za/unesco/unit%2010.htm.

Council on Higher Education (CHE). (2007). Higher education monitor No. 6: A case for improving teaching and learning in South African higher education. Pretoria: CHE.

CHEA. (2002). Accreditation and assuring quality in distance education. Washington, DC: CHEA.

Davis, J.D. (2007). Developing text for web-based instruction. In M.G. Moore (Ed.), Handbook of distance education (2nd ed.) (pp. 285-294). New Jersey & London: Lawrence Erlbaum Associates, Publishers..

Dede, C., Dieterle, E., Clarke, J., Ketelhut, D. J., & Nelson, B. (2007). Media-based learning styles. In M. G. Moore (Ed.), Handbook of distance education (2nd ed.) (pp. 339-352). New Jersey & London: Lawrence Erlbaum Associates, Publishers.

Evans, T., & Pauling, B. (2010). The future of distance education: Reformed, scrapped or recycled in Cleveland-Innes. In M. F. & D.R. Garrison, (Eds). An introduction to distance education: Understanding teaching and learning in a new era. Abingdon and New York: Routledge.

Gunawardena, C.N., Oretgano-Layne, L., Carabajal, K., Frechette, C., Lindemann, K., & Jennings, B. (2006). New model, new strategies: Instructional design for building online wisdom communities. Distance Education, 27(2), 217-232.

Gunawardena, C.N., & LaPointe, D. (2007). Cultural dynamics of online learning. In M.G. Moore (Ed.), Handbook of distance education (2nd ed.). New Jersey & London: Lawrence Erlbaum Associates, Publishers.

Hase, S. & Kenyon, C. (2001. From andragogy to heutagogy. Retrieved from http://www.psy.gla.ac.uk/~steve/pr/Heutagogy.html.

Khan, S. (2012). The one world school house: Education reimagined. London: Hodder & Stoughton Ltd.

Laurillard, D. (2007). Rethinking university teaching: A conversational framework for the effective use of learning technologies (2nd ed.). London: Routledge Falmer.

Laurillard, D. (2006). E-learning in higher education. In P. Ashwin (Ed.) Changing Higher Education: The Development of Learning and Teaching. (pp. 1-12). London: Routledge.

Mays, T. (2004). From policy to practice: an evaluation of the Unisa National Professional Diploma in Education from the perspective of social critical theory. (Unpublished MEd dissertation) Unisa, South Africa.

Mays, T. (2011). Developing practice: Teaching teachers today for tomorrow. US-China Education Review, 1(7). McPherson, M., & Nunes, M.B. (2004). The role of tutors as an integral part of online learning support. 3rd EDEN Research Conference, Oldenberg.

Moore, M.G. (1993). Theory of transactional distance. In D. Keegan (Ed.) Theoretical principles of distance education. London: Routledge.

Moore, M.G., & Kearsley, G. (1996). Distance education: A systems view. Belmont, CA: Wadsworth.

Oliver, R. (1999). On-line teaching and learning: New roles for participants. Retrieved from http://www.monash.edu.au/groups/flt/1999/online.html

Plomp, T. (1999). Higher education for the 21st century and the potential of ICT. In H.W. Maltha J.F. Gerrissen, and W. Veen (Eds.). The means and the ends: ICT and third world education. Amsterdam: Nuffic.

Richardson, W.U.D. (2013). Why school? New York: TED Books.

Salmon, G. (2004). The five stage model (2nd ed.). London: Routledge. Retrieved from http://www.atimod.com/e-moderating/5stage.shtml

SAIDE. 2006. Appendix 2. Quality assurance and e-learning project. The learning promise of ICTs in the academy: A literature review. Johannesburg: SAIDE.

SAIDE. (2012). Considering mode of delivery. Retrieved from http://www.oerafrica.org/design-guide/.

Simpson, O. (2004). Access, retention and course choice in online, open and distance learning. 3rd EDEN Research Conference. Oldenberg.

Strydom, J. F., & Mentz, M. (2010). South African survey of student engagement: Focusing the student experience on success through student engagement. Pretoria: CHE.

University of Idaho. (1985). Distance education: An overview. Retrieved from http://www.uidaho.edu/eo

Welch, T., Drew, S., & Randall, C. (2010). What makes the difference? A case study examining online tutoring and tutoring in conventional distance education. (Draft discussion document). Johannesburg: SAIDE.

Williams, R., Karousou, R., and Mackness, J. (2011). Emergent learning and learning ecologies in Web 2.0. International Review of Research in Open and Distance Learning, 12(3), pp.39-58.

Woodhouse, D. (2009). QA for distance and e-learning. Presentation made in Abu Dhab.

www.ingramcontent.com/pod-product-compliance
Lightning Source LLC
LaVergne TN
LVHW061302060426
835510LV00014B/1846